TOEFL® Test iBT Reading: Practice for Success

TOEFL® Test iBT リーディング 実践編

Jim Knudsen
生井健一

TOEFL is a registered trademark of Educational Testing Service (ETS).
This publication is not endorsed or approved by ETS.

はじめに

　使える英語力を測るテストとしての TOEFL の歴史は、1964 年に遡る。主に北米での大学教育を受けるに足りるだけの英語力があるかどうかを見るためのテストだが、国際的な高評価とともに少なからず批判を受けてきたのも事実である。しかし、その都度改良を繰り返し、様々なバージョンのペーパーテストの後、コンピュータ版（CBT）を経て、近年インターネット版（iBT）に進化した。ここにおいて独立した文法セクションが廃止され、代わりにスピーキングが導入されるに至った。また、ライティングとスピーキングでは、読んだり聞いたりした内容について書く、話す、といった複数技能を同時に使って答える問題形式（integrated task と呼ばれる）も取り入れられるようになった。まさに「使える」英語力を測ろうとする TOEFL 製作者たちの努力の結晶とも言えるだろう。いずれにせよ、TOEFL は長期にわたり（今年で 46 年）広く国際的に通用してきた英語試験であり、その信頼性は非常に高い。日本では TOEIC が流行っているが、留学および海外インターンのパスポートにもなり得る TOEFL で高得点をあげることは、それだけ将来多くのドアが開くことを意味する。ここにこそ TOEFL 受験の大きな魅力があるとも言える。
　さて本書は、TOEFL iBT のリーディング・セクションの効果的な練習教材である。マルティプル・チョイスはもちろん、iBT より始まった新しい形式の設問（情報を類別する、サマリーを完成する等）をも備えている。比較・対照、因果関係など、北米大学での勉強の際に必ず読むことになる文章のパターンを研究し、様々な読解難易度のオリジナル・パッセージを多様な分野から用意した。iBT では難しい単語はクリックしてその定義を参照できるようになっているが、本書でも Glossary を付けたので、必要に応じて活用し、受験準備をしてほしい。また、以前とは違い、試験中にノートを取ることも自由なので、メモをとりながら練習されても構わない。本番では 3 つから 5 つのパッセージがそれぞれ 12 〜 14 の設問とともに出題される。1 つのパッセージに費やすべき時間の目安は 20 分なので、本書をリーディング・セクションの模擬試験のように使う場合は、この時間を念頭に置かれるとよいだろう。
　英語力を上げるには、継続した練習あるのみ。繰り返し本書にあたり、知らない単語がなくなるくらいになれれば理想的だ。また、その手助けになるべく、

すべてのパッセージの音声 CD も用意した。リーディングとリスニングの違いは、情報が目から入ってくるか耳から入ってくるかに過ぎず、脳で行う作業に変わりはない。もちろんリスニングでは、聞き逃した場合に前には戻れないので、英語をそのままの語順で理解せざるを得ないのだが、だからこそリスニングの訓練は、リーディングにおいても英語を英語の語順で理解するのに役立ち、その結果、読解速度の大幅な向上が可能になるのである。また、音読やシャドウィングも並行して行ってみてほしい。そうすれば（当たり前のことだが）次に CD を聞いたときには、全部簡単に分かるようになる。結局英語を理解する脳を作るには、これらの作業をいかに多くの英文で行えるかにかかっているのだ。本書を手始めに、皆さんが効率良く「英語脳」を開発されることを心からお祈りする次第である。

生井　健一

PREFACE

As we're sure you know, TOEFL stands for *Test of English as a Foreign Language*, and if you plan to study at a university in the United States, you have to do very well on it. The first and, to our mind, the most important part of the TOEFL exam is the reading section, which measures your ability to read fairly lengthy reading passages (500 to 600 words) and to answer some pretty "tricky" and sophisticated questions about them. The passages are similar in content and level of difficulty to the type of material you would be assigned to read in an introductory course in an American college or university.

This book's primary aim is to help you boost your score on the TOEFL reading section. And, if you make the effort, we're confident that it will do just that. But the book will also help to make you a much more adept reader of English all round, which, in this Age of Information and the World Wide Web, has become an increasingly vital skill and attribute. And, we might add, the ability to read and comprehend English well is the foundation on which the development of all your other language skills—listening, speaking, writing—depends. Become a better reader, with a larger vocabulary, greater grasp of grammar and usage, and a broader range of general knowledge, and overall English fluency will never be far behind.

This book is made up of twenty practice reading passages that take up the very topics—science and technology, history and biography, politics and culture, art and literature, social science and psychology—you will encounter on the TOEFL and in the American undergraduate classroom. Although some passages deal with some rather weighty technical and abstract subjects and ideas, we have tried to write them in clear, accessible, natural, even lively English for ease of understanding and, we like to think, enhanced enjoyment. Each passage is followed by twelve mostly multiple-choice, TOEFL-type questions. What this means is that many of the must-have vocabulary items (listed alphabetically and clearly defined in the handy Glossary), nearly all of the essential sentence patterns and grammatical structures, and much of the background information you will need to "ace" the TOEFL can be found right here within these pages.

What is the best way to use this book? Our advice to you is to take your time. Don't think of the reading passages and follow-up questions as mere practice tests to take once and then forget, but as texts for slow, thorough, repeated study—as valuable learning opportunities. Read each passage over and over, absorbing everything it has to offer so that when you do move on to the practice questions, you can do so with complete confidence. Then, a week or two weeks later, do it all over again. This kind of follow-up study is the best way we know of to guarantee maximum comprehension and retention.

To make sure you get the most out of the readings, we have provided an Answer Key with detailed explanations for all the correct as well as all the incorrect answers. Always include this Answer Key in your study plan and schedule: not only will it increase your understanding of the readings but it will also show you exactly where your English reading strengths and weaknesses lie—where you need to improve and work harder to come out a winner. We suggest that you pay special attention to chapters 1 and 2, as well as chapter 7, which deal specifically with the language arts: critical reading and thinking; essay types and their accompanying writing strategies; author intention and style; the basic elements of fiction and drama. The "tips" you pick up in these early chapters will make it that much easier for you to work your way through the remaining chapters and, at the same time, give you a running head start up the path to becoming a much sharper, deeper, more active reader of English—and a surefire TOEFL success story.

Jim Knudsen

Table of Contents

1. ENGLISH 101: CRITICAL THINKING AND READING — 10
2. ENGLISH 102: ESSAY TYPES AND STRATEGIES — 16
3. COLOR — 22
4. BATS — 28
5. PAINTING AND OIL PAINTING — 34
6. ENERGY AND ENERGY SOURCES — 40
7. THE ELEMENTS OF FICTION AND DRAMA — 46
8. THE HOAX — 52
9. PHILOSOPHY AND THE GOOD LIFE — 58
10. MYSTERIOUS FORCES — 64
11. LIES AND LIE DETECTION — 70
12. SOCIOLOGY AND RELIGION — 76
13. THE BLACKING FACTORY — 82
14. BEFORE IT'S TOO LATE — 88
15. PTSD — 94
16. ZOOS: FOR AND AGAINST — 100
17. THE PANAMA CANAL — 106
18. JOHN DEWEY'S LABORATORY SCHOOL — 112
19. THE END OF APARTHEID — 118
20. TRANSFORMING BUSINESS — 124

1. イングリッシュ 101：批判的思考と読書	130
2. イングリッシュ 102：エッセイのタイプとストラテジー	136
3. 色	142
4. コウモリ	148
5. 絵画と油絵	154
6. エネルギーとエネルギー源	160
7. フィクションと演劇の初歩	166
8. ホウクス	172
9. 哲学と良い人生	178
10. 未知の力	184
11. 嘘とその発見	190
12. 社会学と宗教	196
13. 靴墨工場	202
14. 手遅れになる前に	208
15. PTSD	214
16. 動物園：賛成と反対	220
17. パナマ運河	226
18. ジョン・デューイの実験学校	232
19. アパルトヘイトの終焉	238
20. ビジネスの転換	244
アンサーキー	251
GLOSSARY	287

Lesson 1

ENGLISH 101: CRITICAL THINKING AND READING

Reading: Carefully read this passage.

1 The need for critical thinking and reading has never been so acute as it is today. Day in and day out, bombarded with reams and reams of information by the mass media—print, broadcast, and now the World Wide Web—we are asked to absorb and digest news reports from sources of all kinds. Which are reliable, which aren't? Politicians of all parties and every <u>persuasion</u> promise us the same peace and prosperity. Who are we to believe? Advertisements and commercials plug every product under the sun. Can they all be as beneficial and necessary to our lives as the advertisers say <u>they</u> are? Hollywood and television present us with docudramas and biopics that tread a very thin line between historical fact and historical fiction. What's true and what isn't? Browsing the Internet, we find ourselves faced with a growing number of "blogs," websites that profess to be the new, alternative journalism—the "people's" answer to the mainstream media. But can we trust the information the bloggers give us? How much is objective fact, and how much personal opinion?

2 1. To sort through all this information, we need to think more critically. 2. To do this, we must develop sound skills and reliable standards for analyzing and evaluating not only information, but our own individual thought patterns and motives as well. 3. We must then habitually apply these skills and standards in such a way that allows us to continue to grow and improve intellectually. 4.

3 This isn't easy to do. We are all products of our upbringing and cultural environment. These often instill in us a narrow or slanted way of seeing the world, giving us a set of assumptions, beliefs, and prejudices that we are loath to part with—that we believe *are* us. Threatened by new information or ideas, we do whatever we can to protect our hard-won knowledge, preserve our <u>precious</u> beliefs, stand by our old opinions. In other words, we think uncritically.

4 Non-critical thinkers take a simplistic, black-white, yes-no view of the world. They close their minds to the world's possibilities and complexities, missing subtle connections and relations and failing to <u>discern</u> deeper meanings. They insist that *their* facts are the only relevant ones, believe that *their* interests and perspectives are the only valid ones.

5 Critical thinkers, on the other hand, are characterized by open-mindedness, honesty, self-awareness, and rationality. They have a sense of curiosity about the world and remain open to new and different interpretations of it. They listen carefully to others, adjusting their viewpoint when presented with new and better evidence. When the need arises, they are willing to acknowledge that their information or understanding may be faulty or lacking, or their motives driven by self-delusion and self-interest. When confronted with sufficient evidence, critical thinkers can see through their prejudices and biases. <u>They rely on reason rather than emotion and strive to find the best explanation for something rather than stubbornly insist that they are right</u>. Critical thinkers also realize that critical thinking doesn't come overnight; it is a skill that is acquired gradually through trial and error, a habit of mind that builds on itself over the course of a lifetime.

6 Critical thinking and critical reading go hand in hand. Critical reading is a technique for uncovering information and ideas within a text. **1.** Critical readers are active readers who have developed certain skills that allow them to engage directly with a piece of writing. **2.** They pre-read or skim a text to see what its main topics are, what its overall purpose or strategy is, how it is organized, and what key words and phrases are italicized, boldfaced, or otherwise highlighted. **3.** Then, as they read slowly and carefully through the text, they underline key ideas and information, circle important or unfamiliar words. As they go along, they ask questions and make observations that occur to them about the author's choice of words, citing of details, and use of supporting evidence for his/her arguments. **4.**

7 Finally, having read actively through a text using these techniques, the critical reader is then ready to go back through it and apply his/her critical-thinking skills to it.

Exercises: Complete the sentences or answer the questions below with the correct choices, or follow the instructions.

1. In paragraph 1, all of the following are mentioned as sources of information today EXCEPT

    (A) Web logs
    (B) radio and TV
    (C) university lectures
    (D) newspapers and magazines

2. The underlined word **persuasion** in paragraph 1 is closest in meaning to

    (A) influence
    (B) nationality
    (C) ethnicity
    (D) creed

3. The underlined word **they** in paragraph 1 refers to

    (A) products
    (B) advertisements
    (C) parties
    (D) the mass media

4. It can be inferred from paragraph 1 that the author believes that

    (A) people should be skeptical about the information that is presented to them
    (B) there is simply too much information, and it should be limited
    (C) the mass media can never be trusted to tell the truth
    (D) blogs speak for the people and will one day replace traditional media sources

5. Look at the four numbers that indicate where the following sentence could be added to paragraph 2.

   Critical thinking may be defined simply as our ability to think for ourselves.

   Where would the sentence best fit?
   (1)   (2)   (3)   (4)

6. In paragraph 3, what does the author say non-critical thinking often leads us to do?

   (A) look down on other people
   (B) despise our own upbringing and culture
   (C) look for relevant or new facts and evidence
   (D) see the world in a narrow, prejudiced way

7. In paragraph 3, why does the author use the underlined word **precious** to describe people's beliefs?

   (A) to emphasize why people don't like to part with them
   (B) to cast doubt on the beliefs themselves
   (C) to show how our beliefs really do define who we are
   (D) to connect this paragraph with the one that follows

8. The underlined word **discern** in paragraph 4 is closest in meaning to

   (A) make judgments about
   (B) recognize
   (C) sympathize with
   (D) approve of

9. In paragraph 5, the author mentions curiosity about the world as an example of

   (A) honesty
   (B) self-awareness
   (C) open-mindedness
   (D) rationality

10. Which sentence below best expresses the essential information in the underlined sentence in paragraph 5? Incorrect choices change the meaning in important ways or leave out essential information.

    (A) Critical thinkers are more rational than non-critical thinkers.
    (B) The best explanation isn't always the right or rational explanation.
    (C) Critical thinkers don't let pig-headedness, pride, and self-righteousness get in the way of finding rational explanations for things.
    (D) It is not always necessary to be right.

11. In paragraph 5, what does the author say that critical thinkers realize?

    (A) that critical thinking is an emotional habit of mind
    (B) that their ideas and information are always faulty and need to be replaced
    (C) that they cannot expect to develop critical-thinking skills easily and quickly and must learn from their mistakes
    (D) that most people's understanding is a product of self-delusion and self-awareness

12. Look at the four numbers that indicate where the following sentence could be added to paragraph 6.

They annotate the text, too, using the margins to record their doubts about and reactions to what they are reading, noting down how the text differs from or resembles their own beliefs and values.

Where would the sentence best fit?
(1)   (2)   (3)   (4)

Lesson 2

ENGLISH 102: ESSAY TYPES AND STRATEGIES

Reading: Carefully read this passage.

1 An essay is a short, non-fiction prose composition which takes up a wide variety of subjects using a diversity of writing strategies and techniques. The "father" of the modern essay is usually said to be Michel de Montaigne, a 16th-century French aristocrat and civic leader who, repulsed by the violent religious quarrels then tearing France apart, retired from public life at the age of 38 to devote himself to reading and reflection and to the composition of what he called "essais," a word coined from the French verb for "to attempt." And attempt is what Montaigne did—attempt to understand himself and human nature, attempt to discover a more humane and rational way of living.

2 Built up on the foundation laid by Montaigne, the essay today has evolved into one of the most flexible of all literary forms, adaptable to almost any authorial aim or intention. An essay can entertain, inform, persuade, argue a point, tell a story. It can be informal and personal, dealing with everyday topics and experiences in a relaxed, colloquial style; or it can be formal and academic, exploring such weighty subjects as art, philosophy, history, and literature.

3 There are many different types of essay, each with a specific writing strategy adopted to carry out its overall purpose. *Descriptive* essays aim to convey, using words only, the perceptions of the five senses—to paint a verbal picture of a person, place, or thing. Some descriptive essays are objective and try to present as factual a picture as possible of the object being described, subordinating the author's personal response to it. Subjective essays are more impressionistic, with the writer's thoughts and feelings about the object more prominently displayed.

4 Another type of essay adopts *illustration*, or example, as its main strategy to explain or clarify the ideas it is putting forth. **1.** An example can be a telling anecdote such as a story from the author's own life, or one he or she has heard or read about, that brings an idea to life. **2.** It can also be a list of specific details—important facts and figures that make a generalization more interesting and convincing. **3.** It is essential that the example be both relevant to the point the writer is making and representative enough to strike a familiar chord in the reader's mind. **4.**

5 Asking questions about why things happen in the way they do is an outgrowth of people's natural curiosity about important relationships between circumstances or events. The *cause and effect analysis* essay attempts to answer such questions and to understand such relationships. This is often easier said than done. <u>The writer must look beyond the immediate causes of, say, a nation's declining birthrate, to the remote causes which might be less obvious but equally important.</u> The writer may also need to trace what is known as a causal chain, going back from the particular effect that is the subject of the essay through a long series of events to the initial cause that put the <u>process</u> in motion.

6 The *process analysis* essay is similar to the cause and effect essay in that it outlines a series of steps or stages—a process—that follow each other in a specific order, leading to a particular end or goal. Each step of the process—how to conduct a multicultural management meeting, for example, or how plants generate oxygen—is separated and described in precise detail and arranged in its proper order.

7 Perhaps the most common type of essay is that which examines the similarities and differences between two or more objects, concepts, people, or places. Good writers know that in such *comparison and contrast* essays, they can influence or persuade the reader most effectively by making sure the things being discussed have a strong basis for comparison, that is, that they belong to the same general category (four video camera models, for example, or baseball in Japan, South Korea, and the United States). Such essays are also more memorable and effective when they avoid the obvious by comparing objects usually considered dissimilar and by contrasting objects normally thought to be nearly the same.

8 Other essay types include the *narrative* essay, which narrates a story or sequence of events, and the essay of *classification*, an example of which is the one you are reading right now. Although there are many different kinds of essay, most are a blend of various types and utilize a variety of strategies to get their point across and fulfill their purpose.

Exercises: Complete the sentences or answer the questions below with the correct choices, or follow the instructions.

1. It can be reasonably inferred from paragraph 1 that

    (A) Montaigne was a regular churchgoer
    (B) an essay can be of book length as well
    (C) Montaigne's essays were originally published in France
    (D) Montaigne was a fairly wealthy man

2. The underlined word **repulsed** in paragraph 1 is closest in meaning to

    (A) disgusted
    (B) affected
    (C) threatened
    (D) turned away

3. According to paragraph 2, which of the following is true?

    (A) Montaigne's influence on the modern essay has been negligible.
    (B) Authors choose to write essays for diverse reasons and purposes.
    (C) Compositions that look into serious subjects like art and philosophy are too formal to be considered real essays.
    (D) Essays are meant to enlighten and inform the reader, not provide pleasure.

4. The underlined word **its** in paragraph 3 refers to

    (A) writing
    (B) strategy
    (C) each
    (D) essay

5. The underlined word **subordinating** in paragraph 3 can be paraphrased as

   (A) eliminating altogether
   (B) replacing in part
   (C) lessening in importance
   (D) re-emphasizing

6. All of the following are mentioned in relation to a descriptive essay EXCEPT that it

   (A) is usually informal in style
   (B) is either impressionistic or detached in point of view
   (C) draws a picture verbally
   (D) shows how an object appears to the senses

7. Look at the four numbers that indicate where the following sentence could be added to paragraph 4.

   To illustrate an assertion that a new school policy has caused an increase in bullying, for example, an author must choose a story or statistic that not only directly supports the assertion, but that is also something that readers can readily relate to and identity with.

   Where would the sentence best fit?
       (1)   (2)   (3)   (4)

8. Which sentence below best expresses the essential information in the underlined sentence in paragraph 5? Incorrect choices change the meaning in important ways or leave out essential information.

   (A) The causes of some phenomena are readily apparent and require no further examination by the author.
   (B) A nation's declining birthrate may be an example of the immediate cause of something rather than its immediate effect.
   (C) The more remote a cause, the less important it becomes to both reader and writer.
   (D) An essay is not successful if it takes the cause of something for granted and overlooks other significant causes which may at first not be apparent.

9. Why most likely does the author use the underlined word **process** at the end of paragraph 5?

   (A) as a transitional concept leading into the next paragraph
   (B) to re-emphasize what the subject of the essay is
   (C) in order to show that every effect is the result of a long series of actions or events
   (D) as an efficient way of summarizing the general contents of the entire paragraph

10. The author makes all of the following points about the process analysis essay EXCEPT that

    (A) it resembles the cause and effect essay
    (B) it breaks the process down into specific steps
    (C) it reverses the order of the process to make it easier to understand
    (D) it shows how a particular end is achieved

11. In paragraph 7, why does the author say that avoiding obvious comparisons and contrasts makes a comparison essay more effective?

    (A) Because it makes a more vivid impression on the reader.
    (B) Because readers prefer not to have to read between the lines.
    (C) Because it satisfies the formal requirements of literary writing.
    (D) Because the more obvious things are, the more memorable they become.

12. An introductory sentence for a brief summary of the passage is provided below. Complete the summary by selecting the THREE answer choices that express the most important ideas in the passage. Some sentences do not belong in the summary because they express ideas that are not presented or are minor ideas in the passage.

    Essays are one of the most varied and adaptable of literary forms and can be familiar or formal, colloquial or academic.

    (A) An example of a process analysis essay would be one that shows how plants generate oxygen.
    (B) Montaigne retired from public life to read, reflect, and write.
    (C) The word *essai*, from the French for "to attempt," was coined by Michel de Montaigne to describe the type of writing he was doing and aptly defines the modern essay as well.
    (D) The personal essay is no longer as popular as it once was, having been replaced by essays that discuss weightier subjects.
    (E) Although essays come in a wide variety of types, most essays combine cause and effect analysis, description, illustration, comparison and contrast, and other strategies.
    (F) The good essayist always keeps in mind the effect he or she wants to make on readers and tries to convey his or her ideas as clearly and memorably as possible.

Lesson 3

COLOR

Reading: Carefully read this passage.

1 The sun's electromagnetic radiation, more commonly referred to simply as light, is distinguished by a physical property known as wavelength, or frequency. A wavelength is the distance between two <u>adjacent</u> rays of light. The light human beings can perceive, or visible light, is only a miniscule fraction of all the light that makes up the electromagnetic spectrum. Wavelengths of perceivable light are measured in billionths of a meter, or nanometers (nm), with the normal human eye only being able to detect the range of wavelengths from approximately 400 nm to 700 nm.

2 Color is defined as the effect produced on the eye of a human observer caused by different wavelengths of light. As Sir Isaac Newton first discovered when he used a diffracting prism to separate sunlight into all the colors of the rainbow, people perceive light beams of specific frequencies as specific colors—from blue-violet at the lower end of the visible spectrum (400 nm) to red-orange at the higher (700 nm). <u>It is important to remember that light is described in terms of wavelength only, while color exists only in a person's interpretation of those wavelengths.</u>

3 Everything we see around us absorbs and reflects wavelengths of light at different intensities. The light transmitted by an object—a ripe tomato, say, or a painting by Paul Gauguin—stimulates the various "color-coded" receptors, known as cones, in the eye's retina. The retina then sends signals to the brain, which processes the information encapsulated in the light and allows us to see <u>it</u> as a certain color. An <u>opaque</u> object that *reflects* all wavelengths of light appears to us as white, while an object that *absorbs* all wavelengths of light is experienced as black. Black and white, however, are not normally considered true colors; the former is said to be the absence of color, the latter all colors mixed together. Incidentally, scientists estimate that the human eye and brain can discriminate up to seven million different colors, though of course we are only capable of labeling a tiny number of them.

4 Colors, and how we perceive them, are important to people in untold ways. (A) Throughout history colors have played an indispensable role in our personal and social lives. Color is the primary means by which we identify physical objects and bring order to the world. (B) Although the significance of particular colors may vary from one culture to another, color itself is the <u>impetus</u> behind much of our symbolic thought. (C) Red, green, and blue are known as the additive primaries, while yellow, magenta, and cyan are subtractive primaries. Colors help define our loyalties and affiliations and religious beliefs, organize our ceremonial and ritualistic practices, and describe our moods. (D) Colors can shock, warn, delight, frighten, soothe, anger, impress. Color-based idioms and metaphors form a rich and essential part of the everyday lexicon, enabling us to vividly express our thoughts and emotions: seeing red, feeling blue, green with envy, a yellow-bellied coward, and purple prose are just a few of hundreds of such expressions.

5 1. In western culture, black and white, though, as mentioned above, not technically colors at all, are rich with symbolic connotation. 2. Black is associated with primeval darkness, chaos, anguish, wickedness, the unconscious mind, and death. 3. Black is the color of mourning, a sign that the wearer of the black garment has suffered irreversible loss and inconsolable hopelessness and despair. 4. A black mood is a feeling of depression and disaffection. The black sheep of a family is the member who never amounts to anything and often brings opprobrium and ruin on the entire clan.

6 Symbolically speaking, the color white is the antithesis of black, positive in meaning and rich with potential. White is associated with daylight and dazzling brightness and thus serves as a symbol of revelation and enlightenment, of intellectual awakening. White represents purity and innocence, as in a bride's wedding gown. White, like the first food, milk, is emblematic of birth and fertility—the promise of plenty. White is order, maturity, and responsibility.

7 Although black and white respectively have their contradictory positive and negative emblematic significance—a black tuxedo is the epitome of elegance and prestige, for example, while to wave a white flag is to submit and surrender—it is in their most commonly recognized symbolic connotations that, when applied to skin pigmentation and race, they breed prejudice and discrimination and have given birth to some of the most deplorable and regrettable aspects of human history.

Exercises: Complete the sentences or answer the questions below with the correct choices, or follow the instructions.

1. The underlined word **adjacent** in paragraph 1 is closest in meaning to

    (A) similar
    (B) perceivable
    (C) contrasting
    (D) neighboring

2. The author's purpose in describing and defining light in paragraph 1 is to

    (A) point out that wavelengths are measured in nanometers, or billionths of a meter
    (B) emphasize how important the sun's electromagnetic radiation is to us
    (C) make sure that readers understand what light is before introducing the concept of color
    (D) stress that only a small fraction of what makes up the electromagnetic spectrum is visible to humans

3. The author mentions Sir Isaac Newton in paragraph 2 as

    (A) the first scientist to observe a rainbow
    (B) a pioneer in the study of light and color
    (C) an example of the average human observer
    (D) the inventor of a diffracting prism

Lesson 3

4. Which sentence below *most effectively* summarizes the main idea of the underlined sentence in paragraph 2?

    (A) In fact, we see wavelengths, not colors.
    (B) It is essential that we endeavor to never forget that when it comes to the method of the description of light, this can only be accomplished by means of measuring or distinguishing what its different wavelengths are, while, on the contrary, it is only in the mind and imagination of the human observer that the concept of color is actually seen, recognized, and remembered.
    (C) Keep in mind that light comes in wavelengths, while color is how we *perceive* those wavelengths.
    (D) Let me remind you that light cannot be described; it can only be perceived.

5. The underlined word **it** in paragraph 3 refers to

    (A) the retina
    (B) the brain
    (C) the information
    (D) the light

6. The underlined word **opaque** as used in paragraph 3 may be paraphrased as

    (A) impenetrable by light
    (B) clear and transparent
    (C) easily visible
    (D) unintelligible

7. The author makes all of the following points in paragraph 3 EXCEPT
    (A) different objects transmit and absorb light differently
    (B) the eye's retina contains cones, or receptors, for picking up light signals
    (C) because of their special properties, black and white are considered the only genuine colors
    (D) we can name only a miniscule fraction of the colors we are capable of distinguishing

8. The underlined word **impetus** in paragraph 4 is closest in meaning to
    (A) stimulus
    (B) similarity
    (C) difference
    (D) explanation

9. Look at the four lettered sentences in paragraph 4. Which one does not belong in the paragraph or is out of place in it?

    (A)   (B)   (C)   (D)

10. Look at the four numbers that indicate where the following sentence could be added to paragraph 5.

    In the English language, black has yielded an extensive list of phrases and metaphors to express the dark, gloomy, negative side of life.

    Where would the sentence best fit?
    (1)   (2)   (3)   (4)

Lesson 3

11. Match the symbolic meanings below to the color they are derived from, black or white. Write the letters of the choices in the parentheses. TWO of the choices will NOT be used.

    (A) evil and suffering
    (B) defeat
    (C) grief
    (D) anger and envy
    (E) sophistication and influence
    (F) knowledge and wisdom
    (G) fear and cowardice
    (H) future prosperity
    (I) failure and shame
    (J) virginity

    Black ( ), ( ), ( ), ( )

    White ( ), ( ), ( ), ( )

12. Which of the following sentences would make the best introductory sentence for a brief summary of the passage?

    (A) The history of color goes back to Sir Isaac Newton, who was the first to use a diffracting prism to observe all the various colors of the rainbow.
    (B) Color, which is how humans perceive the different frequencies of light, not only helps us make sense of the world we live in, but has many symbolic and linguistic uses as well.
    (C) Though they are respectively the absence of all color and a blend of all colors, white and black are rich in color symbolism.
    (D) Not everyone sees colors in the same way since the perception of color is a complicated process involving light, the cones in the retina, and the color-processing center of the human brain.

Lesson 4

BATS

Reading: Carefully read this passage.

1 Bats, leathery-winged mammals of the order Chiroptera, distinguished by their furry bodies and mouse-like features, are the second most numerous mammal after rodents, with an estimated 900 to 1,100 living species. They are found in forests, deserts, open fields, and urban and suburban environments throughout the world (excluding extreme polar regions), with the greatest distribution in tropical areas.

2 Bats range greatly in size. The Malayan flying fox, for example, has a wingspan of up to six feet. The blossom bat of Australia measures only an inch or two across. Most species of bat are nocturnal, doing their hunting and feeding at night and spending their days hanging upside down in hollow trees, caves, or other dark places. Some bat species hibernate during the winter months; others migrate to more comfortable climates. Some bats are solitary, while others are communal, with thousands, even millions, grouping together in colonies for warmth and security, communicating warnings and other messages to one another through a variety of meaningful sounds. Bats also exhibit <u>altruistic</u> behavior, with colony members helping feed and protect ill or injured fellows.

3 Though some 25 percent of bat species are now on the verge of extinction owing to habitat destruction, as a group, bats have shown amazing environmental adaptability, having survived for 50 to 100 million years. <u>Bats are surprisingly long-lived, since longevity in mammals generally correlates with body size.</u> Even the tiniest can live as long as 30 years in the wild.

4 Bat species are traditionally divided into two major groups. Megachiroptera, or megabats, are primarily vegetarian, feeding on fruits, plants, pollen, and nectar. Microchiroptera, or microbats, are either insectivores or carnivores. Of the latter, three known "vampire bat" species survive exclusively on the blood of other vertebrates.

5 Megabats and microbats differ in other important ways, particularly when it comes to perception and navigation. Megabats orient with their eyes,

Lesson 4

which are large and prominent. Microbats, whose eyes are generally very small, navigate by means of *echolocation*. This is an echo-based radar system that enables a bat to calculate how far away an object is by, first, "shouting" out high-pitched sounds through its mouth or nose, then listening carefully for echoes that reverberate back to it, and, finally, determining how long the noise takes to return. Echolocation also tells the bat how big the object is, whether it's to the right or left, and in what direction it is heading.

6 Female bats give birth to one or two "pups" a year. Newborn bats are completely dependent on their mothers for protection and <u>nourishment</u>. When a bat mother goes out foraging for fruit or insects, her pup stays behind, clustered together with the thousands of other pups in the colony to keep warm. When the mother returns, she immediately picks her own pup out of all the others through scent and sound.

7 Of course, the bat characteristic that most obviously distinguishes it from other mammals is flight. While some mammals, lemurs and the so-called flying squirrels, for instance, can glide through the air for short spans, bats have a special wing structure that makes them the only mammal capable of sustained, <u>maneuverable</u> flight. This distance and control are accomplished by means of a specially-structured wing, which more resembles a human arm and hand than a bird's wing. This "hand and arm" is connected to the bat's body by a thin membrane of skin (called the patagium), and it is this that allows it to fly. The bat's "hand" also has a sharp claw at the end for climbing trees and other structures, which is convenient because, unlike birds, bats cannot take flight from a standing position. To fly, bats have to climb to a high location, hang upside down, and then swoop into flight.

8 Legend and rabies fears have given bats a reputation as being harmful and dangerous. But bats actually benefit humans in a variety of ways. For one, they prey omnivorously on insects that damage crops or transmit disease. For another, their feces (guano) provide farmers with a rich <u>organic</u> fertilizer. For a third, fruit-eating bats help maintain biodiversity by dispersing seeds, while pollen- and nectar-eating bats are active plant pollinators. Bats, in other words, are more friend than foe.

Exercises: Complete the sentences or answer the questions below with the correct choices, or follow the instructions.

1. According to paragraph 1, which of the following statements is true?

    (A) Bats tend to avoid areas where people live.
    (B) Bats can even survive in extremely cold climates.
    (C) Bat species outnumber rodent species by two to one.
    (D) Most bats are found in regions near the equator.

2. According to paragraph 2, what do bats do at night?

    (A) look for food
    (B) hang upside down in caves
    (C) look for a place to sleep
    (D) migrate to warmer regions

3. According to paragraph 2, bats live in colonies

    (A) in order to send messages to each other
    (B) because they are solitary by nature
    (C) to stay warm and safe
    (D) to secure food

4. The underlined word **altruistic** in paragraph 2 is closest in meaning to

    (A) needing constant care and attention
    (B) competitive
    (C) loving and generous
    (D) remarkable

Lesson 4

5. Which sentence below best sums up the point being made in the underlined sentence in paragraph 3?

    (A) Despite being mammals, bats live longer than their small size would lead you to expect.
    (B) Larger mammals tend to live surprisingly longer lives than bats.
    (C) Surprisingly, the smaller a bat is, the shorter its life expectancy is.
    (D) Bats live as long as most mammals of similar size.

6. In paragraph 4, vampire bats are specifically mentioned as an example of

    (A) a megabat insectivore
    (B) a microbat insectivore
    (C) a megabat carnivore
    (D) a microbat carnivore

7. In paragraph 5, all of the following are mentioned as steps in the echolocation process EXCEPT

    (A) determining the location and size of an object
    (B) emitting sound signals
    (C) heading in the direction of the object
    (D) calculating an object's distance

8. The underlined word **nourishment** in paragraph 6 is closest in meaning to

    (A) food
    (B) security
    (C) care
    (D) warmth

9. According to paragraph 6, bat mothers can distinguish their children by

    (A) sending out echolocation signals
    (B) their sight and appearance
    (C) the noises and smells they give off
    (D) shouting for them

10. The underlined word **maneuverable** in paragraph 7 may be paraphrased as

    (A) capable of changing courses and directions
    (B) continuous and long-lasting
    (C) bird-like
    (D) high-altitude

11. The most important point that the author makes in paragraph 7 about the bat's ability to fly is that

    (A) the bat has a sharp claw at the end of its wing
    (B) the bat must fall into flight, not lift into it
    (C) the bat has a wing similar to the human hand and arm
    (D) the bat does not resemble the flying squirrel or lemur

12. Which sentence below would make the best introductory sentence for a brief summary of the passage?

   (A) Unlike other squirrels, bats can really fly as well as be vegetarians, insectivores, and carnivores.
   (B) Bats, the only flying mammal, exhibit a variety of unusual characteristics and capabilities that make them both feared by and useful to humans.
   (C) In addition to their agricultural importance, bats have also had great cultural and symbolic significance throughout man's history.
   (D) Bats are found all over the world, particularly in tropical climates, and many migrate from place to place in large colonies as well.

Lesson 5

PAINTING AND OIL PAINTING

Reading: Carefully read this passage.

1. In 1940, some adventurous boys were out exploring the limestone hills near the village of Lascaux in southern France. One of the boys' dogs wandered off, and they all went looking for it. Their search took them down a narrow ravine into a dark, winding cave. Deep inside, the boys shone their flashlights on the white limestone walls and ceilings, and there, to their astonishment, was a tremendous "gallery" of animal paintings—horses, stags, cattle, and even a rhinoceros—caught in amazingly lifelike motion. The boys had <u>inadvertently</u> stumbled across the greatest exhibit of Paleolithic cave art ever discovered. Dating back some 15,000 years, the paintings represent human beings' first known attempts to recreate images of the world they live in—to express themselves through art and, in particular, painting.

2. Painting is the application of pigment to a surface in order to produce, by means of color, composition, and the interplay of dark and light, either a naturalistic representation of the "real" world or a more abstract manifestation of the artist's personal vision. Stone Age artists achieved their paintings by first using a sharp rock or shattered bone to <u>etch</u> the animal figures into the limestone. They then colored them with dyes made from things found in nature—red from iron oxide, blue from indigo, yellow from saffron, black from charcoal, white from ground fossil shells, and so on. <u>Ever since, artists have endeavored to come up with media and techniques that more effectively reproduce their desired effects and more stubbornly withstand the ravages of time and the elements.</u>

3. Artistic paints require both a pigment to give them color and a binder to make them adhere to a surface. Ancient Egyptian painters mixed their pigments with a resin derived from the acacia tree. Greek and later artists bound color with egg and beeswax. It wasn't until the 15th century, however, that the Dutch artist Jan van Eyck (c. 1390-1441) invented oil paint, the artistic medium still regarded today as the "standard" for all painters and the centerpiece of all the visual arts.

Lesson 5

4 Van Eyck's new medium quickly caught on and spread throughout Renaissance Europe. Italian artists welcomed it as the answer to their need for a type of paint that would be less affected by high temperature and moisture. Northern artists saw it as an alternative to the fresco (painting on fresh, moist plaster), which was difficult to pull off in colder climates.

5 **1.** Oil paint is a slow-drying paint in which pigment particles are bound or suspended in various oils, most commonly linseed oil from the flax plant. **2.** Other binders can distort the purity of the pigment, tinting a painting with unwanted hues and dulling its surface sheen. Not oil. **3.** Oil is what gives an oil painting its unsurpassed luminosity, depth, and brilliance. **4.** It is also what makes oil paint such a flexible and versatile medium.

6 Van Eyck himself, using painting techniques more suitable to previously employed media such as tempera, applied the new paint he had invented very thinly, almost transparently, with delicate, hidden brushstrokes, building up one thin layer of paint over another, a technique known as glazing. But other artists, less <u>inhibited</u> by formal rules and restraints, soon recognized oil's great potential and began experimenting with new techniques that took advantage of its inherent qualities. For example, in his religious paintings, the Italian master Titian (c. 1488-1576) introduced the more energetic use of color and bolder, more visible brushstrokes, while van Eyck's 17th-century compatriot, Rembrandt, caused shockwaves when he produced portraits and landscapes with thick, textured, almost sculptured surfaces, leaving gaps in the paint and brush marks for all to see.

7 Today, artists use oil paint in such diverse ways that it is often hard to recognize it as oil. But most oil paintings are still done in stages according to the old "fat over lean" principle. This stipulates that less oily (lean) paint, usually thinned with turpentine, should be applied to the canvas first, with progressively oily (fat) paints added as the lower layers dry. In contrast, *alla prima*, or "wet into wet" paintings, are usually done in one sitting, allowing the artist to record his or her impressions quickly and spontaneously and the colors to bleed and blend into each other.

Exercises: Complete the sentences or answer the questions below with the correct choices, or follow the instructions.

1. The author starts the passage off with a short anecdote

   (A) to show how far back in history man's urge for art, especially painting, goes
   (B) to emphasize that boys will always be boys and seek adventure wherever and whenever they can
   (C) to show how fortunate it was that the boys had brought flashlights with them for exploring the cave
   (D) to point out that the animal we know as the rhinoceros was already in existence even in Paleolithic times

2. The underlined word **inadvertently** in paragraph 1 is closest in meaning to

   (A) mistakenly
   (B) carelessly
   (C) incredibly
   (D) accidentally

3. According to paragraph 2, which of the following statements best sums up what artists hope to create in their paintings?

   (A) color and composition
   (B) contrasts between light and shadow
   (C) products of their observation and imagination
   (D) more effective techniques

Lesson 5

4. The underlined word **etch** in paragraph 2 is closest in meaning to

    (A) scratch
    (B) dye
    (C) trace
    (D) stain

5. Which sentence below best expresses the essential information in the underlined sentence in paragraph 2? Incorrect choices change the meaning in important ways or leave out essential information.

    (A) Artists needed paints that would not be affected by weather and the passing of time.
    (B) Time and climate can crack the paint, dull its colors, and warp the canvas to the point where the painting no longer looks like the original.
    (C) Subsequently, painters have sought paints and methods that would better express their vision and resist aging and deterioration.
    (D) Since then, artists have known that without the proper materials and methods, they cannot accurately express what they want to express in their paintings.

6. In paragraph 3, the author mentions the acacia tree as

    (A) a pigment used in ancient Egypt
    (B) an Egyptian resin
    (C) the source of a binder used by Egyptian artists
    (D) a common plant found in ancient Egypt

7. In paragraph 3, by calling oil paint the "standard," the author implies that of all the artistic media it is the

   (A) most interesting
   (B) most respected
   (C) most traditional
   (D) most experimental

8. It can be inferred from paragraph 4 that

   (A) Van Eyck traveled throughout Europe himself promoting his new medium
   (B) fresco painting soon died out all over Europe
   (C) Italian and northern artists used oil paint in precisely the same way
   (D) Italy's climate is characterized by heat and humidity

9. Look at the four numbers that indicate where the following sentence could be added to paragraph 5.

   What makes oil paint so effective as an artistic medium is the oil itself.

   Where would the sentence best fit?
   (1)   (2)   (3)   (4)

10. The underlined word **inhibited** in paragraph 6 is closest in meaning to

    (A) affected
    (B) impressed
    (C) restrained
    (D) shaped

11. All of the following are explained in paragraph 6 EXCEPT

 (A) what "glazing" refers to
 (B) what exactly "tempera" painting is
 (C) Rembrandt's country of origin
 (D) the thematic nature of Titian's art

12. The most salient feature of the "wet into wet" style of painting described in paragraph 7 is that

 (A) it is known as *alla prima* in Latin
 (B) it can take up to several months to complete
 (C) it is done offhand without waiting for the paint to dry
 (D) it allows the artist to record his or her impressions

Lesson 6

ENERGY AND ENERGY SOURCES

Reading: Carefully read this passage.

1 Without energy, nothing would ever happen, nothing would ever change. No work would ever get done. * Indeed, the English word "energy" has its roots in the ancient Greek term *energos*, meaning "activity" or "work." But the fact is, as the Nobel Prize-winning physicist Richard Feynman confessed in his book, *Lectures on Physics*, "It is important to realize that in physics today, we have no knowledge of what energy is. We do not have an accurate picture that energy comes in little blobs of a definite amount."

2 Generally speaking, then, energy is an abstract concept used to explain a variety of natural phenomena, and though an accurate picture of what it really is may elude us, we can state with confidence that energy is a property or characteristic inherent in all matter that makes, or has the potential to make, things happen.

3 Energy is usually grouped into two broad categories, *potential* and *kinetic*. Potential energy is the capacity for doing work that a resting body possesses because of its condition or position relative to other bodies or objects. The classic example is a boulder sitting on the edge of a steep cliff. The boulder has potential energy due to its position in earth's gravitational field. If, however, some force (an earthquake, for example) should cause it to fall, gravity will act on it, pulling it downward until it crashes to the ground. During the boulder's descent, its potential energy changes to kinetic energy, which is the energy a body or object has because it is in motion. (The kinetic energy of a moving body can be measured using the formula $KE = 1/2 mv^2$, where KE stands for kinetic energy, m equals the body's mass or weight, and v is its velocity.) Once the boulder comes to rest at the bottom of the cliff, its kinetic energy reverts to potential energy, though its capacity for making things happen has been reduced because its circumstances have changed—from teetering precariously on a precipice to sitting solidly on a flat surface.

4 (A) The ability to be transformed or converted from one form to another—from chemical energy into heat and light, as in combustion, for example—is what gives energy its great practical importance. (B) The development of civilized society, the progress of science, and the quest for energy have always gone hand in hand. (C) Although energy can be converted from one form to another, the Law of the Conservation of Energy states that energy can neither be destroyed nor created. (D) It is no exaggeration to say that it is in the search for new and better sources of energy—starting with animal, wind, and water power and up through the development of the internal combustion engine, hydroelectric dams, and nuclear reactors—that man's ingenuity has manifested itself most prominently and his understanding of the natural world most significantly deepened.

5 Modern society, with its burgeoning populations and vast array of sophisticated technological goods, has developed an almost <u>insatiable</u> demand for energy. Until recently, it has been primarily fossil fuels that have lit our homes, powered our factories, run our appliances, driven our planes, trains, and automobiles. But fossil fuels are a finite energy source—and an environmental nightmare. Arguably, the greatest challenge facing us today is to find renewable, non-polluting, alternative cheap sources of energy that can free us from our slavish dependence on gas and oil.

6 While advances in solar power and geothermal energy technology are making these an increasingly viable alternative, the most exciting prospect for a virtually infinite source of energy is the hydrogen fuel cell. Imagine a battery that never runs down. Though challenges still remain to perfect it, a fuel cell is just that. Like a conventional battery, it produces electricity through a chemical reaction. But unlike a conventional battery, it can keep on generating power indefinitely as long as it is supplied with hydrogen. And the only waste product it gives off is pure water. The fuel cell's potential as the motive power for all our domestic, transportation, and industrial needs is immeasurable.

Exercises: Complete the sentences or answer the questions below with the correct choices, or follow the instructions.

1. Look at the * in paragraph 1 where one of the sentences below could be added. Which sentence would best fit?

    (A) Of course, we must also define what we mean by the word "happen."
    (B) In physics, "work" is defined as "the transfer of energy from one body to another by means of a certain force."
    (C) The standard textbook definition of energy takes this into account when it calls energy "the ability or the capacity to cause change or to do work."
    (D) But of course, there is energy—and lots of it.

2. The author mentions Richard Feynman as an example of

    (A) a Nobel Prize winner
    (B) someone who might be expected to know what energy is
    (C) a well-known science author
    (D) a popular lecturer on science matters

3. The underlined word **elude** in paragraph 2 is closest in meaning to

    (A) cause confusion
    (B) be difficult to come up with
    (C) compromise
    (D) run away from

Lesson 6

4. Which sentence below best expresses the essential information in the underlined clause in paragraph 2? Incorrect choices change the meaning in important ways or leave out essential information.

   (A) It is a fact that energy is found in all matter and can work to bring about change.
   (B) Obviously, everything contains energy for a variety of purposes.
   (C) As a matter of fact, energy is potentially useful to us and comes in many forms of matter.
   (D) Energy makes things happen, no matter what its characteristics are.

5. In paragraph 3, what important point does the author make about potential energy?

   (A) Its capacity for work depends on where the body that contains it is situated and what it is near.
   (B) It is one of the various natural phenomena that the concept of energy is used to explain.
   (C) It is subject to earthquakes.
   (D) A falling boulder will eventually crash to the ground and come to a stop on a flat surface.

6. All of the following apply to kinetic energy EXCEPT

   (A) it is the energy a body has while in motion
   (B) it can be abbreviated as KE in formulas for measuring it
   (C) it is always equal to one-half the mass of the body it is contained in
   (D) the speed at which a body moves must be calculated into the measurement of its kinetic energy capacity

7. The underlined word **precariously** in paragraph 3 is closest in meaning to

   (A) unsteadily
   (B) temporarily
   (C) securely
   (D) high

8. Look at the four lettered sentences in paragraph 4. Which one does not belong in the paragraph or is out of place in it?

   (A)   (B)   (C)   (D)

9. The underlined word **insatiable** in paragraph 5 is closest in meaning to

   (A) growing
   (B) greedy
   (C) amazing
   (D) disgusting

10. In paragraph 5, the author mentions gas and oil as examples of

    (A) fossil fuels
    (B) environmental pollution
    (C) a cheap source of power
    (D) mankind's slavish dependence

11. It can be inferred from paragraph 6 that

    (A) hydrogen fuel cells are less expensive than conventional batteries
    (B) fuel cells convert electric energy to chemical energy, just like regular batteries
    (C) all other sources of energy will be rendered unnecessary by fuel cells within a very few years
    (D) ways to improve fuel cell design and efficiency are still being sought

12. Which of the sentences below would be the best introductory sentence for a brief summary of the passage?

    (A) As far back as ancient Greece, energy was associated with the ability to cause change and get things done.
    (B) The quest for energy, which is, in many ways still a mystery despite its ability to be measured and put to use, has been the prime motive force behind the advance of science and civilization.
    (C) Energy is usually classified into two types or categories, potential and kinetic, that can be transformed from one into the other, but neither created nor destroyed.
    (D) Today, population pressure and environmental problems have made the demand for energy greater than at any time in history.

Lesson 7

THE ELEMENTS OF FICTION AND DRAMA

Reading: Carefully read this passage.

1 Although drama in ordinary usage represents an independent branch of literature, it shares many of the fundamental elements of fiction, or prose narrative. Of these, many consider *character* to be preeminent. **1.** The concept of character has two senses. **2.** In the first, a character is a person (or sometimes an animal or even inanimate object) in a novel, story, or play who makes things happen or to whom things happen. **3.** For example, Ahab and Ishmael are characters or protagonists in Herman Melville's *Moby Dick*, as is the <u>eponymous</u> heroine of Charlotte Bronte's *Jane Eyre*, or the people who populate the nightmarish imaginary world of Franz Kafka. **4.**

2 The second sense of character has to do with a fictional being's personality, appearance, and, ultimately, value or meaning. Character in this sense is what makes the hero or heroine of a story or play come alive for the reader or theatergoer. What does Jane Eyre look, think, and feel like? What is it about Hamlet that makes him act the way he does? What moral principles does Leopold Bloom embody? Nearly 100 years ago, E.M. Forster, the author of *A Passage to India*, defined fictional characters as either flat or round, and his classification is still widely accepted. Flat characters, he said, "are constructed round a single idea or quality" and remain static. Round characters, on the other hand, <u>encompass</u> many different ideas and traits, and change and grow significantly over the course of the story.

3 *Plot*, the sequence of events in a story and how they relate to one another, is a second essential element of fiction and drama. In most narratives, the plot involves conflict between opposing forces and can be broken down into five phases. The exposition phase sets up the conflict or problem that the protagonist must deal with, without which there would be no story. In the middle phase, often called the rising action, the plot "thickens," becoming more intense and complicated. In the climax phase, the plot builds to an emotional high or turning point, after <u>which</u> it begins to wind down and head towards resolution. Finally, the sequence of related events comes to a satisfying end by means of a logical and <u>plausible</u> conclusion.

4 A third attribute shared by drama and fiction is *setting*, the time and place of the events of the story. <u>Sometimes the setting is merely the backdrop for the action.</u> At other times, the setting of a story or play is a prime mover for the action and has a significant effect on character and plot, helping articulate the story's general meaning or *theme*, the fourth basic element of both fiction and drama.

5 It is in the fifth element of storytelling, *point of view*, however, where drama and prose narrative usually part ways. Point of view refers to the way a story gets told. In a novel or short story, this most often means either a first-person type narrative, where a subjective narrator, like Nick Carraway in *The Great Gatsby*, uses the pronoun "I" to relate the events, or a third-person narrative, where the story is told by an objective observer who refers to the main character as "he" or "she," as in most great 19th-century novels. Although some plays do have a narrator who comments on and guides the action (Thornton Wilder's American classic *Our Town* is a case in point), plays are not told, but are acted out before a live audience. Thus, point of view in a play is not a technique chosen by the author to tell the story. It is more like a point of reference supplied or taken up by the audience.

6 The most salient feature of the theater is that plays are a communal event in time. Unlike a prose narrative, which is most often told in the past tense to report events that have already happened, a play always unfolds in the present—right before the audience's very eyes, so to speak. And while the writer of fiction is the sole creator of the fixed work of art known as a novel or short story, the playwright knows that his or her play is not a finished product, nor is it his or hers alone. It is an outline or suggested script for the director and actors and set designers, who bring to <u>each</u> performance their own special talents and experience and interpretations of human nature.

Exercises: Complete the sentences or answer the questions below with the correct choices, or follow the instructions.

1. Look at the four numbers that indicate where the following sentence could be added to paragraph 1.

   In this sense, a character is also sometimes called a protagonist, though the term usually refers to the main or leading character in a work of drama or fiction, not the minor characters.

   Where would the sentence best fit?
   (1)   (2)   (3)   (4)

2. The underlined word **eponymous** in paragraph 1 could best be defined as

   (A) famous for a negative reason
   (B) working as a governess and servant
   (C) giving one's name to the title of a work
   (D) involving differences among social classes

3. Which statement below best summarizes the two senses of character described in paragraphs 1 and 2?

   (A) Character refers to a person's personality as well as his or her appearance and view of life.
   (B) Character refers to both an individual in a story and the characteristics that make that person appear to the reader as an individual.
   (C) Character is just another word for protagonist.
   (D) Characters don't necessarily have to be human beings, but can also be animals and things.

4. Which of the following can be inferred from paragraph 2?

   (A) Leopold Bloom embodied sound moral principles.
   (B) The characters in E.M. Forster's novel *A Passage to India* were all round characters.
   (C) It is in the details that the author chooses that a character is made to come alive for the reader.
   (D) The author of the passage prefers round characters to flat characters.

5. The underlined word **encompass** in paragraph 2 is closest in meaning to

   (A) comprise
   (B) accept
   (C) discover
   (D) seek

6. Which of these is the most important point the author makes about plot in paragraph 3?

   (A) It is a sequence of events.
   (B) It is another essential element of fiction.
   (C) It has rising action.
   (D) It involves problems and conflict.

7. In paragraph 3, the underlined word **which** refers to

   (A) the plot itself
   (B) the emotional high point
   (C) the middle phase of the sequence
   (D) the original problem or conflict

8. The underlined word **plausible** in paragraph 3 is closest in meaning to

    (A) unexpected and surprising
    (B) positive and forward-looking
    (C) natural and believable
    (D) deep and significant

9. Which of the clauses below could be added to the underlined sentence in paragraph 4 to make the sentence more complete?

    (A) and has little effect on plot and character
    (B) because the story is so interesting in itself
    (C) despite the writer's best intentions
    (D) in which the events take place

10. By using the underlined word **each** in the final sentence of paragraph 6, the author suggests that

    (A) every play is different
    (B) every performance of a particular play is different
    (C) the actors and director often change the plot before a performance
    (D) the performance depends on the reaction of the audience

11. The author mentions all of the following as being fundamental elements of fiction EXCEPT

    (A) the story's overall theme
    (B) the course of action a story follows
    (C) when and where a story takes place
    (D) the author's voice and tone

12. Match the answer choices below to the following categories. Write the letters of the choices in the parentheses. TWO of the answer choices will NOT be used.

Attributes of both drama and fiction
(   )
(   )

Attributes of fiction alone
(   )
(   )

Attributes of drama alone
(   )
(   )

(A) preeminent among storytelling elements
(B) immediate but also transitory
(C) the product of a single person working alone
(D) "living" characters
(E) set in a certain time and place
(F) constructed around a single quality or idea
(G) first- or third-person narrator
(H) no set or fixed point of view

Lesson 8

THE HOAX

Reading: Carefully read this passage.

1. A hoax is an act intended to trick people into believing that something phony is genuine. The word is said to be rooted in the expression "hocus-pocus"—a sleight-of-hand performed by a magician—<u>which</u>, in turn, is thought to be a corruption of the Latin term *hoc est corpus* used during the Eucharist in the Catholic Mass. But this explanation may itself be <u>apocryphal</u>—an etymological hoax so to speak—since no evidence has yet been found to substantiate it.

2. Hoaxes are perpetrated for many reasons. Some are motivated by malice or mischief or committed as a practical joke. Others are done out of revenge or to cause pain and embarrassment. Many hoaxes have serious intentions, aiming to debunk media "hype," to reveal people's gullibility, or to expose the absurdity of a popular trend or idea. Politicians and government leaders often initiate hoaxes, as well, either to discredit opponents or to justify unpopular—or illegal—decisions and policies. For example, some critics have labeled the stated Bush-Blair rationale for going to war in Iraq—to locate and destroy Iraq's weapons of mass destruction and to root out Al-Qaeda terrorists harbored by Saddam Hussein—a costly and deadly hoax, even an impeachable one, since no such weapons or terrorists were ever found.

(A)

3. History abounds with hoaxes. One of the most notorious is the Piltdown Man. In 1912, an amateur British archeologist named Charles Dawson presented some fossil fragments of a skull and jawbone to the paleontology department of the British Museum. **1.** Dawson claimed that the remains had been dug up in a gravel pit near the village of Piltdown in southern England. **2.** The fragments were immediately pronounced the real thing and hailed as a major anthropological breakthrough: a previously unknown form of human being—the million-year-old "missing link" between man and monkey—had at last been unearthed! **3.** The discovery caused a sensation, and not a little controversy and skepticism. **4.** It took another 40 years, however, for the truth to come out. In 1953, X-ray analysis revealed that the bones were a forgery, an artificially aged <u>amalgam</u> made up of a human skull glued to the jawbone of an orangutan and studded with the teeth of a chimpanzee.

(B)

4 Art forgery is another type of hoax, most often carried out solely for financial gain. There are exceptions, however. During World War II, when Nazi leaders were plundering much of the treasured artwork of Europe, forgers were hard at work giving their unsuspecting customers what they wanted. One was Hans Van Meegeren, who specialized in faking the works of the Dutch artist, Jan Vermeer. When Hitler's right-hand man Hermann Goering approached Van Meegeren, who Goering believed was a legitimate Vermeer collector, to buy a particular masterpiece, he brought along a team of Vermeer experts to validate it, and they did. Years later, while serving time in prison for collaborating with the Nazis, Van Meegeren finally came clean. The painting (and many others like it) was a fake he had forged himself, not for money, he said, but because it <u>rankled on</u> him that his own original paintings were repeatedly scorned by the critics. Duping the experts through fake art was a way of getting his revenge.

(C)

5 In 2006, British author A. N. Wilson was the victim of what must have been a particularly mortifying literary hoax. While working on a biography of the poet John Betjeman, Wilson received a letter purportedly written by his subject that revealed a previously unknown love affair. Thrilled to have come across this new bit of literary gossip, Wilson quickly added the letter to his manuscript, making no attempt to verify its authenticity. But when Wilson's biography came out in 2006, so did the truth. Bevis Hillier, an old rival of Wilson's who was about to publish his own Betjeman biography, contacted a leading London newspaper and admitted that he had written and sent Wilson the letter as a venomous practical joke.

Exercises: Complete the sentences or answer the questions below with the correct choices, or follow the instructions.

1. The underlined word **which** in paragraph 1 refers to

    (A) sleight-of-hand
    (B) *hoc est corpus*
    (C) a magician
    (D) "hocus-pocus"

2. In paragraph 1, the author uses the Eucharist as an example of

    (A) a religious rite
    (B) the Catholic Mass
    (C) a Latin expression
    (D) an etymological explanation

3. The underlined word **apocryphal** in paragraph 1 is closest in meaning to

    (A) authentic
    (B) verifiable
    (C) unacceptable
    (D) fallacious

4. All the following are mentioned in paragraph 2 as being motives for perpetrating a hoax EXCEPT

    (A) showing how easily fooled people can be
    (B) ridiculing social phenomena
    (C) making a good impression on others
    (D) bringing scandal on rival political candidates

5. The tone of the last sentence of paragraph 2 suggests that

    (A) the author agrees that the reasons for going to war in Iraq were not valid
    (B) there are no Al-Qaeda terrorists in Iraq
    (C) Saddam Hussein destroyed all his weapons of mass destruction before they could be found
    (D) the author believes that the war in Iraq is justified

6. Look at the four numbers that indicate where the following sentence could be added to paragraph 3.

    Many scientists smelled a rat and challenged the remains' authenticity.

    Where would the sentence best fit?
    (1)   (2)   (3)   (4)

7. In paragraph 3, what point does the author make about the fossil fragments?

    (A) They were a major anthropological discovery.
    (B) They were thought to be at least a million years old.
    (C) They were unearthed by a British Museum paleontologist named Charles Dawson.
    (D) They provided evolution's missing link.

8. The underlined word **amalgam** in paragraph 3 is closest in meaning to

    (A) forgery
    (B) fossil
    (C) composite
    (D) fragment

9. In paragraph 4, the author mentions Hermann Goering as an example of

   (A) a Nazi leader buying up art treasures
   (B) a legitimate collector of Van Meegereen's art
   (C) a Dutch art forger
   (D) a Vermeer expert

10. The underlined phrase **rankled on** in paragraph 4 is closest in meaning to

    (A) infuriated
    (B) embarrassed
    (C) confounded
    (D) amused

11. It can be inferred from paragraph 5 that

    (A) Bevis Hillier's biography of John Betjeman is more scholarly than A. N. Wilson's
    (B) the phony letter was included in Wilson's published biography
    (C) doing what he did gave Hillier a great deal of satisfaction
    (D) news of Betjeman's secret love affair turned Wilson's book into a bestseller

12. Look at the three places marked (A), (B), and (C) that indicate where the following paragraph might be added to the passage.

   Literature has its hoaxes, too. In 1983, the German magazine *Stern* announced the discovery of over 60 volumes of diaries kept by Adolph Hitler throughout the rise and fall of the Third Reich. Several historians, including Hugh Trevor-Roper, a renowned Hitler expert, gave the diaries their stamp of approval. But tests divulged that the paper on which the diaries were written was of recent origin. The diaries were, in fact, the work of a handwriting forger.

   Where would the paragraph best fit?
   (A)   (B)   (C)

Lesson 9

PHILOSOPHY AND THE GOOD LIFE

Reading: Carefully read this passage.

1. Fittingly, the English word "philosophy," or "love of wisdom," comes down to us from the language of ancient Greece. Philosophy is usually defined as the study of the ultimate reality, causes, and principles of the universe. The origins of Western philosophy can be traced back to 600 B.C., when Greek thinkers established a method of inquiry independent from <u>theological</u> ideas. Thus, while the subject matter of theology is faith and dogma, philosophy rejects <u>these</u> in favor of the objective or logical search for truth. Philosophy differs from science as well: science bases its theories on empirical evidence; philosophy deals with uncertainty and problems where no such evidence is available.

2. As the British philosopher Bertrand Russell expressed it in his classic book, *The Problems of Philosophy*, "To a great extent, the uncertainty of philosophy is more apparent than real: those questions which are already capable of definite answers are placed in the sciences, while those only to which, at present, no definite answer can be given remain to form the residue which is called philosophy."

3. As for the uses or purpose of philosophy, its study is commonly thought to lead to wisdom, virtue, or happiness—to a better, richer, more significant life. According to Russell, philosophical contemplation makes us "citizens of the world." It is in this citizenship, he believes, that "man's true freedom, and his liberation from the <u>thralldom</u> of narrow hopes and fears" consists.

4. Western philosophy is traditionally divided into different branches that seek answers to questions related to different areas of inquiry. *Metaphysics* speculates on the nature and significance of the universe, and, ultimately, being itself. *Epistemology* conducts investigations into the nature of knowledge, how it is acquired and possessed by individuals. Epistemology also looks into such related concepts as perception (how we distinguish reality from appearance and illusion), memory (how knowledge is processed and held in the mind), and belief and imagination.

Lesson 9

5 *Ethics* is the branch of philosophy that examines how we ought to live. It tries to answer questions about what makes an action right (moral) or wrong (immoral). Ethical principles take two distinct forms: as standards of conduct inherent within individual human beings; and as a set of moral rules and obligations imposed by society on its members. Today, moral philosophers usually classify ethics into two general fields. *Meta-ethics* examines ethics itself. It aims to establish the origins of our ethical principles—whether morality exists independently of human beings or is a totally human construct—and speculates on the meaning of such words as "good," "ought," and "just."

6 *Normative ethics*, in contrast, deals with the creation of a body of moral standards, or norms, that aim to regulate people's behavior. Within normative ethics, there are three theories of how this can be done. **1.** *Obligation theories* base human morality on specific fundamental principles of duty and responsibility. **2.** Some of these principles are religious in nature, involving duties to a Supreme Being. **3.** Some involve obligations to oneself—for example, improving personal virtue and intelligence through discipline and study—while others involve responsibilities towards other people: the duty to keep promises, for example, or to improve others' living conditions and to work to relieve general human suffering. **4.**

7 *Virtue theories* emphasize the importance of developing good habits of character, such as generosity, tolerance, and courage, and the avoidance of bad habits such as ill-temper and <u>vanity</u>. The Greek philosopher Aristotle came up with eleven specific virtues for humans to foster, but also argued that it is necessary for us to develop "virtue balance," as well. <u>For example, exhibiting a lack of courage in the face of adversity means giving in to the vice of cowardice, he pointed out, but, on the other hand, showing an excess of courage can just as readily give rise to the vice of rashness.</u>

8 The third branch of normative ethics is *consequentialism*. Consequentialists don't ask us to adhere to long lists of rules or obligations, or to develop specific virtues, but rather advise us to think about the ultimate consequences of our actions before we carry them out. We must first, based on experience and evidence, add up the bad and good consequences of a planned action. If the "goods" outweigh the "bads," to us personally and for others, then the action can be considered morally proper.

Exercises: Complete the sentences or answer the questions below with the correct choices, or follow the instructions.

1. The author uses the word **Fittingly** at the beginning of the essay to

    (A) show why philosophy is the love of wisdom
    (B) explain how the word *philosophy* entered the English language
    (C) emphasize how appropriate it is that the word *philosophy* should come from the Greek language
    (D) make certain the word *philosophy* is not misunderstood

2. The underlined word **theological** in paragraph 1 is closest in meaning to

    (A) religious
    (B) purposeful
    (C) theoretical
    (D) absolute

3. The underlined word **these** in paragraph 1 refers to

    (A) causes and principles
    (B) philosophers and theologians
    (C) ideas and subjects
    (D) faith and dogma

4. Which of the following can be inferred about Bertrand Russell?

    (A) He believes philosophy will eventually answer all questions about the nature of reality.
    (B) He feels philosophy is superior to science.
    (C) He thinks philosophy should be a required course for world citizenship.
    (D) He believes the study of philosophy is valuable, despite its inability to find definite answers.

Lesson 9

5. The underlined word **thralldom** in paragraph 3 is closest in meaning to

    (A) fascination
    (B) slavery
    (C) significance
    (D) effects

6. All of the following are mentioned in paragraph 4 as being subjects for epistemological inquiry EXCEPT

    (A) virtue
    (B) imagination
    (C) memory
    (D) perception

7. In paragraph 5, what does the author say about ethical principles?

    (A) They examine the field of ethics itself.
    (B) They exist independently of human beings.
    (C) They originate in the individual as well as in society.
    (D) They define the terms related to morality.

8. Look at the four numbers that indicate where the following sentence could be added to paragraph 6.

    A good example is found in the Book of Exodus in the Christian Bible, where the Ten Commandments are handed down from God to the prophet Moses.

    Where would the sentence best fit?
    (1)   (2)   (3)   (4)

9. Which statement best describes normative ethics?

   (A) a set of standards or principles that aim to improve human conduct
   (B) the objective study of duty and responsibility
   (C) an examination of where ethical principles originate
   (D) an attempt to relieve human suffering

10. The underlined word **vanity** in paragraph 7 is closest in meaning to

    (A) pride
    (B) uselessness
    (C) confidence
    (D) appearance

11. Which sentence below best expresses the essential information in the underlined sentence in paragraph 7? Incorrect choices change the meaning in important ways or leave out essential information.

    (A) Cowardice in the face of danger is the worst of all vices, excluding of course, rashness.
    (B) Cowardly people are apt to give in too quickly to vices of all kinds, including rashness when trouble strikes.
    (C) While having too little courage when faced with danger is bad and cowardly, having too much can be just as bad because it can lead to hasty, mistaken actions.
    (D) Once a person gives in to vices, it is almost impossible for him or her to develop a strong sense of morality.

12. Match the answer choices below to the type of ethical theory they describe. Write the letters of the choices in the parentheses. TWO of the answer choices will NOT be used.

Obligation and virtue theories
(   )
(   )
(   )

Consequentialism
(   )
(   )

Answer choices
(A) avoidance of vices and bad character habits like anger and taking hasty actions
(B) making moral decisions by looking ahead to the results of one's actions
(C) avoiding people who you think are bad influences
(D) weighing the evidence for personal choices based on past experience and observation
(E) developing a desire to help others whose living conditions are less fortunate than one's own
(F) speculating on the nature and significance of the universe at large
(G) belief in God and His moral guidance

Lesson 10

MYSTERIOUS FORCES

Reading: Carefully read this passage.

1 The universe is the totality of all matter and energy in existence. Cosmology, or astrophysics, the branch of science that attempts to devise a comprehensive theory of the structure of the universe, is concerned with fundamental questions about its formation and evolution, and its eventual fate: How did the universe come into being? What is it made up of? Where is it heading?

2 Throughout most of human history, the answers to these questions were mere <u>conjecture</u>—the subject of metaphysics, not astrophysics, theology, not science. But in the 20th century, aided by powerful new telescopes, computers, and other technological advances, scientists have formulated various theories and made many discoveries that are slowly but surely bringing us closer to a true scientific understanding of the cosmos and our place in it.

3 So, how *did* the universe originate? One explanation holds that the universe has always existed and always will, that it had no beginning and has no foreseeable end, that it is truly infinite. <u>Although it still has a few stubborn adherents, this "Steady-State" theory has by and large been relegated to the history books.</u>

4 Today, the dominant explanation for the creation of the universe is the Big Bang Theory. At a certain "time zero"—somewhere between eight and 15 billion years ago—all energy and matter was concentrated into a dense single point which suddenly exploded—the Big Bang—setting the universe in motion. In the aftermath of that explosion, thought to have lasted a mere three minutes, the universe rapidly expanded. Interactions between matter and energy, carried out in the extremely high temperatures generated during the Big Bang, formed common elements like hydrogen and helium. The stretching of the new cosmos continued, and, over the next few billion years, gave birth to stars, galaxies, planets, moons, life—everything.

5 An underlying assumption of the Big Bang Theory is that the universe has been expanding ever since that original explosion, an idea first propounded by the American astronomer Edwin Hubble after observing the movement of distant galaxies. Hubble discovered that the further a galaxy is from our galaxy, the Milky Way, the faster it moves, indicating that every galaxy in the universe, no matter where it is, took the same amount of time to get to its current position from a central starting point. Other evidence corroborating the Big Bang Theory is based on <u>the concept of cosmic radiation, noise left over from the initial explosion that reaches earth equally from all directions from the remotest regions of the universe</u>.

6 But if the universe is constantly expanding, why, over such vast amounts of time, hasn't it ballooned itself to destruction? Until very recently, the standard view held that gravitation, the mutual attraction of all the visible matter in the universe (that is, the ordinary matter that makes up everything we have ever observed with the naked eye and with all our scientific instruments) was the only force slowing the expansion down and keeping everything from flying apart. In the 1970s, however, a few scientists proposed that "dark matter" may also play a role in decelerating the expansion. These are invisible particles of unknown composition that surround and somehow determine the motion of all galaxies. Scientists now speculate that dark matter accounts for as much as 75 percent of the universe's total make-up.

7 Then, in 1998, astrophysicists made an astounding discovery, calling all previous assumptions into question. **1.** Observations of distant supernova—exploding stars—revealed that they were much dimmer, and therefore much farther away from Earth, than the standard calculations indicated. **2.** This could only mean that the space between them and us had stretched out much further than expected. **3.** What could account for such a phenomenon? **4.** There must be some mysterious force at work. But what could it be?

8 The latest hypothesis is that some form of "dark energy" is <u>repelling</u> gravity, pushing against it, causing the universe to grow ever faster. Although virtually nothing is known about this dark force, the very possibility of its existence is helping scientists interpret diverse pieces of information that so far they have not been able to make sense of. Just having the concept of this mysterious form of energy is helping us formulate even better questions about the nature and fate of the universe.

Exercises: Complete the sentences or answer the questions below with the correct choices, or follow the instructions.

1. All of the following are given as examples of fundamental questions about the nature of the universe in paragraph 1 EXCEPT

    (A) What is its origin?
    (B) What is its structure?
    (C) What is its purpose?
    (D) What will happen to it?

2. The underlined word **conjecture** in paragraph 2 is closest in meaning to

    (A) speculation
    (B) faith
    (C) miscalculation
    (D) anticipation

3. Which of the following words best describes the kind of progress science is making towards a true understanding of the nature of the universe?

    (A) hypothetical
    (B) inevitable
    (C) irrefutable
    (D) gradual

Lesson 10

4. The author believes the "Steady-State" theory is not valid. What word or phrase in the underlined sentence in paragraph 3 best indicates how he feels?

    (A) still
    (B) stubborn
    (C) relegated to
    (D) history books

5. From the information in paragraph 4, what can reasonably be inferred about the Big Bang Theory?

    (A) It will probably never be disproved.
    (B) It is accepted by most scientists.
    (C) It leaves few questions unanswered and involves little speculation.
    (D) No new theories about the origin of the universe will emerge to rival it.

6. In paragraph 4, how does the author say the Big Bang was set off?

    (A) He says that the universe expanded rapidly once it was set in motion.
    (B) He offers no explanation concerning what caused the explosion to occur in the first place.
    (C) He points out that it started from a single dense point.
    (D) He explains that it started from interactions between matter and energy.

7. The author's main purpose in paragraph 5 is to

    (A) emphasize that the universe is still expanding
    (B) point out that it was an American, Edwin Hubble, who first came up with the Big Bang idea
    (C) offer evidence that gives credence to the theory of the Big Bang
    (D) show that all galaxies move at the same speed away from the earth

8. Which sentence below best expresses the essential information in the underlined clause in paragraph 5? Incorrect choices change the meaning in important ways or leave out essential information.

   (A) Cosmic radiation is the noise that was originally generated during the Big Bang itself.
   (B) The Big Bang gave off noise, known as cosmic radiation, traces of which can still be heard throughout the universe.
   (C) Cosmic radiation, or the noise that was emitted during the Big Bang itself, is still evident in the farthest corners of the cosmos and can be heard on Earth at the same intensity no matter which angle it arrives from.
   (D) The noise reaches earth evenly, transformed into cosmic radiation after traveling such great distances across space.

9. Which of the following is the most important point that the author makes about "dark matter" in paragraph 6?

   (A) No one knows what it is made of.
   (B) It was conceived of in the 1970s by a few scientists.
   (C) It has been thought to play a role in slowing down cosmic expansion.
   (D) It's an invisible force about which little is known.

10. Look at the four numbers that indicate where the following sentence could be added to paragraph 7.

    In other words the swelling of the universe was actually speeding up, not slowing down.

    Where would the sentence best fit?
    (1)   (2)   (3)   (4)

11. The underlined word **repelling** in paragraph 8 is closest in meaning to

   (A) offending
   (B) repulsing
   (C) eliminating
   (D) adhering

12. An introductory sentence for a brief summary of the passage is provided below. Complete the summary by selecting the THREE answer choices that best express the most important ideas in the passage. Some sentences do not belong in the summary because they express ideas that are not presented or are minor ideas in the passage.

   Although other theories for the origin of the universe have been put forth, the generally accepted scientific theory today is that the universe was set in motion by a violent explosion billions of years ago.

   (A) Over 100 years ago, Albert Einstein proposed the concept of "dark energy," which he named the "cosmological constant," though he later refuted the idea, calling it his "biggest blunder."
   (B) The Steady-State Theory maintains that the universe is virtually infinite, with no beginning and no end.
   (C) Known as the Big Bang, the theory states that the universe began as a single, dense point from which everything burst forth.
   (D) The universe is usually defined as the sum of all matter and energy and the space in which all events take place.
   (E) The theory that universal expansion is occurring at an accelerating rate because of a hidden force dubbed "dark energy" has both increased our understanding of the universe and raised new questions about it.
   (F) Until recently it was thought that the universe had been expanding steadily ever since the Big Bang, but that the rate of expansion was held in check by gravity, and, possibly, by "dark matter."

Lesson 11

LIES AND LIE DETECTION

Reading: Carefully read this passage.

1 A lie is defined as a false statement deliberately presented as being true with the intention to deceive. Lying is as old as humanity itself, and appears to be universal. Indeed, the propensity to lie may even be programmed into our genes. <u>In one study of personality traits running in families, researchers found that it was in the tendency to lie that family members most closely resemble each other.</u>

2 Some people excel at lying; others are, as Daniel McNeil puts it in his study of human <u>physiognomy</u>, *The Face*, "true Pinocchios" (after the classic Italian children's story of the boy whose nose grows longer whenever he tells a fib). Natural liars are aware of their "talent" and feel no fear or guilt about using it, while for the Pinocchios, "their very worry about detection" shows up on their faces and exposes them.

3 If lying is as old as civilization, so is the attempt to detect it. Early lie-detection methods were both crude and cruel. A suspect might be forced to stick his hand in a pot of boiling water or to walk over a bed of red-hot stones; if his hand or feet didn't burn, he was telling the truth. An ancient Chinese method, more humane, but equally <u>arbitrary</u>, used rice as a lie detector. While listening to accusations against him, a suspect held dry, uncooked rice in his mouth. Because salivation was believed to stop during times of emotional distress, the person was deemed guilty if the rice remained dry. Pity the innocent!

4 It wasn't until 1895 that the Italian criminologist Cesare Lombroso approached lie detection scientifically and developed a device that recorded changes in a person's blood pressure that were supposed to indicate lying. In 1917, William Marston, an American psychologist, invented the first true polygraph, a lie-detecting instrument based on the old assumption that a person guilty of lying will, when asked incriminating questions, exhibit strong emotional reactions accompanied by detectable physiological responses.

5 1. Before the test, the subject is hooked up to a series of wires, tubes, and sensors which will measure his or her respiratory rate, blood pressure, and electrodermal activity (sweatiness). **2.** During the test, a professional polygraph examiner asks the examinee simple yes-no questions about a certain event or incident. **3.** The polygraph machine records the subject's responses on a scrolling paper, or, today, on a computer monitor. **4.** These responses are then analyzed and interpreted by the examiner.

6 The polygraph doesn't actually detect lies; it can only detect whether an examinee is displaying deceptive behavior. In fact, there is little scientific evidence that polygraphs are reliable indicators of deception, with accuracy predictions varying widely. Also, the test can be beaten. The readings can be skewed by, for example, anyone who knows such simple relaxation techniques as meditation or yoga. Thus, while thousands of people take polygraph tests every year, polygraph evidence is rarely admissible in a court of law.

7 In recent years, the quest for an infallible lie detector has been aided by advances in technology, particularly brain imaging. The most intriguing development is the use of "brain fingerprinting" to determine whether specific information related to a crime or event is stored in a suspect's brain. This new technology measures electric brain responses using a headband equipped with sophisticated sensing devices. When the brain receives information it recognizes, it emits a brain-wave response called a MERMER (the so-called brain fingerprint), which the sensing devices can detect and measure. During a brain-fingerprinting interview, a crime suspect is fitted with a headband and presented details of a crime that only the real perpetrator would know. If a particular detail incites a suspect's brain to emit a MERMER, it proves that he or she is guilty. An innocent person's brain would not emit the incriminating wave because the information would mean nothing to him or her.

8 Meanwhile, the U.S. Department of Defense is working on a lie detector that uses invisible microwaves or laser beams reflected off people's skin to assess their physiological condition—and to detect prevarication. The device will be utilized mainly at airports as a weapon in the war on terrorism. Such a detector, if perfected, is sure to raise civil rights and privacy issues, however, since it can be used remotely and secretly without the subject's knowledge or permission.

Exercises: Complete the sentences or answer the questions below with the correct choices, or follow the instructions.

1. In paragraph 1, the author uses the word **deliberately** in his definition of a lie

    (A) to indicate how much he disapproves of lying
    (B) to emphasize that a lie must be intentional for it to be classified as a lie
    (C) as a means of making his writing style more convincing
    (D) in order to show how motivated liars are

2. Which sentence below best expresses the essential information in the underlined sentence in paragraph 1? Incorrect choices change the meaning in important ways or leave out essential information.

    (A) One study showed that the personality trait most often shared by members of a family is the propensity to lie.
    (B) The study tried to find out which personality traits run in which families.
    (C) Family members who lie tend to resemble other members of the family more closely.
    (D) It was revealed by researchers that liars run in families whose personality traits are similar.

3. The underlined word **physiognomy** in paragraph 2 has to do with

    (A) psychological problems
    (B) body shape
    (C) facial features
    (D) lying

Lesson 11

4. In paragraph 2, what is given as the main reason that "Pinocchios" are so easily exposed?

   (A) their feelings of guilt about lying
   (B) their anxiety about being exposed
   (C) their tendency to be detected
   (D) their lack of talent for lying

5. The underlined word **arbitrary** in paragraph 3 is closest in meaning to

   (A) cruel
   (B) fortunate
   (C) capricious
   (D) inessential

6. In paragraph 4, all of the following are mentioned concerning Cesare Lombroso EXCEPT

   (A) how his device actually recorded body changes
   (B) how he looked at lie detection
   (C) what his lie detector did
   (D) what he did for a living

7. In paragraph 4, what point does the author make about William Marston's polygraph?

   (A) It answered people's incriminating questions.
   (B) It was based on Cesare Lombroso's discovery.
   (C) It detected true guilt accurately.
   (D) It was based on the belief that guilty people react emotionally and physically.

8. Look at the four numbers that indicate where the following sentence could be added to paragraph 5.

   Since Marston's day, the polygraph machine itself and the lie-detecting test centered around it have undergone continual refinement and improvement.

   Where would the sentence best fit?
   (1)   (2)   (3)   (4)

9. In paragraph 6, the underlined phrase **The readings** refers to

   (A) predictions
   (B) simple yes-no questions
   (C) responses indicated on paper or computer monitor
   (D) reliable indicators

10. The explanation of brain fingerprinting in paragraph 7 is an example of

    (A) cause and effect analysis
    (B) process analysis
    (C) narration
    (D) comparison and contrast

11. The author mentions civil rights and privacy issues in paragraph 8 to show that the new lie detector may

    (A) be controversial in the future
    (B) be used as evidence in courts of law
    (C) be perfected by the U.S. Department of Defense
    (D) secretly use the latest microwave and laser-beam technology

Lesson 11

12. An introductory sentence for a brief summary of the passage is provided below. Complete the summary by selecting the THREE answer choices that express the most important ideas in the passage. Some sentences do not belong in the summary because they express ideas that are not presented or are minor ideas in the passage.

Lying and attempts at lie detection have gone hand in hand throughout human history.

(A) Today, scientific progress, particularly brain-scanning techniques, is intensifying the search for a foolproof lie detector.
(B) Children lie, too, from a very early age, though they don't develop a sense of right and wrong about it until later in life.
(C) Ancient lie-detecting methods were based on certain beliefs and superstitions and not on scientific evidence.
(D) A few people have built-in lie detectors that allow them to see subtle signs that people exhibit when they try to deceive others.
(E) Daniel McNeil's book, *The Face*, uses Pinocchio as an example of a person who is not good at lying.
(F) While the polygraph, a 20th-century invention, uses scientific knowledge and can detect deceptive behavior, it cannot really determine whether a person's answer to a particular question is true or false.

Lesson 12

SOCIOLOGY AND RELIGION

Reading: Carefully read this passage.

1 Sociology is the scientific study of human society that attempts to construct abstract explanatory theories of social behavior supported by factual and statistical evidence. It is the youngest of the social sciences, having emerged as a discipline in its own right only in the middle of the 19th century when the French positivist philosopher Auguste Comte undertook to examine human social life in all its manifestations—cultural, economic, and political—with a view to uncovering its unifying principles and promoting social harmony.

2 Throughout the 19th century, the field was further developed and refined by several other major figures. Emile Durkheim (1858-1917) pioneered the use of empirical and statistical evidence, inspiring sociologists to think of themselves as true scientists and challenging them to look at society as it really is, not as they would like it to be. Max Weber (1864-1920) devised the concept of "ideal types," which are working conceptual models that serve as tools for understanding social forces by offering a fixed basis for comparison. Philosopher Karl Marx (1818-1883) took a historical approach and theorized on how societies evolve and develop, concluding that social change comes about primarily as a result of contradictions and conflicts within economic systems.

3 Today, the scope of sociology is extremely, sometimes <u>bafflingly</u>, wide, encompassing analysis of everything from casual social encounters between two people to the social causes and implications of crime and divorce—from village life to globalization and cross-cultural conflict. Sociology is interested in society in all its aspects, most fundamentally perhaps in social structure, the preexisting patterns of social reality that strongly influence personal behavior and relationships. <u>Sociologists also investigate social class, an individual's relative position within the overall social structure, as well as the dynamics of social groups and social interaction.</u> Vital to the sociologist is the ability to develop what the American social theorist C. Wright Mills called the "sociological imagination," the capacity to overcome narrow personal

Lesson 12

circumstances and beliefs and to cultivate a way of seeing the world in a new and broader light.

4 Sociology is particularly concerned with probing into the <u>ins and outs</u> of social institutions, and the field itself is divided into a wide array of sub-studies devoted to how <u>each</u>—the family, the economy, schools and education, politics and government, and religion—is organized and functions, and how it affects an individual's life and behavior.

5 Of these, religion poses a unique challenge to the sociological imagination. It demands that the social scientist put on hold his or her own religious beliefs—or non-beliefs—and look at the institution of religion dispassionately and with great sensitivity to the needs and feelings of believers. To the sociologist, then, religion is <u>necessarily</u> defined as nothing more than a cultural system comprising the shared beliefs, values, and norms of a particular group of people, beliefs and values that provide them with a sense of purpose and meaning and answer fundamental questions or allay fundamental fears about life and death by creating a vision of existence that is sacred, ritualistic, and, above all, supernatural.

6 Thus, sociologists are not concerned with whether a particular religious belief is true or false, or a religious practice good or bad. Sociologists examine religion from its human and not its divine or transcendental aspects. Sociologists ask questions like how a religious group or cult is organized, what are its most salient features and principal beliefs, how it is related to and influences the society of which it forms a sub-group, how it actually functions and manages to survive. Sociology aims to discover what a religion's main attractions are and how it recruits its adherents—even how it raises money. It wonders how, at times, religious beliefs can contribute to social harmony and how, at other times, they can give rise to social conflict and sectarian violence. In other words, instead of looking at personal religious phenomena such as conversion, mysticism, and saintliness from a purely psychological point of view, as did the psychologist/philosopher William James in his classic *The Varieties of Religious Experience*, sociology seeks more worldly explanations for such experiences, and focuses on factors in the social structure that give rise to them.

Exercises: Complete the sentences or answer the questions below with the correct choices, or follow the instructions.

1. It can be inferred from paragraph 1 that until the 19th century

    (A) sociology formed part of other fields of study
    (B) social life had not been studied before
    (C) all theories of social life were based on speculation, not facts
    (D) there were no fixed unifying societal principles

2. The essay mentions all of the following as pioneers in the field of sociology EXCEPT

    (A) Karl Marx
    (B) William James
    (C) Emile Durkheim
    (D) Auguste Comte

3. In paragraph 2, the author says that Max Weber's "ideal types" are useful because

    (A) they understand social forces
    (B) they are tools for contrasting real social conditions against ideal models
    (C) they are based on empirical and statistical evidence
    (D) they explain the process of social change

4. The underlined word **bafflingly** in paragraph 3 is closest in meaning to

    (A) amazingly
    (B) confusingly
    (C) critically
    (D) intentionally

Lesson 12

5. In paragraph 3, the author defines social structure as

    (A) the underlying patterns of social life
    (B) a fundamental necessity for sociologists
    (C) the broad scope of sociology
    (D) being deeply influenced by an individual's behavior

6. Which sentence below best expresses the essential information in the underlined sentence in paragraph 3? Incorrect choices change the meaning in important ways or leave out essential information.

    (A) Social class tells where a person stands in society in relation to other members of that society.
    (B) Sociology is interested in how the members of groups communicate with and view each other.
    (C) Sociology also studies how and where people fit into society at large, how groups are organized and function, and how people communicate and get along with each other.
    (D) Sociology attempts to do away with the concept of social class, showing how it undermines social organization, group formation, and interpersonal relationships.

7. Why does the author mention C. Wright Mills in paragraph 3?

    (A) to show that sociology is not only a European field of study
    (B) to emphasize the fact that sociology encompasses a broad range of aims and interests
    (C) to offer readers an example of a sociologist who exemplifies the "sociological imagination"
    (D) to reiterate that sociologists must develop a special, non-subjective way of looking at reality

8. The underlined phrase **ins and outs** in paragraph 4 is closest in meaning to

   (A) various divisions
   (B) structure and function
   (C) deeper meaning
   (D) problems

9. The underlined word **each** in paragraph 4 refers to

   (A) sociology
   (B) social institution
   (C) sub-study
   (D) individual

10. In paragraph 5 the author uses the underlined word **necessarily** to

    (A) emphasize that sociologists should confine themselves to examining what religion means to believers, not what it means to them
    (B) emphasize how essential an institution religion is to society
    (C) imply that all sociologists must accept the definition of religion that the discipline gives them
    (D) link the definition with the needs of true believers

11. The author probably feels that the most important point about the vision of life offered by a religion or cult is that

    (A) its rituals are social not cultural in origin
    (B) believers actually accept it as true
    (C) it encompasses the idea of a supernatural being
    (D) it makes its members feel superior to members of other religious groups

Lesson 12

12. Choose the FOUR sentences below that best summarize the main ideas expressed in the concluding paragraph.

    (A) For the sake of objectivity, it is far better if sociologists do not follow any particular religion.
    (B) Sociologists must refrain from making value judgments about particular religions.
    (C) Sociologists must try to discover what holds a religious organization together and what makes it work.
    (D) Religious beliefs sometimes give rise to conflicts and violence.
    (E) Things such as conversion and mysticism matter to the sociologist only in that they relate to social causes and factors.
    (F) Sociologists must examine both the positive and the negative influences that religion can have on society.

Lesson 13

THE BLACKING FACTORY

Reading: Carefully read this passage.

1 Just two days after his twelfth birthday, Charles Dickens (1812-1870), the future author of *Oliver Twist, Great Expectations,* and some fifteen other classics of English literature, began working in a blacking (boot polish) factory in a rundown, rat-infested warehouse near the River Thames in central London. Every night after work, an exhausted young Charles walked the three miles back to the tiny room where he lived on his own all alone, separated from his family, wondering how he "could have been so easily <u>cast away</u> at such an age."

2 The period of servitude in the blacking factory was deeply humiliating for "a child of singular abilities, quick, eager, delicate, and soon hurt, bodily or mentally," as Dickens later described himself. Six days a week, ten hours a day, Charles glued labels on pots of bootblack, working side by side with poor working-class children ("common companions," he called them), <u>convinced that his great expectations of becoming a learned and distinguished gentleman had been crushed forever.</u>

3 And yet, just a few months earlier, Charles had been happier than at any other time in his young life. He was living with his parents and seven brothers and sisters in a large, comfortable, middle-class home. An Oxford scholar tutored him in his lessons, and Charles spent his free time attending the theater and devouring the classics of Western literature. John Dickens, Charles's father, was a clerk in the Navy Pay Office, a respectable position with a good salary. But John, an amiable man who often entertained his many friends with lavish parties and dinners, was unable to live within his means, and the family's debts steadily mounted. To help pay off these debts, the Dickens family moved into a one-room flat and pawned off all their possessions—and young Charles was put to work. But it was too little, too late. In the end, John Dickens was imprisoned for debt.

4 This traumatic episode in the bottling factory is of <u>crucial</u> importance in understanding both the man and his fiction. According to Peter Ackroyd,

Lesson 13

Dickens's biographer, <u>it</u> was the formative experience of Dickens's life and contributed in many ways to his becoming a novelist—and to the type of novelist he was to become. **1.** For one thing, the experience brought out Dickens's native diligence and conscientiousness. **2.** Despite his hatred for the work itself, Charles early on made up his mind to become as adept at it as any of the other boys there, and he did. For the rest of his life, Dickens was an <u>indefatigable</u> worker, devoting himself wholeheartedly to whatever task was at hand. **3.** The blacking factory thus became the source of the future novelist's incomparable energy and ambition. **4.**

5 At the same time, living apart from his parents and family forced Charles to learn how to manage his time and control his own affairs, thereby developing the habits of organization and careful planning that eventually made him such a prolific novelist and journalist.

6 That dreary riverside factory was also, says Ackroyd, the birthplace of Dickens the storyteller. It was here that his genius for attention to detail and his uncanny descriptive powers first manifested themselves. To entertain his co-workers and console himself, Charles would make up elaborate, humorous tales based on his appalling family life and the things he observed and experienced while walking the streets of London. In these fairy-tale-like stories, Charles "rewrote" the world he lived in. He would put himself at the center of the action, re-imagining himself as an ambitious young boy who overcomes injustice and cruelty to become a pillar of society. This early storytelling impulse surely led to Dickens' decision to become a writer of fiction, just as the blacking factory incident surely explains why some of Dickens's most memorable characters are orphans and abandoned children, and why he used his novels to champion the cause of the poor and downtrodden.

7 Some readers, however, shine a less favorable light on Dickens's blacking factory episode, contending that he childishly never stopped feeling sorry for himself over it. This refusal to grow up accounts not only for the sentimentality of some of Dickens's novels, they say, but also explains the tone of profound self-pity that pervades them.

Exercises: Complete the sentences or answer the questions below with the correct choices, or follow the instructions.

1. The author uses the quotation from Charles Dickens in paragraph 1 to

    (A) give an example of Dickens's writing style
    (B) place blame on Dickens's parents
    (C) show the young boy's state of mind at the time
    (D) emphasize how young Dickens was then

2. The underlined phrase **cast away** in paragraph 1 is closest in meaning to

    (A) overlooked
    (B) taken advantage of
    (C) manipulated
    (D) abandoned

3. Which sentence below best expresses the essential information in the underlined clause in paragraph 2? Incorrect choices change the meaning in important ways or leave out essential information.

    (A) Dickens was convinced that he would end up working in the blacking factory for the rest of his life.
    (B) Dickens believed that all a person needed to become an important member of society was to be well educated.
    (C) Becoming a learned person was the only thing the young boy wanted, and he believed that if he couldn't realize this ambition, he would be a failure.
    (D) He felt that he would never have the chance to grow up to be the educated, important person he had always dreamed of becoming.

4. Based on the information in paragraph 2, all of the following refer to the conditions that Dickens worked under in the blacking factory EXCEPT

   (A) toiling side by side with people he thought were beneath him
   (B) being easily hurt
   (C) doing work that was boring and repetitive
   (D) working long hours with only one holiday

5. In paragraph 3 the author mentions all of the following about Dickens's happiest time of life EXCEPT

   (A) where his home was located
   (B) what kind of home he lived in
   (C) how he was educated
   (D) what his reading habits were

6. Based on the information in paragraph 3, which of the following CANNOT be inferred about John Dickens?

   (A) He was often forced to borrow money.
   (B) He was not concerned for his son's future welfare.
   (C) His salary wasn't enough to cover his household expenses.
   (D) He was popular and well-liked.

7. The underlined word **crucial** in paragraph 4 is closest in meaning to

   (A) chronic
   (B) critical
   (C) relative
   (D) recognized

8. The underlined word **it** in paragraph 4 refers to

    (A) the blacking factory itself
    (B) the traumatic episode in the factory
    (C) Dickens's hatred for the work
    (D) the man and his fiction

9. The underlined word **indefatigable** in paragraph 4 is closest in meaning to

    (A) dedicated
    (B) adept
    (C) willing
    (D) tireless

10. Based on the information in paragraph 4, which statement below best describes Dickens's attitude once he started working in the factory?

    (A) He thought he should make the best of a bad situation.
    (B) He believed he would never be able to compete with the other boys.
    (C) He thought it was a good chance to show everyone how clever he was.
    (D) He decided that the job wasn't as bad as he thought it would be.

11. Look at the four numbers that indicate where the following sentence could be added to paragraph 4.

    ("Do everything you do," Dickens later characteristically told an aspiring novelist, "as if there were nothing else to be done in the world.")

    Where would the sentence best fit?
    (1)   (2)   (3)   (4)

12. An introductory sentence for a brief summary of the importance of the blacking factory episode in Dickens's life and work is provided below. Complete the summary by selecting the THREE answer choices that express the episode's most important effects.

In 1824, Charles Dickens was put to work in a dreary blacking factory, an experience that in many ways formed Dickens's adult character as well as the character and style of his writing.

(A) Dickens never forgave his parents for putting him to work at such an early age.
(B) Dickens was also forced to take his family's possessions to the pawn shop.
(C) The work brought out the boy's native industry, and the boy's long, lonely walks around London helped develop his powers of observation.
(D) Dickens may have been overly affected by the episode, however, which some say weakened his fiction.
(E) Although at the time, Dickens looked down on his poor colleagues in the factory, he later became sympathetic with the plight of the disadvantaged and stood up for them in his writing.
(F) Dickens was too ashamed to tell anyone about his appalling family life.

Lesson 14

BEFORE IT'S TOO LATE

Reading: Carefully read this passage.

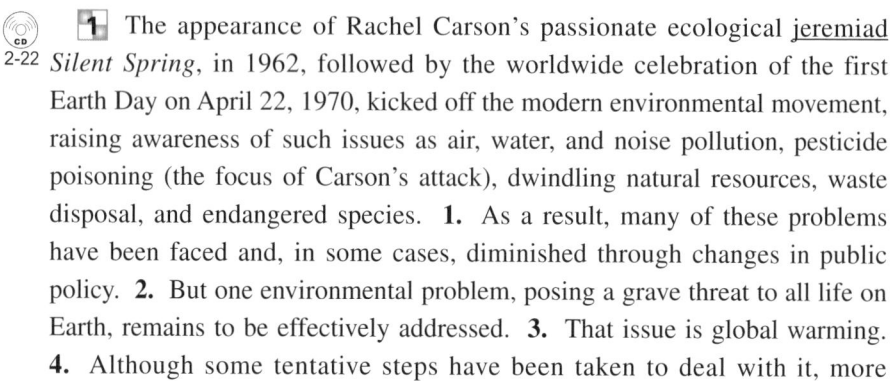

1 The appearance of Rachel Carson's passionate ecological <u>jeremiad</u> *Silent Spring*, in 1962, followed by the worldwide celebration of the first Earth Day on April 22, 1970, kicked off the modern environmental movement, raising awareness of such issues as air, water, and noise pollution, pesticide poisoning (the focus of Carson's attack), dwindling natural resources, waste disposal, and endangered species. **1.** As a result, many of these problems have been faced and, in some cases, diminished through changes in public policy. **2.** But one environmental problem, posing a grave threat to all life on Earth, remains to be effectively addressed. **3.** That issue is global warming. **4.** Although some tentative steps have been taken to deal with it, more decisive action has been hampered by the debate that surrounds it.

2 That the average temperature of the earth's atmosphere and oceans is rising is not at issue. The evidence overwhelmingly says that it is. According to research conducted by NASA's Goddard Institute of Space Studies, the average worldwide temperature in 2005 was 14.6 degrees centigrade, making it the hottest year since recordkeeping began back in the mid-1800s. Furthermore, the warming trend is accelerating. The five warmest years on record have all occurred since 1998. So there can be little doubt about it: the earth is getting hotter.

3 What the experts have disagreed on are the causes of this climate change. Some climatologists (swayed perhaps by pressure from business and political leaders) have contended that there are too many variables and unknown factors to make accurate predictions about present and future climate trends. Perhaps, they say, the warming is merely a normal fluctuation in surface temperatures caused by variations in the amount of sunlight reaching the earth. Or, they speculate, perhaps the earth is just emerging from a previous cooling period—the so-called Little Ice Age.

4 But these arguments are no longer tenable. The prevailing scientific opinion is that the majority of the earth's warming is attributable to human activities, in particular, to the burning of fossil fuels—coal and petroleum

Lesson 14

products for industry and transportation—and the spewing of gases like carbon dioxide, methane, and nitrous oxide into the air.

5 Normally the earth's surface temperature is maintained through a process known as the greenhouse effect. Shortwave light from the sun arrives at the planet's surface after being filtered through a thermal blanket composed of water vapor, carbon dioxide, ozone, and other so-called greenhouse gases. This light then bounces off the earth and heads back towards space. But by then, this light and heat have lost some of their intensity and cannot pass so easily back through the gassy protective blanket, and are trapped by it. Under ideal conditions, this process keeps the earth's surface at just the right temperature to sustain life—just like in a greenhouse. But with the increased concentrations of greenhouse gases now in the atmosphere, this thermal blanket is thicker and heavier, allowing it to trap more heat close to the earth's surface. Hence, global warming.

6 Why do rising atmospheric temperatures pose such a danger? Scientists now predict that if the heating trend continues, if world leaders don't take immediate action to halt and reverse it by drastically cutting greenhouse-gas emissions, the consequences will be catastrophic—igniting social and economic disruption on a scale equivalent to global war or depression. (See Al Gore's *An Inconvenient Truth* for a frightening preview of what we can expect.)

7 Already, some of these effects are making themselves known. Climate change is melting glaciers in mountain ranges and shrinking the polar ice caps, causing ocean levels to rise and some Pacific island nations to "sink" further beneath the sea each year. Before long, low-lying continental coastal regions will be threatened as well. Unprecedented heat waves are altering weather patterns worldwide, sparking off increasing numbers of forest fires, followed by torrential rains and severe flooding. Meanwhile, to survive, entire communities are being forced to migrate to other areas. According to the Worldwatch Institute, Chinese farmers near the expanding Gobi Desert and Inuit populations in sub-polar North America are being particularly hard hit. Many animal species are also losing their natural habitats to global warming, and dying out as a result. These and other trends will only be <u>exacerbated</u> by further temperature increases.

Exercises: Complete the sentences or answer the questions below with the correct choices, or follow the instructions.

1. The underlined word **jeremiad** in paragraph 1 is closest in meaning to

    (A) quarrel
    (B) diatribe
    (C) bestseller
    (D) non-fiction book

2. In paragraph 1, the author points out that pesticide poisoning

    (A) is the main subject of *Silent Spring*
    (B) is a problem that has been effectively addressed
    (C) helped bring about the modern environmental movement
    (D) is a type of air pollution

3. Look at the four numbers that indicate where the following sentence could be added to paragraph 1.

    Recycling has gone a long way toward preserving resources and cutting waste, while mandatory emission-control standards on automobiles and factories have helped clean up our skies.

    Where would the sentence best fit?
    (1)   (2)   (3)   (4)

4. Which sentence below best expresses the essential information in the underlined sentence in paragraph 2? Incorrect choices change the meaning in important ways or leave out essential information.

   (A) Rising temperatures around the world are not really the problem.
   (B) The average global temperature is indeed higher.
   (C) No one is claiming or arguing that global temperatures are not rising.
   (D) The real issue is whether the earth is actually warming up.

5. In paragraph 2, the author cites NASA's Goddard Institute of Space Studies to

   (A) show that he is talking about a problem unique to the United States
   (B) introduce authoritative statistics to back up his argument
   (C) bring the information in the essay up to date
   (D) prove that recordkeeping is still being carried out

6. In paragraph 3, all of the following are mentioned as suggested explanations for global warming EXCEPT

   (A) normal surface temperature ups and downs
   (B) most information on global warming is based on temperature readings taken in big cities only
   (C) changes in the volume of light reaching the earth from the sun
   (D) the earth is coming out of a colder period

7. In paragraph 3, the author mentions pressure from business and political leaders

   (A) to hint that climatologists are not all completely impartial
   (B) because he believes that economics is as important as the environment
   (C) in order to urge government leaders to take action
   (D) for reasons of fairness and objectivity

8. It can be inferred from the information in paragraph 4 that the author

   (A) supports the prevailing scientific opinion
   (B) doubts the prevailing scientific opinion
   (C) believes that global warming is not necessarily man-made
   (D) is not sure what to believe

9. Ozone is mentioned in paragraph 5 as an example of

   (A) infrared radiation from the sun
   (B) a normal atmospheric condition
   (C) a component of the atmosphere's thermal blanket
   (D) the greenhouse effect

10. Which of the following statements is most likely true based on the information in paragraph 7?

    (A) Some Chinese farmers' land is drying up and is no longer suitable for farming.
    (B) Torrential rains are forcing Eskimos to move.
    (C) Many Pacific islands have already disappeared.
    (D) Animals no longer can survive on the polar ice caps.

11. The underlined word **exacerbated** in paragraph 7 is closest in meaning to

    (A) relieved
    (B) worsened
    (C) misunderstood
    (D) concerned

12. An introductory sentence for a brief summary of the passage is provided below. Complete the summary by selecting the THREE answer choices that express the most important ideas in the passage. Some sentences do not belong in the summary because they express ideas that are not presented or are minor ideas in the passage.

    Global warming is getting worse and is already negatively affecting life on Earth, with even direr consequences sure to come about in the near future if something isn't done about it very soon.

    (A) Evidence points overwhelmingly to emissions caused by burning fossil fuels as the primary—and man-made—cause of the phenomenon.
    (B) It is the United States that is the largest spewer of greenhouse gases into the earth's atmosphere.
    (C) Scientists now believe that the ozone layer over the polar ice caps is getting thinner.
    (D) Some people are being forced out of their homelands and numerous animal species are becoming endangered because of loss of habitat.
    (E) The pace of warming is heating up, too, with five of the world's hottest years on record coming since 1998, which has led to heat waves, flooding, and rising sea levels.
    (F) Some environmental problems are being effectively dealt with and even diminished.

Lesson 15

PTSD

Reading: Carefully read this passage.

1 Life today seems to be fraught with dangers of all kinds, maybe more so than at any other time in history. From war and acts of terror to jumbo jet crashes and natural calamities; from mysterious viruses to horrific crimes of violence—disaster (or so television and the papers would have us believe) is lurking around every corner. Whether life is indeed riskier than ever before may be open to debate, but statistics do show that post-traumatic stress disorder (PTSD) is on the rise. Perhaps this alone proves it.

2 Post-traumatic stress disorder is a mental affliction arising in an individual from an experience involving extreme psychological stress. <u>The stressful event is usually followed by lengthy periods of emotional numbness, avoidance, and denial.</u> Sufferers are subject to insomnia, memory loss, severe depression, and chronic irritability. They also persistently relive the traumatic episode through hallucinations, nightmares, and flashbacks. Alcoholism and drug dependency are not uncommon.

3 The events that <u>trigger</u> the disorder usually involve actual or threatened death or serious physical injury. **1.** These include: childhood physical, emotional, or sexual abuse; being involved in an automobile or other accident; living through natural disasters such as earthquakes, tsunami, and violent storms; and rape. Loss of personal dignity and psychological integrity (as with torture victims and hostages) can be another factor in causation. **2.** Rescue workers in disaster areas are also highly susceptible to PTSD. **3.** Even some people who viewed the September 11, 2001, World Trade Center attacks on television have exhibited symptoms. **4.** Doctors now estimate that nearly ten percent of Americans will suffer from PTSD in their lifetime.

4 Not surprisingly, however, the most frequent immediate cause of PTSD is being sent off to war. Following World War I, the syndrome was called "shell shock" (the British author Pat Barker's *Regeneration Trilogy* of novels memorably brings to life the efforts of <u>pioneering</u> psychologists to treat victims of the then little understood affliction); after World War II, the term "battle fatigue" was coined to describe it. But it wasn't until the 1980s that the term PTSD and its diagnosis came into wide use on the heels of extensive studies of Vietnam War veterans. <u>These</u> showed that nearly 30 percent of the American men and women who served in Vietnam developed symptoms of PTSD. Soldiers who have returned from the Gulf War and the current wars in Iraq and Afghanistan have shown similar rates of incidence.

5 Although men and women are equally likely to experience traumatic events, women are twice as likely to develop post-traumatic stress disorder, with childhood traumas being the most common cause. Certain personality traits like shyness and a history of depression and anxiety disorders have been found to increase a person's risk of coming down with the affliction. Some people may also have a genetic predisposition to suffer traumatic stress more intensely.

6 But not all individuals who experience traumatic events develop symptoms of PTSD. Using neuroimaging techniques like fMRI to find out why some people are more at risk than others, researchers now suggest that there are distinct differences in brain activity—particularly in areas responsible for dealing with fear and processing memory and emotions—between those trauma survivors who suffer from PTSD and those who don't. For example, the hippocampus, a part of the brain associated with <u>perception retention</u>, has been found to be smaller in PTSD sufferers. In fact, evidence is mounting that sudden traumatic stress actually causes physical changes in the brain's makeup, thereby leading to its own disorder.

7 PTSD is now commonly and very often successfully treated using a combination of psychotherapy and psychotropic drugs such as anti-anxiety medications and anti-depressants. Group therapy—talking with others who have experienced similar trauma—is especially helpful in educating victims and getting them to come to terms with their problem. The key to recovery, however, seems to be early intervention. The sooner a victim can be reached after a traumatic incident and enrolled in Critical Incident Stress Management (CISM), the better his or her chances of avoiding a severe onset of PTSD.

Exercises: Complete the sentences or answer the questions below with the correct choices, or follow the instructions.

1. In paragraph 1, the author suggests that

    (A) air accidents are the worst natural calamities
    (B) there is a danger waiting on every corner
    (C) the media might exaggerate the dangers of modern life
    (D) post-traumatic stress disorder is caused by watching too much television

2. Which sentence below best expresses the essential information in the underlined sentence in paragraph 2? Incorrect choices change the meaning in important ways or leave out essential information.

    (A) A traumatic event can cause people to withdraw into themselves, lose feelings for others, and refuse to admit they have a problem.
    (B) The symptoms of experiencing a traumatic event usually don't show up for a long time afterwards.
    (C) Victims of a traumatic event have few friends and seldom leave the house.
    (D) The sooner a person forgets about a traumatic event, the longer it takes him or her to recover from it.

3. In paragraph 2, all of the following are mentioned as symptoms of post-traumatic stress disorder EXCEPT

    (A) inability to sleep
    (B) terrifying dreams
    (C) marital difficulties
    (D) feelings of despair and hopelessness

4. The underlined word **trigger** in paragraph 3 is closest in meaning to

   (A) discharge
   (B) precipitate
   (C) undergo
   (D) release

5. Look at the four numbers that indicate where the following sentence could be added to paragraph 3.

   Individuals don't necessarily need to experience a traumatic event themselves to develop PTSD; witnessing others being victimized can also give rise to symptoms.

   Where would the sentence best fit?
   (1)   (2)   (3)   (4)

6. In paragraph 4, the author uses the underlined word **pioneering** in order to

   (A) show how successful the psychologists' efforts were
   (B) emphasize that the doctors didn't have any idea what "shell shock" was
   (C) remind readers that it is World War I that he is discussing
   (D) point out that the psychologists were the first to try to treat war veterans suffering from trauma

7. The underlined word **These** in paragraph 4 refers to

   (A) men and women in Vietnam
   (B) studies
   (C) symptoms of PTSD
   (D) the term PTSD and its diagnosis

8. All of the following are mentioned in paragraph 5 as factors predisposing people to post-traumatic stress disorder EXCEPT

    (A) being a woman
    (B) being born with the disorder
    (C) being naturally bashful
    (D) having suffered a bad childhood

9. The underlined term **perception retention** as used in paragraph 6 refers to

    (A) emotion
    (B) memory
    (C) a physical change in the brain
    (D) a cause of PTSD

10. Anti-depressants are mentioned in paragraph 7 as an example of

    (A) psychotropic drugs
    (B) psychotherapy
    (C) combined treatment
    (D) a medication for treating anxiety

11. In paragraph 7, what point does the author make about group therapy?

    (A) It is only successful when used in combination with psychotherapy.
    (B) It won't work unless started immediately after the traumatic event.
    (C) It helps victims understand and face up to their problems.
    (D) It is the key to full recovery.

Lesson 15

12. An introductory sentence for a brief summary of the passage is provided below. Complete the summary by selecting the THREE answer choices that express the most important ideas in the passage. Some sentences do not belong in the summary because they express ideas that are not presented or are minor ideas in the passage.

   Post-traumatic stress disorder is a psychological problem that afflicts nearly one in ten Americans.

   (A) The quicker victims can be started on stress management counseling, the better their chances of recovery.
   (B) Novels have been written about the disorder, which was once known as "battle fatigue."
   (C) The disorder's symptoms include hallucinations, nightmares, loss of emotional feeling, and severe depression.
   (D) The event that triggers symptoms is usually a near-fatal one, involving serious psychological and/or physical damage.
   (E) PTSD is not only an American problem, but is suffered by people all over the world.
   (F) Men who have suffered childhood trauma rarely experience PTSD.

Lesson 16

ZOOS: FOR AND AGAINST

Reading: Carefully read this passage.

1 Zoos have been around for at least 3500 years, ever since the 15th-century-B.C. Egyptian queen Hatshepsut kept a private menagerie of monkeys, lions, leopards, and other African animals to attract eligible suitors and impress visiting dignitaries. A thousand years later, Alexander the Great of Macedonia amassed a collection of over 300 animal specimens, which the Greek philosopher Aristotle closely observed and made the subject of the first scientific zoological treatise, *History of Animals*.

2 But the most <u>assiduous</u> collectors were the citizens of Imperial Rome, who brought back tens of thousands of creatures that had been captured during far-flung military conquests or received as gifts of tribute from <u>subjugated</u> rulers. Many of these animals were only displayed temporarily, however—the more ferocious ones were soon moved out of their cages and into "sporting" arenas, where gladiators engaged them in mortal combat before crowds of bloodthirsty spectators.

3 Throughout the Age of Imperialism (15th to 18th centuries), the kings and queens of Europe maintained large private collections of exotic animals from around the globe as displays of colonial wealth, power, and prestige. It wasn't until the 19th century, however, that the zoo as a place of popular entertainment was born. Zoos sprang up in most major metropolitan areas, and, following the example of the London Zoological Society, began claiming for themselves scientific and educational as well as amusement purposes.

4 1. Today, zoos still thrive, attracting millions of visitors annually. 2. The days when the animals were locked up in tiny iron cages or cold concrete enclosures have thankfully disappeared. 3. Those cruder zoos have given way to more enlightened parks that endeavor to replicate as closely as possible the animals' natural habitats by creating mini-swamps, artificial rivers, special climate conditions, and mixed-specie exhibits. Today's best zoos are also actively involved in studying wildlife diseases and reproduction, developing new veterinary surgical techniques, and carrying out other serious-minded research projects. 4.

5 Despite these welcome improvements, zoos remain highly controversial, with many animal-rights activists advocating their total abolishment. Zoos, they say, are inherently unethical and inhumane. <u>Keeping wild animals in custody not only demeans the animals, it demeans us</u>. Animals in captivity, they argue, display such "mad" behaviors as staring, pacing, circling, and bar-biting—all caused by the boredom, frustration, and dislocation of loss of freedom. No matter how loudly zoos assert their right to existence, activists maintain, they cannot deny <u>this basic fact</u>. What exactly are the zoos' assertions? And what are the activists' arguments against them?

6 Today's more advanced zoos claim to play a key role in educating the public about wild animal life, habits, and problems. Opponents of zoos don't see it like this. To them, zoos' educational efforts, though <u>laudatory</u> in a way, are misguided, self-deceiving, and superficial at best. Animals in captivity soon lose their natural characteristics and are no longer representative of their species. What, ask animal welfare groups, can we learn from such tame, sanitized animals? If zoos really want to educate people about animals, and to arouse compassion for their plight, wouldn't it be better, for example, to give public screenings of documentary films that show how man has exploited our animal cousins and destroyed their native surroundings?

7 Zoos also claim to be centers of scientific research on animal behavior, disease, and so on. Not so, say the animal rights groups, and for the same reason cited above. Zoo animals are not wild animals. Any research conducted on them cannot be truly scientific or useful because it applies only to animals in zoos.

8 The most important pretext for their existence that zoos proffer, however, is that they are there for the animals' protection and preservation. Through captive-breeding programs, zoos claim to be saving many endangered animal species from extinction. These animals are then being reintroduced into the wild, where it is hoped they will repopulate their species and help maintain biodiversity.

9 Animal supporters disagree. These repopulation programs have had very little success, they say. In fact, zoos continue to remove more animals from the wild than they return to it. The idea of captive breeding is misguided for another reason: in most cases, the animals' habitats have been destroyed, so that even if the animals are "saved," there is no "wild" for them to return to. Thus, they are doomed to a life in captivity. The only true way to save these animals from extinction, say the activists, is to protect and restore their original habitats.

Exercises: Complete the sentences or answer the questions below with the correct choices, or follow the instructions.

1. In paragraph 1, the author mentions Aristotle as an example of

    (A) a famous Greek philosopher
    (B) a pioneer in animal studies
    (C) Alexander the Great's private tutor
    (D) a gatherer of hundreds of animal specimens

2. The underlined word **assiduous** in paragraph 2 is closest in meaning to

    (A) enthusiastic
    (B) cruel
    (C) notorious
    (D) systematic

3. The underlined word **subjugated** in paragraph 2 is closest in meaning to

    (A) distant
    (B) deceased
    (C) conquered
    (D) captured

4. All of the following are mentioned in paragraphs 1, 2, and 3 about zoos in history EXCEPT

    (A) they were displays of wealth and power
    (B) they were places where animals were slaughtered by armed warriors
    (C) their animals were gathered during military expeditions
    (D) they were mostly private collections

Lesson 16

5. It can be inferred from the information in paragraph 3 that

   (A) in the 1800s, no zoos existed outside the large cities
   (B) the first 19th-century zoos received their animals from the kings and queens of Europe
   (C) the London Zoological Society established the world's first public zoo
   (D) the general public didn't have many opportunities to see wild animals until the 19th century

6. Look at the four numbers that indicate where the following sentence could be added to paragraph 4.

   The modern zoo, however, is for the most part a far cry from the zoos of yesterday.

   Where would the sentence best fit?
   (1)   (2)   (3)   (4)

7. In paragraph 4, the author mentions mixed-specie exhibits as an example of

   (A) special climate conditions
   (B) a zoo practice that has long since disappeared
   (C) an attempt to reproduce natural habitats
   (D) a serious-minded research project

8. Which sentence below best expresses the essential information in the underlined sentence in paragraph 5? Incorrect choices change the meaning in important ways or leave out essential information.

    (A) By locking animals in cages, we both abuse them and bring shame on ourselves.
    (B) Many zoo officials confess that they feel sorry for the animals they are in charge of.
    (C) Since animals don't feel shame or embarrassment, taking away their freedom doesn't really bother them that much.
    (D) Staring at captive animals is one of the most degrading things people can do.

9. The underlined phrase **this basic fact** in paragraph 5 refers to

    (A) the abolition of zoos
    (B) animals' "mad" behavior caused by boredom and frustration
    (C) zoos' right to existence
    (D) the immorality of keeping animals in captivity

10. The underlined word **laudatory** in paragraph 6 is closest in meaning to

    (A) unintentional
    (B) praiseworthy
    (C) explicable
    (D) unforgiveable

11. All of the following are cited by zoos in paragraph 8 as aims of captive-breeding programs EXCEPT

    (A) observing animals' reproductive habits
    (B) reintroducing threatened animal species to the wild
    (C) keeping species from dying out
    (D) helping to maintain biodiversity

Lesson 16

12. An introductory sentence for a brief summary of animal rights activists' call for an abolishment of zoos is provided below. Complete the summary by selecting the THREE answer choices that express their main arguments. Some sentences do not belong in the summary because they express ideas that are not mentioned or are minor ideas in the passage.

Despite zoos' claims to the contrary, keeping animals in captivity is inherently immoral.

(A) Zoos pay high prices to animal hunters who bring them specimens of endangered species.
(B) There is a very high incidence of death and disease among animals kept in zoos.
(C) Zoos cannot be truly educational or conduct genuine scientific research if the animals in them are practically domesticated.
(D) Since many of the animals' original habitats have long since been destroyed, plans to reintroduce them to "the wild" are both futile and hypocritical.
(E) Studying captive animals is the only way we have to learn about how animals behave in nature.
(F) Animals kept in captivity not only lose their natural characteristics, but they also lose their minds in the process.

Lesson 17

THE PANAMA CANAL

Reading: Carefully read this passage.

1 Civil engineering is the profession devoted to altering the geographical landscape to accommodate the needs of business, industry, and daily life. Civil engineers design, construct, and maintain structures of all kinds, including offices, factories, bridges, tunnels, railroads, dams, highways, and irrigation and water-supply systems.

2 The Panama Canal, built by the United States in the early years of the 20th century on land leased from the Republic of Panama, is one of the greatest civil engineering projects ever undertaken. The 50-mile waterway consists of seventeen artificial lakes, an <u>intricate</u> system of man-made channels, and three sets of hydraulic locks for lowering and raising water levels. It neatly bisects the Western Hemisphere, linking the Pacific and Atlantic oceans, enabling ships to avoid the treacherous waters of Cape Horn at the tip of South America, and affording them huge reductions in sailing time, distance, and expense.

3 Building a waterway across the Isthmus of Panama was first suggested in the early 16th century, when Spain was actively exploiting the rich resources of its newly established American colonies and increasing its trade with the Orient. Although Spanish officials did draw up some preliminary plans for such a project, wars in Europe kept <u>them</u> from being realized. It wasn't until the mid-19th century, following the discovery of gold in California in 1848 and the ensuing Gold Rush, that plans for connecting the two oceans were seriously revived. <u>In 1881, a French civil engineering firm inaugurated work on a canal, but poor planning, financial and machinery problems, and rampant disease among workers doomed the project to failure.</u>

4 Then, in 1903, the United States acquired the rights to a Panama concession, and, the next year, began construction in earnest, with American engineers picking up where the French had left off. Officials spent the first three years determining the most suitable kind of canal for the location (eventually opting for an elevated system of locks), conducting land surveys, and planning the overall project. Of particular importance was disease

Lesson 17

control. The deadly French experience had shown that in order for the project to succeed, the workers must be well fed, well housed, and disease free. Whole towns sprang up out of the Panamanian jungle to accommodate them, complete with shops, churches, schools, and hospitals. Stagnant swamps were drained, drainage ditches built, and plumbing and sanitation facilities installed. Armed with recently acquired knowledge about the prevention of malaria and yellow fever, health officials constantly sprayed the site with pesticides and disinfectants.

5 Nevertheless, the going was rough. Using dynamite, clumsy steam shovels, and horse- and ox-drawn wagons, workers, <u>toiling</u> in torrid heat and fighting off insects and snakes of all kinds, had to excavate and haul away over 100 million cubic yards of earth and rock. Torrential rains caused frequent—and frequently lethal—mud and landslides. To build the canal's locks, dams, and retaining walls, workers mixed and poured millions of tons of concrete made from crushed rock.

6 In the end, the canal took the efforts of over 200,000 people and nine years to construct, at a cost of $340 million and nearly 6,000 lives. The first ship to use the canal—the merchant freighter *Ancon*—sailed through on August 15, 1914.

7 Today, the Panama Canal remains a vital channel for international trade and shipping. **1.** Some 14,000 ships carrying approximately 250 million tons of cargo sail through the Panama Canal each year. **2.** But most of the ships for which the canal was originally built are a thing of the past. **3.** Modern shipping has greatly increased the size of vessels, with some capable of carrying 300,000 tons of cargo. **4.** These gargantuan freighters and liners, which are expected to account for a full one-third of the world's shipping by 2010, have raised serious questions about the canal's future. Other locations, through Mexico, Nicaragua, or Columbia, have been proposed as sites for a bigger, better canal. Meanwhile, Panama, whose economy and welfare depend absolutely on the income the canal brings in, is ambitiously going ahead with expansion and modernization plans.

Exercises: Complete the sentences or answer the questions below with the correct choices, or follow the instructions.

1. All of the following are mentioned in paragraph 1 as projects undertaken by civil engineers EXCEPT

    (A) industrial plants
    (B) domestic housing
    (C) structures for business
    (D) transportation facilities

2. The underlined word **intricate** in paragraph 2 is closest in meaning to

    (A) elaborate
    (B) complete
    (C) practical
    (D) efficient

3. The most important idea expressed by the author in paragraph 2 is that

    (A) the canal is 50 miles long
    (B) the canal's locks raise and lower water levels
    (C) the canal is a great civil engineering project
    (D) the canal saves shippers time and money

4. The underlined word **them** in paragraph 3 refers to

    (A) Spanish officials
    (B) plans for a canal
    (C) wars in Europe
    (D) resources exploitation

Lesson 17

5. In paragraph 3, what reason is given for the revival of interest in a canal project in the mid-19th century?

    (A) the establishment of colonies in the New World
    (B) the discovery of gold in California
    (C) competition from Spain
    (D) increasing trade with Asia

6. Which sentence below best expresses the essential information in the underlined sentence in paragraph 3? Incorrect choices change the meaning in important ways or leave out essential information.

    (A) The French company that worked on the project in 1881 should have spent more time and money on planning.
    (B) The 1881 French project ran out of money before it could successfully complete the canal's construction.
    (C) The French construction company that started building a canal in 1881 might have pulled it off if it had had better disease control, better equipment, and more money and foresight.
    (D) The machines that the 1881 project used were inadequate for the conditions, as were the workers and medical personnel.

7. It can be inferred from paragraph 4 that

    (A) the Americans both took advantage of what progress the French had made and also learned from their mistakes
    (B) America obtained the concession through military and diplomatic means
    (C) the canal was built by foreign workers
    (D) disease ceased to be a problem altogether

8. The underlined word **toiling** in paragraph 5 is closest in meaning to

   (A) working
   (B) sweating
   (C) suffering
   (D) living

9. All of the following are mentioned as examples of working conditions during the canal construction project EXCEPT

   (A) high temperatures
   (B) bad weather
   (C) pests
   (D) making concrete out of crushed rock

10. Look at the four numbers that indicate where the following sentence could be added to paragraph 7.

    The canal can accommodate vessels ranging in size from small yachts to merchant freighters with a maximum cargo capacity of 65,000 tons.

    Where would the sentence best fit?
    (1)　(2)　(3)　(4)

11. According to paragraph 7, what will happen in the next few years?

    (A) The Panama Canal will become a thing of the past.
    (B) A bigger and better canal will be constructed across Mexico.
    (C) Giant ships will make up a large portion of the world's fleet.
    (D) Panama will maintain its income by raising the toll charge for passage through the canal.

Lesson 17

12. Which of the following sentences would make the best introductory sentence for a brief summary of the main ideas in the passage?

   (A) Every year, some 14,000 vessels sail through the Panama Canal, which is now owned and operated not by the United States but by the Republic of Panama.
   (B) Construction of the Panama Canal was carried out in two stages, the first undertaken by a French firm starting in 1881, and the second begun in 1904 by the American government.
   (C) A great feat of engineering skill and human labor and sacrifice that revolutionized the international shipping business, the Panama Canal is now faced with an uncertain future.
   (D) Today, many ships are so large that they must bypass the Panama Canal and make the long and expensive trip around South America and through the dangerous waters of Cape Horn.

Lesson 18

JOHN DEWEY'S LABORATORY SCHOOL

Reading: Carefully read this passage.

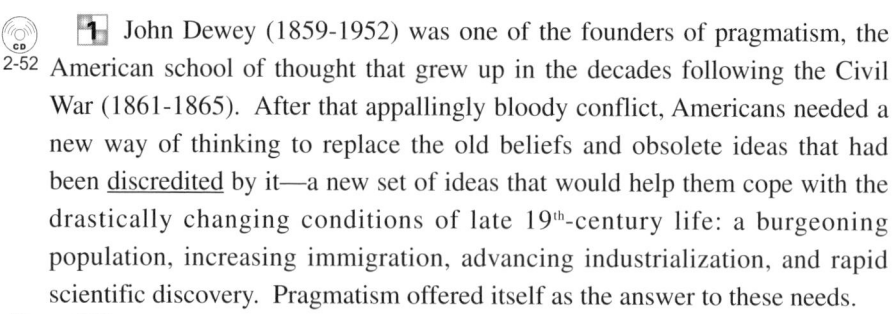

1 John Dewey (1859-1952) was one of the founders of pragmatism, the American school of thought that grew up in the decades following the Civil War (1861-1865). After that appallingly bloody conflict, Americans needed a new way of thinking to replace the old beliefs and obsolete ideas that had been <u>discredited</u> by it—a new set of ideas that would help them cope with the drastically changing conditions of late 19th-century life: a burgeoning population, increasing immigration, advancing industrialization, and rapid scientific discovery. Pragmatism offered itself as the answer to these needs.

2 Dewey and other pragmatists like Willam James held that ideas are not absolute, permanent entities existing on their own, but are ever-changing, <u>provisional</u> human responses to specific circumstances. An idea's truth lies in its usefulness as a tool for better living and can only be determined through experience and observation.

3 Pragmatists also taught that assumptions and beliefs should never be allowed to deteriorate into hardened dogma or ideology. <u>They</u> should constantly be reexamined for error and revised to fit changing circumstances. Dewey and his fellow pragmatists hoped that this new way of thinking would help foster tolerance towards differences among peoples and cultures, making it more difficult for old, hardened ideas to be used as an excuse for hatred and violence.

4 Early on in his career, John Dewey wrote several books on pedagogy that reflected his pragmatic beliefs. In 1896, to put his theories and beliefs to the test, he opened an experimental primary and secondary school in Chicago, Illinois, that became known as the Laboratory School.

5 Dewey was convinced that the conventional, desk-bound approach to education was ineffective and futile. He believed that traditional teaching, with its emphasis on completion of assignments through isolated private study, was "static in subject matter, authoritarian in methods, and mainly passive and receptive." Teachers of the time had little or no special training in educational methods or theory and were in school mainly to impose ideas and to instill specific habits of thought and discipline. Curricula were made up of

Lesson 18

fixed subjects, which were then divided up into fixed lessons, which, in turn, were broken down into fixed formulas and facts. As Dewey saw it, in such a classroom environment, the child was a mere "ductile and <u>docile</u>" receptacle for bits and pieces of information. The traditional classroom, "with its rows of ugly desks placed in geometrical order, crowded together so that there is as little moving room as possible," was arranged to reflect this rote, passive approach to learning. Education in such a classroom was also cut off from the community at large, instead of being an integral part and extension of it.

6 Dewey wanted to change all this. <u>Education, he believed, should be a "process of living," not mere "preparation for future living."</u> Thus, the Laboratory School put the child at the center of education. **1.** Self-realization, not the mere accumulation of knowledge and information, was its goal. **2.** Academic excellence was important, but not nearly as important as creative problem-solving. The school was indeed a laboratory in two senses. It was a place where new educational theories and ideas could be both generated and tested. **3.** It was also a place where pupils could take charge of their own learning, developing approaches that fit their individual needs as well as the needs of the group. **4.**

7 Perhaps Dewey's greatest insight was that learning and knowledge begin in doing and activity. The majority of learning at the Laboratory School took place through hands-on projects: exploring nature firsthand rather than reading about it in books; taking trips rather than poring over maps; seeing historical plays instead of memorizing historical facts. Dewey's pupils also sewed their own clothes, worked on carpentry projects, and prepared their own lunches. Cooking, for example, provided learners with lessons in arithmetic (weighing and measuring ingredients), biology (discussing nutrition and digestion), and geography (learning about the natural habitats of plants and animals). It also involved cooperation for the good of all.

8 The Laboratory School folded after a few years, when John Dewey moved from Chicago to New York City. As Laurel Tanner points out in her excellent study of the Laboratory School: "Although influential in its time, the school that John Dewey established … has all but been forgotten …. A century later, the ideas and practices still have been mainly disregarded. They are waiting for us in the records of this school, lessons yet unlearned about things that deeply concern us."

Exercises: Complete the sentences or answer the queastions below with the correct choices, or follow the instructions.

1. The underlined word **discredited** in paragraph 1 is closest in meaning to

    (A) less well known
    (B) less trusted
    (C) less clearly understood
    (D) less doubted

2. All of the following are mentioned in paragraph 1 as social changes taking place at the end of the 19th century in America EXCEPT

    (A) the violence of the Civil War
    (B) population increases
    (C) the influx of foreigners
    (D) progress in science

3. The underlined word **provisional** in paragraph 2 is closest in meaning to

    (A) temporary
    (B) long-lasting
    (C) absolute
    (D) generous

4. The underlined word **They** in paragraph 3 refers to

    (A) dogma and ideology
    (B) pragmatists
    (C) changing circumstances
    (D) assumptions and beliefs

5. In paragraph 3, what does the author say the pragmatists hoped their new way of thinking might do?

   (A) serve as an excuse for hatred and violence
   (B) be constantly reexamined
   (C) educate people about other cultures
   (D) promote open-mindedness

6. It can be inferred from paragraph 4 that

   (A) John Dewey became the first teacher at the Laboratory School
   (B) Dewey's books on education have been very influential
   (C) The Laboratory School was a place where people from different cultures could get to know each other
   (D) Dewey wanted his school to give pupils ideas and tools that would help them cope with real-life problems and conditions

7. The underlined word **docile** in paragraph 5 is closest in meaning to

   (A) friendly
   (B) passive
   (C) rote
   (D) attentive

8. Which sentence below best expresses the essential information in the underlined sentence in paragraph 6? Incorrect choices change the meaning in important ways or leave out essential information.

   (A) Dewey believed that education should be seen as ongoing with life itself rather than as a way to lay the groundwork for the years ahead.
   (B) According to Dewey, schools should help pupils become successful in their chosen careers.
   (C) Dewey wanted education to be more process-oriented.
   (D) Dewey wanted his pupils to stop worrying about the future and to concentrate on their immediate studies.

9. Look at the four numbers that indicate where the following sentence could be added to paragraph 6.

   Children mixed and mingled freely with each other, in the classroom and around the school, which encouraged them to "act as a cooperative member of a unity" and to "emerge from their narrowness of action and feeling."

   Where would the sentence best fit?
   (1)   (2)   (3)   (4)

10. All of the following are mentioned as examples of the Laboratory School pupils' hands-on learning projects EXCEPT

    (A) making trips out into nature
    (B) writing historical plays
    (C) making their own clothes
    (D) making their own lunches

11. Match the answer choices below to the type of school they describe. Write the letters of the choices in the parentheses. TWO of the answer choices will NOT be used.

    Traditional schools
    (   )
    (   )

    The Laboratory School
    (   )
    (   )
    (   )

    (A) The emphasis was on studying alone and completing specific assignments.
    (B) The emphasis was on doing and actively participating in cooperative projects.
    (C) It was a place where teachers received instruction in educational psychology.
    (D) No emphasis was placed on academic excellence or the accumulation of knowledge.
    (E) Teachers imposed ideas on pupils and formed fixed habits of thought in them.
    (F) Education was child-centered and geared toward self-actualization.
    (G) Pupils had some control over how their educations should be conducted.

12. Which of the following statements is most likely true about the main focus of Laurel Tanner's book on John Dewey?

    (A) It tries to make Dewey's ideas less difficult to understand for modern readers.
    (B) It proposes that today's schools should pay more attention to Dewey's ideas and methods.
    (C) It argues that Dewey's ideas have become less relevant and useful over time.
    (D) It is deeply concerned with pragmatism and its insights into how people actually think and learn.

Lesson 19

THE END OF APARTHEID

Reading: Carefully read this passage.

1 Apartheid was the South African caste system that rigidly divided the country along racial lines from 1948 to 1992. Black Africans, who accounted for some 75 percent of the total population, as well as Indians, Asians, and "coloreds" (people of mixed ancestry), were forcibly segregated from the ruling whites, who, despite comprising just 13 percent of the populace, controlled virtually all of South Africa's wealth and resources, owned and operated most of its principal businesses and industries, and monopolized government.

2 Although South African racial separation itself extended back to the 17th century and the first days of white colonial settlement, apartheid was not formalized as official government policy until after the Second World War. While the human rights abuses it <u>engendered</u> were primarily motivated by white supremacist racism, apartheid also had economic causes. Working class whites low down on the social hierarchy feared that they would lose their jobs and livelihoods to cheaper black labor. White farmers needed cheap black labor to plant and harvest their crops and manage their livestock. In the years immediately following the war, these and other interest groups lobbied for severely restricted black freedoms.

3 As a result, throughout the 1950s, the South African government enacted a series of laws <u>entrenching</u> white domination. The Group Areas Act of 1950 assigned races to different geographical districts. Urban blacks were uprooted and relocated to "townships" and "homelands" far outside the city, in effect condemning them to lives of rural poverty. "Pass Laws" and curfews severely curtailed black mobility within the country. All blacks had to carry identity passbooks at all times, and only those holding special permits were allowed to work in white areas. <u>Blacks were denied suffrage, and access to education was effectively curtailed.</u> They could not participate in any kind of political activity, nor could they own land or join unions. Regulations prohibited interracial relations of all kinds and strictly segregated all public transportation, recreation, and medical facilities.

4 The South African government used every means of suppression to

Lesson 19

brutally enforce these laws. Police and military forces enjoyed sweeping powers of arrest and detention. Nevertheless, non-white opposition to apartheid, much of it necessarily underground, grew throughout the 50s and 60s. The country's most powerful black organization, the African National Congress (ANC), encouraged resistance through a variety of tactics—strikes, demonstrations, sabotage, passbook burnings—strategies which often brought swift, violent reprisals from the government.

5 1. The 1961 Sharpeville Massacre, when some 70 unarmed black protestors were shot in the back by police, along with the 1964 jailing of Nelson Mandela, the ANC leader, and other black dissidents, spurred blacks (and their sympathetic white supporters) to step up opposition. Further resistance brought further reprisals. An uprising in the township of Soweto in 1976 resulted in the loss of hundreds of black lives. 2. South African military aid to racist white regimes in Rhodesia, Angola, and other African colonies inflamed anti-apartheid sentiment among the international community. 3. Financial and moral support for black freedom poured in from around the globe. 4. South Africa suddenly found itself a <u>pariah</u> among nations. Important trading partners severed ties and applied <u>sanctions</u>, tourists boycotted, and investors fled.

6 Adding to the South African government's woes was the growing Black Consciousness Movement, which meant that more and more young blacks were committed to revolution—by any means. Thus, by the mid-1980s, the country was plunged into a constant state of emergency, with acts of terrorism and uprisings becoming almost daily occurrences. Something had to give—and it did.

7 In 1986, pressure inside and outside the country compelled leaders to repeal the Pass Laws and allow blacks a greater voice in politics. Three years later, the president of South Africa, Pieter Botha, met in prison with Nelson Mandela, which led to Mandela's release the next year. In 1991, F.W. de Klerk, Botha's successor, and the South African parliament began dismantling apartheid piece by piece, freeing political prisoners and desegregating hospitals, schools, and other public institutions. Apartheid officially came to an end the next year. Within a year, a new constitution that provided for universal suffrage and full participation by blacks in government was proposed and approved. Then, the following year, the country held its first ever democratic elections. By an overwhelming majority, the nation's voters elected Nelson Mandela to be their first black president.

Exercises: Complete the sentences or answer the questions below with the correct choices, or follow the instructions.

1. According to paragraph 1, all of the following statements are true EXCEPT

    (A) whites used coercion to keep the races apart
    (B) Asians and Indians were not classified as "coloreds," but as separate racial groups
    (C) whites were the most populous racial group in the country
    (D) non-whites played little or no role in the political process

2. The underlined word **engendered** in paragraph 2 is closest in meaning to

    (A) gave rise to
    (B) set up
    (C) did away with
    (D) was known for

3. All of the following can be inferred from paragraph 2 EXCEPT

    (A) agriculture in South Africa depended on black labor
    (B) not all whites in South Africa enjoyed equal status
    (C) racism didn't play as important a role in apartheid as most people think
    (D) white farmers and workers exerted considerable influence on the South African government

4. The underlined word **entrenching** in paragraph 3 is closest in meaning to

   (A) improving
   (B) strengthening
   (C) defining
   (D) generating

5. In paragraph 3, the author mentions passbooks as

   (A) a direct result of the Group Areas Act
   (B) an example of restrictions on interaction among the various races
   (C) documents blacks needed in order to find jobs
   (D) a policy restricting black movement

6. Which sentence below best expresses the essential information in the underlined sentence in paragraph 3? Incorrect choices change the meaning in important ways or leave out essential information.

   (A) Blacks couldn't vote and few went to school.
   (B) Schooling for blacks left much to be desired.
   (C) Without voting rights or education, blacks could exercise little political power.
   (D) Because they were uneducated, blacks were not allowed to vote.

7. In paragraph 4, what is mentioned as the main cause of government reprisals?

   (A) sweeping powers of arrest and detention
   (B) the African National Congress
   (C) meetings held in secret by non-whites
   (D) strikes, demonstrations, and sabotage

8. Look at the four numbers that indicate where the following sentence could be added to paragraph 5.

   Meanwhile, external developments exacerbated the crisis.

   Where would the sentence best fit?
   (1)   (2)   (3)   (4)

9. The underlined word **pariah** in paragraph 5 is closest in meaning to
   (A) victim
   (B) suspect
   (C) defendant
   (D) outcast

10. The underlined word **sanctions** in paragraph 5 is closest in meaning to
    (A) tacit approval
    (B) embargoes
    (C) limited conditions
    (D) urgent requests

11. In paragraph 6, the author uses the expression **by any means** in order to
    (A) hint that young blacks increasingly resorted to violence to get what they wanted
    (B) show that the revolution was succeeding
    (C) criticize the Black Consciousness Movement
    (D) show his sympathy for the efforts of young blacks

Lesson 19

12. Based on the information in paragraph 7, match each of the events below with the year that it took place. Write the appropriate letters on the lines.

   1. _____ new constitution proposed and approved
   2. _____ Nelson Mandela meets with Botha
   3. _____ passbooks no longer required
   4. _____ blacks vote for first time
   5. _____ apartheid as official policy abolished
   6. _____ political prisoners freed and schools desegregated

   (A) 1986   (B) 1989   (C) 1991   (D) 1992
   (E) 1993   (F) 1994

Lesson 20

TRANSFORMING BUSINESS

Reading: Carefully read this passage.

1 Given the current state of the world, particularly when it comes to social justice and enviromental matters, and the public's growing awareness of and concern over it, the business case for corporate social responsibility is stronger than ever. <u>It has become increasingly apparent that corporations must adapt their business practices to this new set of circumstances—or else</u>. Recent studies show that the ecosystems on which civilization and society depend are deteriorating to the "do or die" point. This stress and strain on the earth's natural functions is not only <u>jeopardizing</u> the quality and future of human life, but is profoundly affecting business where it hurts most—the bottom line.

2 More and more, today's enlightened consumers, when faced with a choice between two products of comparable price and quality, are buying the one produced by the company that is more sensitive to the needs of society and the environment. When presented with the option of working for a company that acts responsibly towards the community in which it operates and one that doesn't, workers who value personal fulfillment over personal gain are embracing the former. Likewise, when investors who hope to make a significant contribution and not just a quick profit look for some place to put their money, they increasingly choose companies that deal with *all* their stakeholders—employees, customers, local neighborhoods, business partners, and investors—justly and humanely. When concerned consumers, workers, and stockholders discover that a company in which they have a strong stake operates overseas sweatshops using child labor, or is secretly dumping toxic wastes, or is marketing faulty goods, their conscience tells them that it's time to <u>sever</u> their connection with that company.

3 <u>These trends</u> have made it imperative that corporations "clean up their act." They can no longer afford to disregard the truth: they must either behave in an environmentally sustainable and socially beneficial manner, or face declining competitiveness and shrinking profits.

Lesson 20

4 Of course, this is just the opposite of the truth as conventional businesses and capitalists have seen it. Traditionally, corporations have operated under the perception that profit—that is, giving greedy, demanding shareholders maximum short-term return on their investments—is first and foremost. Everything that the traditional corporation does is geared to this end. Everything—ethics, social welfare, the environment—must take a back seat to it. Thus, instead of trying to create a more favorable and sustainable system for doing business, instead of working for the benefit of society as a whole, corporations have worked to promote their own selfish interests: for weaker environmental laws, for example, or for increased tax breaks. This, however, can no longer be tolerated.

5 **1.** Corporations must be made to see—and many already do—that while some sacrifices are unavoidable, switching over to a more socially responsible and sustainable type of operation can, over the long term, substantially improve their financial performance and increase profits. **2.** Global studies show that during employment interviews, today's potential recruits are just as likely to ask questions about a firm's record on social issues as they are questions about benefits and salaries. **3.** Research—and common sense—also indicates that taking pride in their company's community performance gives workers a higher sense of job satisfaction and actually boosts worker productivity. **4.** And when a company makes employee community involvement a part of its corporate culture through charity fundraising and volunteer activities, for example, it becomes known as a "good place to work," helping it to build up a more efficient, loyal, and permanent staff. Meanwhile, by "thinking environmentally" and initiating such responsible policy measures as reducing power consumption, cutting waste, and promoting more efficient use of resources through recycling, a company can both decrease costs and increase competitiveness.

6 Once a company earns a reputation for being eco-, employee-, and socio-friendly, the benefits to it start to <u>accrue</u> immediately. Ethically minded consumers rush out to buy its products. Investors and banks line up to give it money. Social activists and government regulators get off its back. And its shareholders get what they want, too.

Exercises: Complete the sentences or answer the questions below with the correct choices, or follow the instructions.

1. Which sentence below best expresses the essential information in the underlined sentence in paragraph 1? Incorrect choices change the meaning in important ways or leave out essential information.

    (A) More and more obviously, changing social conditions have made it necessary for companies to either find new ways of doing business, or risk going out of business.
    (B) It goes without saying that corporations will never be able to change with the times.
    (C) Companies that want to improve their business performance must work to make the world more suitable to their selfish needs and interests.
    (D) Needless to say, the world needs business in order to make it possible to change present circumstances.

2. The underlined word **jeopardizing** in paragraph 1 is closest in meaning to

    (A) underestimating
    (B) threatening
    (C) ameliorating
    (D) complicating

3. In paragraph 1, how does the author say that business will be most affected by deteriorating ecosystems?

    (A) They will be forced to protect current business practices.
    (B) They will find it more difficult to make a profit.
    (C) They will increasingly depend on society.
    (D) They will find it impossible to hire good workers.

4. In paragraph 2, what point does the author make about how today's consumers choose the products they buy?

   (A) Quality and price no longer concern them.
   (B) They want to have a choice between two comparable companies' products.
   (C) They are as interested in a company's policies as they are in a product's price and quality.
   (D) They buy the higher-priced product if the quality is comparable.

5. The author mentions sweatshops in paragraph 2 as an example of

   (A) a company acting responsibly
   (B) an unjust and inhumane business practice
   (C) a faulty product
   (D) a secret dumping operation

6. The underlined word **sever** in paragraph 2 is closest in meaning to

   (A) renew
   (B) discuss
   (C) strengthen
   (D) discontinue

7. The underlined phrase **These trends** in paragraph 3 refers to

   (A) increasing corporate social responsibilities
   (B) new attitudes among workers, consumers, and investors
   (C) the earth's deteriorating natural functions
   (D) using child labor, dumping toxic wastes, and marketing faulty goods

8. The author discusses traditional corporate business practices in paragraph 4

   (A) as an example of the truth of the situation
   (B) to emphasize how hopeless the situation seems to conventional businessmen
   (C) to stress what needs to be overcome in order for companies to become more responsible
   (D) to prove how evil the corporate system is

9. Look at the four numbers that indicate where the following sentence could be added to paragraph 5.

   By making themselves more openly accountable to society, companies can attract and retain a better-educated, higher-quality, more committed type of worker.

   Where would the sentence best fit?
   (1)   (2)   (3)   (4)

10. In paragraph 5, the author mentions all of the following as ways that being more socially responsible can improve a company's financial performance EXCEPT

    (A) lobbying for weaker pollution laws and lower taxes
    (B) using resources more efficiently
    (C) improving its corporate culture
    (D) reducing waste

Lesson 20

11. The underlined word **accrue** in paragraph 6 is closest in meaning to

    (A) fall off
    (B) mount up
    (C) move forward
    (D) bear out

12. An introductory sentence for a brief summary of the passage is provided below. Complete the summary by selecting the THREE answer choices that express the most important ideas in the passage. Some sentences do not belong in the summary because they express ideas that are not presented or are minor ideas in the passage.

    Environmental and ethical considerations have brought the concept of corporate social responsibility into the spotlight in recent years.

    (A) While becoming more socially responsible may involve some sacrifice for a company, eventually it will pay off in increased profits.
    (B) Children working in overseas sweatshops work in slave-like conditions for very little money.
    (C) Being socially accountable involves making sure that all stakeholders and the community at large benefit from a company's business practices.
    (D) Dumping toxic waste can cause great damage to a company's reputation.
    (E) Customers are more apt to buy a socially committed company's products, banks are more likely to lend it money, and its employees tend to work harder and stay with the company longer.
    (F) Research shows that many employees enjoy getting involved in outside volunteer activities and donating part of their salaries to charity.

Lesson 1

イングリッシュ 101: 批判的思考と読書

リーディング： 以下の文章を注意深く読め。

① 今日ほど批判的思考と読書の必要性が高まったことはかつてない。私たちは、来る日も来る日もマス・メディア —— 印刷物、放送、そして今ではワールド・ワイド・ウェブ —— による大量の情報にさらされ、あらゆる種の筋からのニュース・レポートの吸収・消化を求められている。どれが信頼のおけるものでどれがそうでないのか。すべての政党の政治家、またどんな信条の政治家も、お馴染みの平和と繁栄を約束している。誰を信じればいいのだろう。広告とコマーシャルがこの世のすべての製品を推奨してくる。それらは本当に額面通り私たちの生活に有益で必要なものなのか。ハリウッドとテレビは、歴史上の出来事に関するドキュメンタリー・ドラマと有名人の伝記映画を提供してくれるが、どれも歴史的事実と歴史上のフィクションの微妙な境目に位置するものばかりである。何が本当で、何がそうでないのか。インターネットをブラウズすれば、私たちはどんどん増殖するブログに直面する。これは、新しいもう1つのジャーナリズム —— 主流メディアに対する人々の答え —— だと称されるウェブ・サイトである。しかし、ブロガーがもたらす情報は本当に信じられるのか。どこまでが客観的事実で、どこまでが個人の意見なのか。

② **1.** このすべての情報を分別するには、もっと批判的にものを考えられるようになる必要がある。**2.** そのためには、情報のみならず、我々個人の思考パターンと動機をも分析・評価するための確かな技術と信頼のおける基準を開発しなければならない。**3.** 次に、自らが成長し、より知的になり続けられるように、これらの技術と基準を習慣的に適用していかなければならないのだ。**4.**

③ これは簡単にできることではない。我々の自己はみな家庭のしつけと文化環境によって作られるものである。このため我々は、どうしても捨てられない —— 我々自身を構成しているとまで信じる —— 一連の仮説、信念、偏見を持つようになり、しばしば世界を偏狭に、あるいは歪めて見るようになってしまう。新しい情報や考えを前にすると、これまでに苦労して得た知識を保護し、大切な信念を保存して、以前からの意見を保守するために躍起になる。つまり、我々は反批判的に考えてしまうのである。

④ 批判的に考えられない人たちは、単純な、黒か白か、イエスかノーかの世界観

しか持たない。世界の可能性と複雑さに心を閉ざしてしまい、かすかな繋がりおよび関連性を見逃して、より深い意味など認識できないのである。自分たちの事実が唯一妥当なものであると主張し、自らの興味と観点しか正当なものはないと信じるのだ。

5　一方、批判的に考える人たちに特徴的なのは、心の広さ、知的な誠実さ、自己認識、そして合理性を兼ね備えているということだ。彼らは好奇心を持って世界を見つめ、世界の新しい解釈や異なった解釈にもオープンであり続ける。他人にも注意深く耳を傾け、新しい証拠、より良い証拠を提示されれば、自らの見方のほうを調整するのである。批判的に考える人たちは、必要とあれば、自分の情報や理解が誤っていたり、何かを欠いているのかもしれない、あるいは自分の動機が自己欺瞞と私欲に突き動かされたものであるかもしれないと認めるにやぶさかでない。十分な証拠の前では、自分自身の偏見と先入観を見抜くことができるのである。感情よりも道理を頼りにし、かたくなに自らの正しさを主張しようとするよりも、物事に対する最良の説明を見つけようと努力するのである。批判的に考える人たちは、批判的思考が一夜にして成るものでないことも承知している。試行錯誤を通して徐々に獲得されるものであり、一生をかけて積み重ねていく心の習慣であるのだと。

6　批判的思考と批判的読書は密接に関係している。批判的読書は、テキストの中から情報とアイディアを発掘するテクニックである。1. 批判的に読書をする人は、文章に直接働きかけることを可能にしてくれる、ある種の術を確立したアクティブな読書家である。2. 彼らは予めテキストにざっと目を通し、主題が何であるのか、全体の目的あるいはストラテジーが何であるのか、テキストがどう構成されているのか、どの重要単語・フレーズが斜体や太字などで強調されているのかを調べる。3. そして、テキストをゆっくり注意深く読み進みながら、カギになる詳細とアイディアに下線を施し、重要な単語あるいは見慣れない単語に丸をする。読むに従い、著者による単語の選択、詳細の引用、そして主張の根拠となる証拠について、思いつくままに疑問を投げかけ、観察するのである。4.

7　最後に、これらのテクニックを使って積極的にテキストを読み終えた後、もう一度読み通し、自分の批判的思考のスキルを適用する準備をできるのが批判的読者なのである。

エクササイズ：正しい選択肢をもってして、以下の文を完成させるか、質問に答えよ。あるいは、指示に従え。

1. 第1パラグラフにおいて、＿＿＿＿＿＿＿を除いた以下のすべてが情報の源として言及されている。

    (A) ウェブ・ログ
    (B) ラジオとテレビ
    (C) 大学の講義
    (D) 新聞と雑誌

2. 第1パラグラフにおける下線語 **persuasion** は意味上＿＿＿＿＿＿＿に最も近い。

    (A) influence（影響）
    (B) nationality（国籍）
    (C) ethnicity（民族性）
    (D) creed（信条）

3. 第1パラグラフにおける下線語 **they** は＿＿＿＿＿＿＿を指している。

    (A) products（製品）
    (B) advertisements（広告）
    (C) parties（政党）
    (D) the mass media（マス・メディア）

4. 第1パラグラフから、著者は＿＿＿＿＿＿＿と信じていることが推測できる。

    (A) 人々は提供される情報に懐疑的になるべきだ
    (B) 単に情報が多すぎるので、制限されるべきだ
    (C) マス・メディアが真実を伝えるなど、決して信用できない
    (D) ブログは人々のために発言し、いつか伝統的なメディア筋に取って代わる

Lesson 1

5. 第2パラグラフに以下の文を追加し得る場所を示す4つの番号を見よ。

   批判的思考は、単に自分のために考える我々の能力と定義されるのかもしれない。

   この文がふさわしい場所はどこか。

   (1)　　(2)　　(3)　　(4)

6. 第3パラグラフにおいて、批判的に考えないと、我々はしばしば何をしてしまうと著者は言っているか。

   (A) 他人を見下す
   (B) 我々自身の育てられ方と文化を嫌う
   (C) 関連性がある事実と証拠あるいは新しい事実と証拠を探す
   (D) 世界を偏狭で偏見に満ちた目で見る

7. 第3パラグラフにおいて、なぜ著者は人々の信念を描写するのに下線語 **precious** という単語を使っているのか。

   (A) 人々がその信念を捨てたくないことを強調するため
   (B) 信念自体に疑問を投げかけるため
   (C) 我々が誰であるのかを本当に決定するのは、我々の信念であることを示すために
   (D) このパラグラフを次のパラグラフと結びつけるため

8. 第4パラグラフにおける下線語 **discern** は意味上 _____ に最も近い。

   (A) make judgments about（～についての判断を下す）
   (B) recognize（認識する）
   (C) sympathize with（～に同情する）
   (D) approve of（～を許可する）

9. 第5パラグラフにおいて、著者は世界についての好奇心を _____ の例として言及している。

   (A) 正直さ
   (B) 自己認識
   (C) 開放的な心
   (D) 理性

10. 以下のどの文が、第5パラグラフにおける下線文の主要な情報を最もよく表しているか。誤った選択肢は、重要な点で意味が違うか、大事な情報を欠いている。

    (A) 批判的に考える人はそうでない人よりも理性的である。
    (B) 最良の説明は、いつも正しい、あるいは理性的な説明とは限らない。
    (C) 批判的に考える人は、物事の理性的な説明を見つけるのに、強情、自尊、独善に惑わされることはない。
    (D) いつも正しくある必要はない。

11. 第5パラグラフにおいて、批判的に考える人は何を認識していると著者は言っているか。

    (A) 批判的思考は、心の感情的な習慣であるということ
    (B) 自分の考えと情報はいつも間違っていて置き換えの必要があること
    (C) 批判的思考の技術は、簡単に素早く開拓できるものではなく、間違いから学ぶ必要があるということ
    (D) ほとんどの人の理解というものは、自己欺瞞と自己認識の賜物であるということ

12. 第6パラグラフに以下の文を追加し得る場所を示す4つの番号を見よ。

    彼らは、いかにテキストが自らの信念および価値と異なっているか、あるいは類似しているかを書き留めながら、読んでいるものに対する疑念と反応を余白に記録して、テキストに注釈も付けるのだ。

    この文がふさわしい場所はどこか。

    (1)　　(2)　　(3)　　(4)

Lesson 2
イングリッシュ 102: エッセイのタイプとストラテジー

リーディング：以下の文章を注意深く読め。

1. エッセイとは、多様なライティング・ストラテジーとテクニックを使用し、いろいろな主題を幅広く採りあげた短い散文体の文章のことである。現代エッセイの父は、16世紀のフランス貴族であり、市民リーダーでもあったミシェル・ド・モンテーニュだと言われている。彼は、当時フランスを引き裂いていた攻撃的な宗教的反目にうんざりして、38歳のときに公務員を辞め、読書と熟考および自らが「エセー」── フランス語の動詞「試みる」からの造語 ── と呼ぶものの創作に専念した。そして「試み」こそまさに彼がしたことであった。自分自身と人間の本質を理解する試み、そして、より慈悲深く理性的な生き方を見つける試みである。

2. 現代のエッセイは、ミシェル・ド・モンテーニュによって築かれた基盤をもとにして、あらゆる文芸形式の中でも最も柔軟なものに進化し、著者の目的や意図のほとんどに適応できるものになった。エッセイは娯楽にもなり、情報も与え、説得や論点主張もし、物語にもなり得る。日常の話題と経験をリラックスした口語的なスタイルで論じるという、インフォーマルで個人的なものにもなり得る。また、フォーマルで学問的になることもあり、芸術、哲学、歴史、そして文学といった重々しい話題を探究したりもする。

3. 多くの異なるタイプのエッセイが存在し、各々がそれぞれの全般的な目的遂行のために使われる特定のライティング・ストラテジーを備えている。描写エッセイは、言葉のみを用いて、五感のとらえるものを伝えること ── 人物、場所、あるいはものを言葉で描くこと ── を目的とする。客観的な描写エッセイも存在し、描写対象物への著者の個人的な反応はさておき、可能な限り事実に忠実な叙述の提供を試みている。また、より印象に基づき、対象物についての著者の考えと感情をより前面に出すという主観的なエッセイもある。

4. 例証あるいは実例を、主張する考えの説明や明確化のためのメイン・ストラテジーとする別タイプのエッセイもある。**1.** たとえば、著者自身の人生に基づいた話のような印象的な逸話 ── あるいは、著者が聞いたり読んだりした話 ── などが考えを具体化し、このタイプのエッセイのよい例になり得よう。**2.** 具体的な詳細のリスト ── 一般的なステートメントをより興味深く、より説得力のあるものにしてく

れる重要な事実および数字のリスト —— も例になり得る。**3.** 例は、著者の論点との関連性を持ち、読者の心に馴染みの念が浮かぶくらい典型的なものであることが肝要である。**4.**

⑤ 物事の起こりようについて、なぜそうなのかと疑問を呈することは、状況や事象間における重要な関係に対して人々が抱く自然な好奇心から派生するものである。因果関係分析エッセイは、そのような疑問に答え、そういう関係を理解しようとするものである。と言うのは簡単だが、これらを実際に行うのは難しいことが多い。著者は、たとえば、ある国における少子化現象の現下の原因を超えたところにある、さほど明確ではないかもしれないが等しく重要な遠因にも目を向けねばならないのである。著者にはまた、エッセイの主題を成す特定の結果から、長い一連の事象を遡り、その過程を引き起こした最初の原因にまで引き返すという、いわゆる原因の連鎖をたどる必要もあるかもしれない。

⑥ 過程分析エッセイは、特定の順番で並び、ある目的や目標につながる一連のステップや段階 —— 過程 —— を概説するという点において、因果関係エッセイに似ている。その過程の各ステップ —— たとえば、どう多文化間のマネージメント・ミーティングを行うか、あるいはいかに植物が酸素を生成するか —— は、切り離され、精緻なほど詳細に描写されて、適切な順番に並べられる。

⑦ おそらく最も一般的なエッセイ・タイプは、2つ以上のもの、概念、人あるいは場所等の間における類似点と相違点を考察するものであろう。書くのが上手い人は、そのような比較・対象エッセイの中において、考察対象物には比較に値するだけの強い根拠がある、つまり、それらが同じ一般カテゴリー（たとえば、4つのビデオカメラの機種、あるいは日本、韓国、アメリカの野球）に属しているということを明確にすれば、読者に最も効果的に影響を与え、説得できるということを知っている。そのようなエッセイはまた、当たり前を避けて、ふつう似ていないと思われるものを比べたり、通常ほとんど同じだと思われるものを対比させることによって、より記憶に残り、効果的なものにもなる。

⑧ 他のエッセイ・タイプには、物語や出来事の連続を語る説話式エッセイや、今あなたが読んでいるものが好例となる分類エッセイなどがある。エッセイには多くの様式があるが、そのほとんどが様々なタイプの混合であり、主張を伝え、目的を達成するために多様なストラテジーを利用するのである。

エクササイズ： 正しい選択肢をもってして、以下の文を完成させるか、質問に答えよ。あるいは、指示に従え。

1. 第 1 パラグラフより、＿＿＿＿＿＿ が無理なく推測される。

    (A) モンテーニュは、規則正しく教会に通っていた
    (B) エッセイは、本と同じくらいの長さになり得る
    (C) モンテーニュのエッセイはもともとフランスで出版された
    (D) モンテーニュは、比較的裕福な男だった

2. 第 1 パラグラフにおける下線語 **repulsed** は意味上 ＿＿＿＿＿＿ に最も近い。

    (A) disgusted（うんざりした）
    (B) affected（影響を受けた）
    (C) threatened（脅された）
    (D) turned away（追い払われた）

3. 第 2 パラグラフによると、以下のどれが本当であるか。

    (A) 現代エッセイに対するモンテーニュの影響は取るに足らないものであった。
    (B) 著者は、多様な理由と目的を持ってエッセイを書くことを選ぶ。
    (C) 芸術と哲学のような真面目な主題を研究する創作は、真のエッセイとみなすにはフォーマルに過ぎる。
    (D) エッセイは読者を啓発し情報を与えるためのものであって、娯楽提供のためのものではない。

4. 第 3 パラグラフにおける下線語 **its** は、＿＿＿＿＿＿ を指す。

    (A) writing（ライティング）
    (B) strategy（ストラテジー）
    (C) each（各々）
    (D) essay（エッセイ）

5. 第3パラグラフにおける下線語 **subordinating** は、＿＿＿＿と言い換えられる。

    (A) eliminating altogether（すべてまとめて除去して）
    (B) replacing in part（部分的に置き換えて）
    (C) lessening in importance（重要性を減らして）
    (D) re-emphasizing（再強調して）

6. 描写エッセイに関して、＿＿＿＿ということを除いて以下のすべてが言及されている。

    (A) ふつうインフォーマルなスタイルである
    (B) 印象に基づいた観点あるいは超然的な観点をとる
    (C) 言葉で絵を描く
    (D) 対象がどのように五感に映るのかを示す

7. 第4パラグラフに以下の文を追加し得る場所を示す4つの番号を見よ。

    たとえば、新しい学校方針がいじめ増加の原因になったという主張を例証するのに、著者は、主張を直接サポートするだけでなく、読者が共感し共鳴できる話や統計を選ばなければならない。

    この文はどこに最もふさわしいか。

    (1)　(2)　(3)　(4)

8. 以下のどの文が、第5パラグラフにおける下線文の主要な情報を最もよく表しているか。誤った選択肢は、重要な点で意味が違うか、大事な情報を欠いている。

   (A) 原因が明快にわかり、著者によるさらなる調査を必要としない現象もある。
   (B) 一国の下降する出生率は、何かの直接的な結果というより、その直接的原因の例と言えるかもしれない。
   (C) 原因が疎遠であればあるほど、読者と著者の両方にとってその重要性は低くなる。
   (D) 何かの原因を当然のこととみなし、最初は明らかでないかもしれない他の重要な原因を見落としてしまうと、エッセイは成功しない。

9. 著者は第5パラグラフの最後で下線語 **process** という語を使っているが、その理由として最も無理のないものはどれか。

   (A) 次のパラグラフに続いていく過渡的な概念として
   (B) エッセイの主題を再強調するために
   (C) どの帰結も長い一連の行動や出来事の結果であるということを示すために
   (D) このパラグラフ全体の全般的内容をまとめる効率的な方法として

10. 著者は、過程分析エッセイについて ＿＿＿＿ を除いて、以下のすべてのポイントを指摘している。

    (A) 因果関係エッセイに似ていること
    (B) 過程を特定のステップに分解すること
    (C) 理解しやすくするために、過程の順序を逆にすること
    (D) 特定の目的がいかに達成されるかを示すこと

Lesson 2

11. 第7パラグラフにおいて、なぜ著者は明らかな比較・対照を避けることが、比較エッセイをより効果的にすると言うのか。

    (A) より生き生きした印象を読者に与えるから
    (B) 読者は行間を読む必要がないことのほうを好むから
    (C) 文学創作の形式的必要条件を満たすから
    (D) 物事は明らかであればあるほど、記憶に残るものになるから

12. この文章の簡潔なサマリーのための最初の1文が以下に与えられている。文章中の最も重要な考えを表す3つの選択肢を選び、サマリーを完成させよ。文章中に出てこない考えを表したり、文章中ではさほど重要でない考えであるためサマリーには属さない文も存在する。

    エッセイは、最も変化に富み、適応性のある文学形態の1つであり、気楽なものであるかあるいは形式的であり、口語的であるかあるいは学問的でもあり得る。

    (A) 過程分析エッセイの例には、植物がどう酸素を生成するかを示すものがあろう。
    (B) モンテーニュは、読書し、熟考し、著作するために公職から引退した。
    (C) フランス語の「試みる」から来ているエッセイという語は、ミシェル・ド・モンテーニュにより、彼が行っていたタイプの著作を描写するために作られ、現代エッセイの適切な定義にもなっている。
    (D) 私的エッセイはかつてほどの人気はもうなくなり、より重々しい主題を論じるエッセイに取って代わられた。
    (E) エッセイには広く多様なタイプがあるが、ほとんどが因果関係分析、描写、例証、比較・対照、そして他のストラテジーを組み合わせるものである。
    (F) 上手なエッセイストは、読者に与えたい効果をいつも気に留め、自分の考えをできるだけはっきり、また記憶に残るように伝えようとする。

Lesson 3

色

リーディング：以下の文章を注意深く読め。

⑴　太陽の電磁波放射はふつう単に光と呼ばれているが、波長、つまり周波数として知られる物理的な特質によって分類されるものである。波長とは2つの隣り合う光線間の距離のこと。人間が知覚できる光、つまり可視光線は、電磁波スペクトルを構成するすべての光のほんの一部分に過ぎない。知覚できる光の波長は1メートルの10億分の1、つまりナノメートル(nm)で測られ、通常の人間の目は大体400から700ナノメートルの範囲の波長しか感知できない。

⑵　色は、「異なる波長の光によって観察者の目の上にもたらされる効果」と定義される。サー・アイザック・ニュートンが分散プリズムを使って太陽光を虹の全色に分けたときに最初に発見したことだが、人は特定の周波数を持つ光線を特定の色 —— 可視スペクトルの下の端 (400 nm) における青紫から高いほう (700 nm) の赤橙まで —— として認識するのである。光は波長によってのみ描写されるが、色は人がその波長をどう解釈するかということの中にのみ存在するものだということを覚えておくことが大切である。

⑶　我々の周りに見えるものすべてが、異なった強度で光の波長を吸収・反射している。物体 —— たとえば、熟れたトマトやポール・ゴーガンによる絵画 —— によって伝播される光は、目の網膜にある、錐状体として知られる「色分けされた」感覚器官を刺激する。すると網膜は脳に信号を送り、脳は光に包まれていた情報を処理して我々にそれを特定の色として見せてくれるのである。光のすべての波長を反射する不透明な物質は白に見えるが、光のすべての波長を吸収する物質は黒として認識される。しかし、黒と白はふつう本当の色とはみなされない。前者は色の欠落、後者は全色の混合体とみなされるのである。ちなみに科学者の見積もりでは、人間の眼と脳は700万までの色を識別できるというが、もちろん我々にはそのほんの少数にしか名前をつけることができない。

⑷　色および我々がそれをどう知覚するかということは、人々にとって言葉で表せないほど重要なことである。(A) 歴史上ずっと、色は我々の個人生活および社会生活の中で欠くことのできない役割を果たしてきた。我々が物理的物体を認識し、世界に秩序をもたらすときの主要な手段になるのが色なのである。(B) 特定の色が持つ重

要性は文化によって異なるのかもしれないが、我々の象徴的思考のほとんどが、色そのものに感化されたものなのである。(C) 赤、緑、青は加法混色の原色として、また黄色、マゼンタ、シアンは減法混色の原色として知られている。色は、我々の忠誠・所属心と宗教信仰を明確にし、儀式・儀礼慣行をまとめあげ、気分を描写するのに役立つ。(D) 色は人に対しショックを与え、警告をし、喜ばせ、恐れさせ、落ち着かせ、怒らせ、印象付けたりする。色を基にした慣用・比喩表現が日々の語彙の豊富で重要な部分を占め、おかげで我々は考えと感情を生き生きと表現することができるのだ。「カッとなる (seeing red)」、「憂鬱である (feeling blue)」、「ねたむ (green with envy)」、「臆病な意気地なし (a yellow-bellied coward)」、「華麗な文章 (purple prose)」などが何百とあるそのような表現のほんの数例である。

⑤　**1.** すでに見たように正式にはまったく色ではないのだが、西洋文化では黒と白が多くの象徴的な意味を持っている。**2.** 黒が連想させるものは、原始的な暗黒、無秩序、苦悩、邪悪、無意識の心、そして死である。**3.** 黒は喪の色であり、黒の服をまとった者は、取り戻せない損失、慰めることのできないほどの希望のなさ、そして絶望を経験したというしるしを示していることになる。**4.** 「黒の気分」というのは鬱と不満の感情のことである。「家族の中の黒い羊」とは、将来大した者にならず、しばしば一族全体に不名誉と没落をもたらすメンバーのことを指すものだ。

⑥　白という色は象徴的に黒の反対であり、ポジティブな意味を持ち、多くの可能性を秘めている。白は昼の光と目が眩むほどの明るさを連想させるので、啓示・啓蒙および知的な目覚めのシンボルとなっている。白は、花嫁のウェディング・ガウンのように、純粋さと無邪気さを表す。また最初の食べ物である母乳のように、白は生と豊饒 —— 多産の見込み —— の象徴となっている。白は、秩序、成熟、責任感を指すのである。

⑦　黒と白は、それぞれ矛盾するポジティブ/ネガティブな象徴的重要性 —— たとえば、黒のタキシードはエレガンスと威信の典型である一方、白旗を持つことは屈伏・降参することである —— も持つが、肌の色と人種にあてはめられた際に偏見と差別を引き起こし、人間の歴史における最も嘆かわしく遺憾な状況をいくつか生み出したのは、黒と白が最も一般的に認識される象徴的意味においてである。

エクササイズ：正しい選択肢をもってして、以下の文を完成させるか、質問に答えよ。あるいは、指示に従え。

1. 第1パラグラフにおける下線語 **adjacent** は意味上 ＿＿＿＿ に最も近い。

    (A) similar（似た）
    (B) perceivable（知覚できる）
    (C) contrasting（対照的な）
    (D) neighboring（隣接した）

2. 第1パラグラフにおいて著者が光を描写し定義する目的は ＿＿＿＿ である。

    (A) 波長が1メートルの10億分の1であるナノメートルで測られることを指摘すること
    (B) 太陽の電磁波放射がいかに我々にとって大事であるかを強調すること
    (C) 色の概念を紹介する前に光とは何であるかを読者に理解させておくこと
    (D) 電磁波スペクトルを構成するもののほんの一部分しか人には見えないということを強調すること

3. 第2パラグラフにおいて著者は ＿＿＿＿ としてサー・アイザック・ニュートンに言及している。

    (A) 虹を観察した最初の科学者
    (B) 光と色の研究における開拓者
    (C) 平均的観察者の一例
    (D) 分散プリズムの発明者

4. 以下のどの文が第2パラグラフにおける下線文の主要な考えを最も効果的にまとめているか。

(A) 実際のところ、我々には波長が見えるのであって色が見えるのではない。
(B) 光を描写するメソッドについては、光の異なる波長がどういうものであるかを測定する、あるいは区別することよってのみその描写ができるのだが、一方、色という概念が実際に目に映り、認識され、記憶されるというのは単に観察者の心と想像の中におけるものであるということを忘れないように努力することが大事である。
(C) 光は波長として伝わってくるのであり、色はそのような波長に対する我々の認識であるということを覚えておくように。
(D) 光は描写できず、ただ知覚できるだけであることを思い出してください。

5. 第3パラグラフにおける下線語 **it** は ＿＿＿＿ を指す。

(A) 網膜
(B) 脳
(C) 情報
(D) 光

6. 第3パラグラフにおける下線語 **opaque** は ＿＿＿＿ として言い換えられる。

(A) 光を通さない
(B) クリアで透明な
(C) 簡単に目に見える
(D) 判読できない

7. 第3パラグラフにおいて、著者は _____ を除く以下のすべての点を指摘している。

   (A) 物質が異なれば、それによる光の伝達と吸収も異なる。
   (B) 目の網膜には、光信号を受け取るための感覚器官である錘状体がある。
   (C) その特別な特徴のため、黒と白のみが本物の色とみなされている。
   (D) 我々は見分けることのできる色のうちほんのわずかな部分にしか名前をつけることができない。

8. 第4パラグラフにおける下線語 **impetus** は意味上 _____ に最も近い。

   (A) stimulus（刺激）
   (B) similarity（類似点）
   (C) difference（相違点）
   (D) explanation（説明）

9. 第4パラグラフにおける4つのアルファベットを冠した文を見よ。どれがこのパラグラフに属さない、あるいは場違いなものであるか。

   (A)　　(B)　　(C)　　(D)

10. 第5パラグラフに以下の文を追加し得る場所を示す4つの番号を見よ。

    英語において、黒は、人生における暗く陰気でネガティブな側面を表すフレーズと比喩表現を数多く生み出した。

    この文はどこに最もふさわしいか。

    (1)　　(2)　　(3)　　(4)

Lesson 3

11. 下の象徴的意味を、それらの派生元である黒と白にそれぞれマッチさせよ。答えのアルファベットをカッコ内に示せ。

    (A) 邪悪と苦悩
    (B) 敗北
    (C) 悲嘆
    (D) 怒りと妬み
    (E) 洗練と威光
    (F) 知識と智恵
    (G) 恐れと臆病心
    (H) 将来の繁栄
    (I) 失敗と恥
    (J) 純潔

    黒：（　）,（　）,（　）,（　）
    白：（　）,（　）,（　）,（　）

12. 以下のどの文が、本文の簡潔なサマリーに最適な第1文であるか。

    (A) 色の歴史はサー・アイザック・ニュートンにまで遡るが、虹の多様な色の全てを観察するのに最初に分散プリズムを使ったのが彼であった。
    (B) 色とは人間が光の異なった周波数を知覚した結果なのであるが、我々が住む世界を理解する際の手助けになるだけでなく、それには多くの象徴的・言語的使用法も存在する。
    (C) 白と黒は、それぞれ全色の欠如と全色の混合であるのだが、色に関する象徴的意味も豊富に持ち合わせている。
    (D) 誰もが色を同じように見るわけではない。というのも、色の知覚とは、光、網膜内の錐状体、そして人間の脳における色を処理する中枢を巻き込んだ複雑なプロセスのことだからである。

Lesson 4

コウモリ

リーディング： 以下の文章を注意深く読め。

[1] 革のような羽を持つ翼手目の哺乳動物であり、柔毛で覆われた体とネズミのような特徴が際立つコウモリは、齧歯類に次いで2番目に数の多い哺乳類種で、900から1,100の生存種が見積もられている。コウモリは世界中（極域は除く）の森、砂漠、開けた野原、都会、そして郊外で見られるが、最も分布が多いのは熱帯である。

[2] コウモリは、そのサイズにおいて差異が非常に大きい。たとえば、ジャワオオコウモリは6フィートもの翼幅を持つ一方、オーストラリアのミナミハナフルーツコウモリは1～2インチに過ぎない。コウモリ種はほとんどが夜行性なので、獲物を捕らえて食べるのは夜であり、昼間は、穴のあいた木、洞穴、あるいは他の暗い所で逆さにぶら下がって過ごしている。冬期は、冬眠するコウモリもあれば、もっと心地良い気候を求めて移動するものもある。群居しないコウモリが存在する一方、共同体を好むものもあり、数千、ときに数百万が集まってコロニーを形成し、暖を取り、安全を確保し、意味のある様々な音を使って警告や他のメッセージを互いに伝達している。さらにコウモリは利他的な行動も見せる。コロニーのメンバーは、病気や傷ついた仲間がエサを食べるのを助け、保護してやるのだ。

[3] 居住環境の破壊により、25パーセントものコウモリ種が今や絶滅の危機に立っているが、グループとしてのコウモリは驚嘆すべき環境適応性を示し、5千万から1億年もの間生き残ってきた。哺乳類の寿命は一般に体の大きさに比例するので、コウモリは、驚くほど長生きということになる。最も小さいものでも、野生で30年も生きられるのだ。

[4] コウモリ種は伝統的に2つの主要なグループに分けられる。大翼手亜目、またはオオコウモリ、は主にベジタリアンで、フルーツ、植物、花粉、花蜜を食べる。小翼手亜目、またはコウモリ、は食虫動物か肉食動物のどちらかである。特に後者のほうでは、3種の「吸血コウモリ」が知られていて、他の脊椎動物の血液のみで生きている。

[5] オオコウモリとコウモリは、他にも重要な点で異なるが、特に知覚と飛行の手段において違っている。オオコウモリは、その大きくて際立つ目を使って方向を確認する。コウモリは一般に目がとても小さく、エコロケーションを使って飛行する。こ

れは反響を基にしたレーダーシステムで、これによって物体がどれだけ離れているかを判断できるのだ。コウモリは、まず口や鼻から甲高い音を「叫び出す」。次に、反響して戻って来るエコーを注意深く聴く。そして最後に、音が戻るのにかかる時間を割り出す。エコロケーションによってコウモリはまた物体がどれくらいの大きさであるか、それが右側に位置するのか左側なのか、そしてどの方向に進んでいるのかを知ることができる。

6　メスのコウモリは、年に1～2匹の「子供」を生む。生まれたてのコウモリは、母親の庇護のもとで栄養をもらうしか生きる術がない。コウモリの母親がエサ探しに出ると、子供は後に残り、コロニーの他の何千もの子供たちと寄り添って暖を取る。母親は戻ると、臭いと音を頼りに他のすべての子供たちの中から自分の子供を直ちに見つけ出す。

7　もちろん、他の哺乳類とコウモリを最もはっきり区別する特徴は飛行である。ある哺乳動物、たとえばキツネザルや俗に言う空飛ぶリスも、空中を短い距離だけ滑空することができるが、長く、自在に飛べる哺乳類はコウモリだけである。この飛行距離と操縦操作は、特別の構造を持つ羽によってもたらされるのだが、それは鳥の羽よりも人間の腕や手にとても似ている。この「手と腕」は、皮膚の薄膜（飛膜と呼ばれる）によってコウモリの身体に結びついていて、これが飛行を可能にしている。コウモリの「手」にはまた、その先端に木や他の高所に登るための鋭い爪が付いていて便利である。というのも、鳥とは異なり、コウモリは立った姿勢から飛び立つことができないからだ。飛ぶには高所によじ登って逆さにぶら下がり、それから一気に飛行に移らねばならないのである。

8　伝説と狂犬病の恐れによって、コウモリは有害で危険なものという評判を得るに至った。しかしコウモリは実際には様々な形で人間に恩恵を与えているのである。まず、穀物に害を及ぼしたり、病気を伝染する昆虫をむさぼり食べてくれる。また彼らの糞（グアノ）は、農家にとって豊かな有機肥料となる。さらにフルーツを食べるコウモリは、種をばらまくことによって生物の多様性の維持の手助けになっているし、花粉と花蜜を食べるコウモリは、活発に植物の受粉を行っている。言い換えると、コウモリは敵と言うより味方なのである。

エクササイズ： 正しい選択肢をもってして、以下の文を完成させるか、質問に答えよ。あるいは、指示に従え。

1. 第1パラグラフによると、以下のどのステートメントが本当であるか。

    (A) コウモリは人が住む地域を避ける傾向にある。
    (B) コウモリは極度に寒い気候においてでさえ生きていける。
    (C) 2対1の割合で、コウモリ種のほうが齧歯類より多い。
    (D) ほとんどのコウモリが赤道に近い地域に見られる。

2. 第2パラグラフによると、コウモリは夜何をするというのか。

    (A) エサを探す
    (B) 洞窟で逆さにぶら下がる
    (C) 寝場所を探す
    (D) 暖かい地域に移動する

3. 第2パラグラフによると、＿＿＿＿、コウモリはコロニーを形成して暮らす。

    (A) 互いにメッセージを送りあうために
    (B) 生まれつき単独行動を好むので
    (C) 暖と安全を得るために
    (D) エサを確保するために

4. 第2パラグラフ中の下線語 **altruistic** は意味上＿＿＿＿に最も近い。

    (A) 不断の世話と注意を必要とする
    (B) 競争的な
    (C) 愛情に満ち、寛大な
    (D) 注目すべき

Lesson 4

5. 第3パラグラフにおける下線文のポイントを最もよくまとめているのは以下のどの文であるか。

    (A) 哺乳類であるにもかかわらず、その小さなサイズから我々が想像する以上にコウモリは長生きをする。
    (B) 大きな哺乳動物は、コウモリより驚くほど長生きする。
    (C) 驚いたことに、小さければ小さいほどコウモリの寿命は短い。
    (D) コウモリは、同程度のサイズの哺乳動物のほとんどと同じくらいの寿命を持つ。

6. 第4パラグラフにおいて、吸血コウモリが特に言及されているのは、＿＿＿＿の例としてである。

    (A) 食虫オオコウモリ
    (B) 食虫コウモリ
    (C) 肉食オオコウモリ
    (D) 肉食コウモリ

7. 第5パラグラフにおいて、＿＿＿＿を除いた以下のすべてがエコロケーション過程のステップとして言及されている。

    (A) 物体の場所と大きさを割り出す
    (B) 音声信号を発する
    (C) 物体の方向に向かう
    (D) 物体の距離を計算する

8. 第6パラグラフにおける下線語 **nourishment** は意味上 ＿＿＿＿ に最も近い。

    (A) food（食糧）
    (B) security（安全）
    (C) care（世話）
    (D) warmth（暖）

9. 第6パラグラフによると、＿＿＿＿＿＿＿によって、コウモリの母親は自分の子供を見分けることができる。

   (A) エコロケーション信号を送り出すこと
   (B) 子供を見てその見かけから判断すること
   (C) 子供が出す音と臭い
   (D) 子供を呼ぶこと

10. 第7パラグラフにおける下線語 **maneuverable** は、＿＿＿＿＿＿＿と言い換えられる。

    (A) 進路と方向を変えることができる
    (B) 連続的で長く続く
    (C) 鳥のような
    (D) 高い高度（の）

11. 第7パラグラフにおいて著者がコウモリの飛行能力について指摘する最も重要なポイントは、＿＿＿＿＿＿＿である。

    (A) コウモリが羽根の先端に鋭い爪を持っていること
    (B) 上昇してではなく、落下して飛行に移らねばならないこと
    (C) コウモリの羽が、人間の手と腕に似ていること
    (D) コウモリが空飛ぶリスやキツネザルに似ていないこと

Lesson 4

12. 以下のどの文が、この文章の簡潔なサマリーの第1文として最適であるか。

    (A) 他のリスとは違い、コウモリはベジタリアン、食虫動物、肉食動物であるとともに本当に空を飛べる。

    (B) 唯一の飛行哺乳類であるコウモリは、様々な珍しい特徴と能力を持ち、ゆえに人に恐れられもするが、恩恵も与えている。

    (C) コウモリは、彼らの農業に対する重要性に加え、人間の歴史を通して大きな文化的、象徴的な重要性も示してきた。

    (D) コウモリは世界中、特に熱帯性気候において見られるが、その多くが大きなコロニーを形成して場所から場所へ移動もする。

Lesson 5

絵画と油絵

リーディング：以下の文章を注意深く読め。

[1] 1940年、冒険好きな若者数人が、フランス南部にあるラスコー村近くの石灰岩の丘に探検に出かけた。少年たちの犬が1匹見えなくなったので、彼らはみんなで探しにでかけ、狭い谷間を降り、暗く曲がりくねった洞窟に入っていった。深く中に入ったところで少年たちが白い石灰石の壁と天井を懐中電灯で照らすと、驚いたことに、動物絵画のとても大きな「ギャラリー」が浮かび上がり、馬、鹿、牛、そしてサイまでが、すべて今にも動き出すかのように生き生きと描かれていたのだった。少年たちが偶然に出くわしたのは、これまで発見されたうちで最高の旧石器時代洞窟芸術の展示であった。およそ1万5千年も前のこれらの絵が象徴するのは、我々が知る限りホモ・サピエンスが自分たちの居住する世界のイメージを再生しようとした —— 芸術、特に絵画を通して自らを表現しようとした —— 最初の試みである。

[2] 絵を描くとは、表面に顔料を塗ることであり、色、構成、濃淡の相互作用を用いて、「本当の」世界を写実的に表現したり、芸術家個人の心象をもっと抽象的に表したりすることである。石器時代の芸術家は、最初に鋭い石や砕かれた骨を使って石灰石に動物の姿を刻み込んで洞窟絵画を描いたのだった。次いで彼らは自然に見つかるもの —— 赤は酸化鉄、青は藍、黄色はサフラン、クロは木炭、白にはひいて粉にした貝の化石、etc. —— を使ってそれらに色をつけた。それ以来、芸術家は自らが望む効果を効果的に再現し、時間と風雨による攻撃にも頑として持ちこたえてくれる材料とテクニックを見つける努力をしてきた。

[3] 芸術家の絵具は、色を与えてくれる顔料と表面に付着させるための展色剤とを必要とする。古代エジプトの芸術家は、顔料をアカシアの木から採った樹脂と混ぜた。ギリシャ時代およびその後の芸術家は、卵と蜜蝋で色を定着させた。しかしながら、オランダの芸術家ヤン・ヴァン・アイク (1390-1441) によって油絵具が発明されるまでには、15世紀まで待たねばならなかった。油絵具は、今日でもすべての画家にとっての「標準」であり、あらゆる視覚的芸術の中心とみなされる芸術の材料である。

[4] ヴァン・アイクの新しい材料はすぐに流行し、ルネサンス時代のヨーロッパに広まった。イタリアの芸術家たちは、高温多湿にもっと強い絵の具を必要としていたが、これがその答えであると歓迎した。北部の芸術家たちは、これがフレスコ（塗り

たての湿った漆喰に描く画法）の代わりになると思った。フレスコは、寒い気候のもとで行うのは難しかったのである。

5　**1.** 油絵具は、様々な油 ── 最も一般的なのは亜麻から採れる亜麻仁油 ── から成り、その中で顔料粒子が付着したり、懸濁したりする、乾くのに時間のかかる絵具である。**2.** 他の展色剤だと顔料の純度が落ち、作品に望ましくない色合いをつけて表面の光沢を鈍らせてしまう。油ならそういうことはない。**3.** 油のおかげで油絵は他には見られない光沢、深み、華麗さを得るのである。**4.** また油のおかげで、油絵具は融通の利く多目的な材料にもなっている。

6　ヴァン・アイク自身は、以前使われていたテンペラのような技法により適した絵画テクニックを用い、自らが発明した新絵具をとても薄く、ほとんど透明なくらいに塗り、繊細かつ隠し味的な筆づかいで、絵具の薄層に別の薄層を重ねるのだった（これはグレージングというテクニックとして知られている）。しかし、他の芸術家たちは、形式的なルールや束縛にあまりとらわれず、すぐに油の大きな可能性を認識し、油特有の性質を利用した新しいテクニックを用いて実験を始めた。たとえば、イタリアの巨匠ティツィアーノ (1488-1576) は、宗教絵画において、よりエネルギッシュな色の使い方とより大胆でもっと目立つ筆づかいを紹介した一方、ヴァン・アイクの17世紀の同胞であるレンブラントは、絵具とはけ跡の中に、人の目につくようなギャップを残し、厚く、手ざわりのある、ほとんど型どられたような表面を持つ肖像画と風景画を世に出して、衝撃を与えたのだった。

7　今日では、芸術家が非常に多様に油絵具を使っており、油であると認識するのがしばしば困難なくらいである。しかし、油絵のほとんどが未だに昔からの「ファット・オーバー・リーン」の原則に従って段階を踏んで描かれている。これは、油脂分の少ない（つまり、リーンな）絵具（ふつうテレビン油で薄められる）を最初にキャンバスに塗り、下の層が乾くのに従い、徐々に油脂分の多い（つまり、ファットな）絵具をかぶせていくと規定する原則である。これとは対照的に、「プリマ描き」、つまり「ウェット・イントゥ・ウェット」の絵画は、たいてい一気に描かれるもので、芸術家は自分の印象を素早く、自発的に描き残すことができるし、色はにじみ出して互いに溶け込むようになるのである。

エクササイズ： 正しい選択肢をもってして、以下の文を完成させるか、質問に答えよ。あるいは、指示に従え。

1. 著者は _____ 、問題文を短い逸話で始めている。

   (A) ヒトの芸術、特に絵画への衝動が歴史をどこまで遡るものかを示すために
   (B) 少年はいつも少年であり、可能な限りどこでもいつでも冒険を求めるものであるということを強調するために
   (C) 問題の少年たちが洞窟探検に懐中電灯を用意してきたことがいかに幸運なことであったかを示すために
   (D) 我々がサイとして知っている動物が旧石器時代にすでに存在していたことを指摘するために

2. 第1パラグラフにおける下線語 **inadvertently** は意味上 _____ に最も近い。

   (A) mistakenly（間違って）
   (B) carelessly（不注意に）
   (C) incredibly（信じられないほど）
   (D) accidentally（偶然に）

3. 第2パラグラフにおいて、芸術家が自らの絵画をもってして創造したいものを最もよくまとめているステートメントは以下のどれか。

   (A) 色と構成
   (B) 光と影の対照
   (C) 自らの観察と想像による作品
   (D) より効果的な技法

Lesson 5

4. 第2パラグラフにおける下線語 **etch** は意味上 ＿＿＿＿＿＿ に最も近い。

    (A) scratch（ひっかく）
    (B) dye（染める）
    (C) trace（敷き写す、トレースする）
    (D) stain（しみをつける）

5. 以下のどの文が第2パラグラフにおける下線文の主要な情報を最もよく表しているか。誤った選択肢は、重要な点で意味が違うか、大事な情報を欠いている。

    (A) 芸術家は、天候と経年の影響を受けない絵具を必要としていた。
    (B) 時間と気候は、絵画をもとのものには見えなくなるほどにひびを入れ、色褪せを引き起こし、キャンバスを歪めてしまうことがある。
    (C) 後に画家は、よりよく自らの空想を表現し経年変化と品質低下をはねつける絵具とメソッドを探すようになった。
    (D) それ以来、適切な材料とメソッドがなければ、表現したいことを絵画の中で表現できないことを芸術家は知るようになった。

6. 第3パラグラフにおいて、著者は ＿＿＿＿＿＿ としてアカシアの木に言及している。

    (A) 古代エジプトで使われた顔料
    (B) エジプトの樹脂
    (C) エジプトの芸術家によって使われた展色剤の源
    (D) 古代エジプトでよく見られた植物

7. 第3パラグラフで「標準」と呼ぶことによって、著者はすべての芸術材料の中で油絵具が ＿＿＿＿ ことを暗示している。

   (A) 最も興味深い
   (B) 最も評判が高い
   (C) 最も伝統的である
   (D) 試作的である

8. 第4パラグラフから ＿＿＿＿ と推測できる。

   (A) ヴァン・アイクは自分自身でヨーロッパを旅し、自分の新材料を宣伝した。
   (B) フレスコ画はヨーロッパ中からじきに消滅した。
   (C) イタリアと北部の画家は油絵具をまったく同じ方法で使った。
   (D) イタリアの気候は、暑さと湿気が特徴である

9. 第5パラグラフに以下の文を追加し得る場所を示す4つの番号を見よ。

   油絵具が芸術の材料としてこれほどまで効果的であるのは、油そのもののおかげである。

   この文はどこに最もふさわしいか。

   (1)　　(2)　　(3)　　(4)

10. 第6パラグラフにおける下線語 **inhibited** は意味上 ＿＿＿＿ に最も近い。

    (A) affected（影響を受けた）
    (B) impressed（感銘した）
    (C) restrained（抑制された）
    (D) shaped（形作られた）

11. ＿＿＿＿＿＿＿を除く以下のすべてが第6パラグラフにおいて説明されている。

    (A) 「グレージング」が何のことであるか
    (B) 「テンペラ」画法とは何であるか
    (C) レンブラントの出身国
    (D) ティツィアーノ芸術の主題性

12. 第7パラグラフで描写されている「ウェット・イントゥ・ウェット」様式の画法に最も特徴的な点は＿＿＿＿＿＿＿である。

    (A) ラテン語で「アラ・プリマ」として知られていること
    (B) 完成させるのに数か月かかることがあること
    (C) 絵具が乾くのを待たずに即座に行われること
    (D) 芸術家が自分の印象を記録できるようになること

Lesson 6

エネルギーとエネルギー源

リーディング： 以下の文章を注意深く読め。

1. エネルギーなしでは、まったく何も起こらないし何も変わらない。何の仕事も成し遂げられない。＊ 事実エネルギーという英単語の語源は、「行動」や「仕事」を意味する energos という古代ギリシャ語なのである。しかし実際のところは、ノーベル賞受賞物理学者リチャード・ファインマンがその著書「物理学講義」で告白したように、「重要なのは、今日の物理学においてエネルギーが何なのか我々にはさっぱりわかっていないということを認識することだ。エネルギーが特定の量の小さな塊としてやってくるのか正確にはわからない。」

2. ということなので、一般的には、エネルギーとは様々な自然現象を説明するのに使われる抽象的概念であって、その正体に関する正確なところは把握できないのかもしれないが、エネルギーはすべての物質に内在する、物事を起こすあるいは起こす可能性を持つ特性や特徴のことであるということだけは自信を持って言えよう。

3. エネルギーはふつう2つの大きなカテゴリー、位置エネルギーと運動エネルギーにグループ分けされる。位置エネルギーとは、静止している物体が、その状況あるいは他の物体や物質に対するその相対的な位置により持つことになる仕事容量のことである。その古典的な例として、切り立った崖の縁に座る石が挙げられる。石は、地球の重力場中におけるその位置により位置エネルギーを獲得している。しかし、何らかの力（たとえば地震）により落とされることになると、重力が作用して地面に衝突するまで下向きに引っ張られることになる。降下している間に石の位置エネルギーは運動エネルギーに変化するが、これは物体や物質が動くことによって持つようになるエネルギーのことである。（移動体が持つ運動エネルギーは、$KE=1/2mv^2$ という公式を使って測定できる。ここでの KE は運動エネルギーを表し、m は物体のマスつまり質量、v はその速度のことである。）崖のふもとで静止すると、石の運動エネルギーは位置エネルギーに戻るが、物事を起こす力量は減少してしまう。なぜなら、絶壁の上で不安定にぐらついていたのが平坦な地表に安定して座るようになり、石の状況が変わったからだ。

4. (A) 1つの形から他の形へ、たとえば燃焼において化学エネルギーから熱と光へ変換あるいは転換されるという能力が、エネルギーに大きな実用的重要性をもたら

している。(B) 文明社会の発達、化学の進歩、そしてエネルギーの探究はいつもともに歩んできた。(C) 1つの形から他の形へと転換されることはあっても、エネルギー保存の法則によると、エネルギーは消滅させることも作ることもできないという。(D)人間の創意が最も顕著に表れ、人間による自然世界の理解が特に深まったのは、動物の力、風力、水力に始まり、内燃機関、水力発電ダム、原子炉の開発へと、新しくてより良いエネルギー源の探究を通してのことであったと言っても過言ではない。

[5] 増加する人口と広範に渡る精巧な技術製品を抱える現代社会は、エネルギーに対してほとんど青天井の需要を持つようになってしまった。ごく最近まで我々の家々を照らし、工場に動力供給し、電化製品を作動させ、飛行機、列車、自動車を動かしてきたのは主に化石燃料であった。しかし、化石燃料は有限のエネルギー源であり、環境にとっては悪夢である。今日の人間が直面する最大の課題は、ガスと石油に隷属的に依存している我々を解放してくれる、安くて再生可能であり公害を出さない代替エネルギー源を見つけることであるということはほぼ間違いないであろう。

[6] 太陽エネルギーと地熱エネルギー技術の進歩に従い、これらがますます実用可能な代替エネルギーとして成長してきているが、事実上無限のエネルギー源として最もエキサイティングな見込みがあるのは水素燃料電池である。決して切れることのない電池を想像してみよう。完全なものになるまでにはまだ課題が残るものの、水素燃料電池がまさにそれなのだ。一般の電池と同様に、この電池も化学反応を通して電気を発生させる。しかし一般の電池とは異なり、水素が供給される限り無限にエネルギーを生成し続けることができる。そして発生させる廃棄物は、純粋な水だけだ。家庭、交通、産業における需要に対するすべての動力源としての水素燃料電池の可能性は、計り知れないものなのである。

エクササイズ：正しい選択肢をもってして、以下の文を完成させるか、質問に答えよ。あるいは、指示に従え。

1. 第1パラグラフ中の＊の個所には、以下の文章の1つが入る。どの文が最適であるか。

    (A) もちろん「起こる」という語をどんな意味で使っているのかも定義しなければならない。

    (B) 物理学において、「仕事」は「ある力によって1つの物体から別の物体へエネルギーが変換すること」と定義されている。

    (C) 標準的な教科書がエネルギーを「変化を起こす、あるいは仕事をする能力や力量」と定義しているのは、このことを考慮に入れてのことである。

    (D) しかしもちろんエネルギーは存在している —— それも大量に。

2. 著者は ＿＿＿＿＿＿ の例としてリチャード・ファインマンに言及している。

    (A) ノーベル賞受賞者
    (B) エネルギーの正体を知っているだろうと思われる人
    (C) 有名な科学作家
    (D) 科学事象に関する人気講師

3. 第2パラグラフにおける下線語 **elude** は意味上 ＿＿＿＿＿＿ に最も近い。

    (A) cause confusion（困惑させる）
    (B) be difficult to come up with（思いつくのが難しい）
    (C) compromise（体面を汚す）
    (D) run away from（から逃げ去る）

Lesson 6

4. 以下のどの文が第2パラグラフにおける下線文の情報を最もよく表しているか。誤った選択肢は、重要な点で意味が違うか、大事な情報を欠いている。

   (A) エネルギーはすべての物質内に見出すことができ、作用して変化をもたらすことができるのは事実だ。
   (B) 自明なことだが、あらゆるものが様々な目的でエネルギーを含んでいる。
   (C) 事実、エネルギーは我々にとって潜在的に便利なものであり、物質の様々な形態を通して現れてくる。
   (D) 特徴がどんなものであれ、エネルギーが物事を起こすのである。

5. 第3パラグラフにおいて、著者が位置エネルギーに関して指摘する最も重要なポイントは何であるか。

   (A) その仕事容量は、位置エネルギーを含む物体がどこにあるか、そしてそれが何の近くにあるかということによって異なる。
   (B) それはエネルギーという概念で説明される様々な自然現象の1つである。
   (C) それは地震に左右される。
   (D) 落下する石は最終的には地面に衝突し、平坦な表面に静止する。

6. ＿＿＿＿ を除いた以下のすべてが、運動エネルギーについて当てはまることである。

   (A) それは動いているときに物体が持つエネルギーである。
   (B) それを量るための公式においてはKEと略される。
   (C) それを含む物体の重量の半分にいつも相当する
   (D) 物体が動くスピードはその運動エネルギー容量測定の計算に組み込まれなければならない。

7. 第3パラグラフにおける下線語 **precariously** は意味上 ＿＿＿＿ に最も近い。

    (A) unsteadily（不安定に）
    (B) temporarily（一時的に）
    (C) securely（しっかりと）
    (D) high（高い）

8. 第4パラグラフにおけるアルファベットを施された4つの文を見よ。このパラグラフに属さない、あるいはパラグラフ中で場違いなものはどれか。

    (A)   (B)   (C)   (D)

9. 第5パラグラフにおける下線語 **insatiable** は意味上 ＿＿＿＿ に最も近い。

    (A) growing（増加する）
    (B) greedy（貪欲な）
    (C) amazing（驚嘆すべき）
    (D) disgusting（実にいやな）

10. 第5パラグラフにおいて、著者は ＿＿＿＿ の例としてガスと石油に言及している。

    (A) 化石燃料
    (B) 環境汚染
    (C) 安い電力源
    (D) 人間の隷属的な依存

11. 第6パラグラフから _____ と推測することができる。

   (A) 水素燃料電池は従来の電池より廉価である
   (B) 燃料電池は、ちょうど普通電池のように、電気エネルギーを化学エネルギーに転化させる
   (C) 燃料電池によって、これからほんの数年の間に他のすべてのエネルギー源が不必要になる
   (D) 燃料電池のデザインと能率を向上させる方法が未だに探究されている

12. 本文の簡潔なサマリーの最初の1文として最適なのは以下のどの文であるか。

   (A) 古代ギリシャほどの昔でも、エネルギーは変化を起こしたり物事を成し遂げる能力だと思われていた。
   (B) 測定も実用も可能だが、未だに多くの点において未知の部分を残しているエネルギーの探究が、科学と文明の発展の主要な原動力となってきた。
   (C) エネルギーはふつう位置エネルギーと運動エネルギーという2つのタイプ、あるいはカテゴリーに分類されるが、これらは片方から他方へ変換できる一方、作ることも壊すこともできない。
   (D) 今日、人口によるプレッシャーと環境問題によって、エネルギー需要は過去のどの時代よりも大きなものになってしまった。

Lesson 7

フィクションと演劇の初歩

リーディング：以下の文章を注意深く読め。

1　「演劇」という言葉は、文学の一独立部門として通例使われるが、演劇はフィクションあるいは散文物語の基本的要素の多くを持ち合わせている。これらの要素のうち、「キャラクター」というものが最も顕著であると考える人が多い。**1.**「キャラクター」の概念には、2つの意味がある。**2.** 第一に、キャラクターは小説、物語、あるいは劇中の人物（またはときに動物や無生物でさえあり得る）であり、物事を起こしたり、事件を被ったりする。**3.** たとえば、エイハブとイシュメルは、ハーマン・メルヴィルの『白鯨』におけるキャラクター、または主役、であり、シャーロット・ブロンテ作『ジェーン・エア』の題名と同名のヒロインや、フランツ・カフカの悪夢的な想像の世界に住む人々もそうである。**4.**

2　キャラクターの第2の意味は、フィクション中の人物の性格、容姿、究極的にはその人の価値や意義に関係するものである。この意味でのキャラクターによって、読者や観劇者は、物語や劇中のヒーローあるいはヒロインがあたかも実在するかのように思うのである。ジェーン・エアのものの見方、考え方、感じ方はどのようなものか。ハムレットをハムレットとして行動させるものは何なのか。レオポルド・ブルームはどんな道徳原理を体現しているのか。100年近く前、『インドへの道』の著者であるE.M.フォースターは、フィクション中のキャラクターをフラットかラウンドのいずれかとして定義したが、彼のこの分類は今でも広く受け入れられている。彼が言うには、フラット・キャラクターは「1つの思想や資質を基に作られるものであり」、それは変わることがない。一方、ラウンド・キャラクターは、多様な思想と習性を包含しており、話が進むにつれて大きく変化・成長していく。

3　プロット、つまり物語における出来事の連鎖、またそれらが互いにどう関連しているかということが、フィクションと演劇の第2の重要要素である。ほとんどの物語においてプロットは相反する勢力間の衝突を伴うものであり、5つの段階に分けることができる。序説的説明段階において、主役が立ち向かわざるを得ない衝突や問題が提示されるが、これらがなければ話が成り立たない。しばしば筋の盛り上がりと呼ばれる中間段階では、プロットが「深まり」、より深刻で複雑になる。クライマックス段階において、プロットは感情的頂点あるいはターニング・ポイントに上り詰め、そこから話が落ち着き始めて、解決に向かっていく。最後に、関係する一連の出来事

が論理的かつ妥当と思われる結論をもってして、満足のいく結末を迎えるのである。

④ 演劇とフィクションが共有する第3の要素は舞台背景、つまり物語中の出来事に関する時と場所である。舞台背景は、単に話の展開のための背景に過ぎないこともあるが、ときに物語や演劇の舞台背景が話の展開の原動力になってキャラクターとプロットに多大な影響を与え、物語の全般的な意味あるいは主題をはっきり伝えるのに役立つこともあり、フィクションと演劇の第4の基本要素になっている。

⑤ しかしながら、演劇と散文物語がふつう袂を分つのは物語の第5の要素「視点」においてである。視点とは話の語られ方のことを指す。小説や短編においてこれが意味するのは、『グレート・ギャツビー』におけるニック・キャラウェイのように、主観的なナレーターが出来事を伝えるのに「私」という代名詞を使う1人称タイプの物語か、あるいは19世紀の偉大な小説のほとんどに見られるように、主要なキャラクターを「彼」あるいは「彼女」と呼ぶ客観的な観察者によって話が語られる3人称ナレーションであることが最も多い。話の展開のコメントをし案内役を務めるナレーターが出てくる演劇もあるが（ソーントン・ワイルダーによるアメリカの名著『わが町』がその良い例）、演劇は語られるものではなく、生の観客の前で演じられるものである。よって、演劇における視点というのは、作家が話を語るのに選ぶテクニックではない。どちらかというと観客が補ったり選んだりする判断基準のようなものに過ぎないのだ。

⑥ 劇場劇の最も顕著な特徴は、劇はその時々の共同行事だということである。すでに起きてしまったことを伝えるために過去形で語られることが散文物語では普通であるが、それとは違って、演劇はいつも現在形で、そしていわば観客の眼前で展開する。フィクション作家が小説や物語として知られる確固たる芸術作品を単独で創作するのに対し、劇作家は自分の劇が完成品でないこと、また自分だけのものでないことをわきまえている。それは監督、役者そしてセット・デザイナーのための概略あるいは原稿の提案に過ぎず、彼らが各々の手腕と経験および人間の本質に関する解釈を持ち寄って毎回の上演を完成させるのである。

エクササイズ： 正しい選択肢をもってして、以下の文を完成させるか、質問に答えよ。あるいは、指示に従え。

1. 第1パラグラフに以下の文を追加し得る場所を示す4つの番号を見よ。

   この意味において、キャラクターは、ときにまた「主役」とも呼ばれるが、この用語はふつう演劇あるいはフィクション作品中のマイナーなキャラクターではなく、主要なキャラクターまたは主演キャラクターを指すものである。

   この文はどこに最もふさわしいか。

   (1)　　(2)　　(3)　　(4)

2. 第1パラグラフにおける下線語 **eponymous** は _____ として定義されるのが最も良い。

   (A) 悪い理由で有名である
   (B) 女性家庭教師および使用人として働く
   (C) 自らの名が作品名になっている
   (D) 社会階級間の違いを含む

3. 以下のどのステートメントが、パラグラフ1と2において描写されているキャラクターの2つの意味を最もよくまとめているか。

   (A) キャラクターは人の性格および外見と人生観のことである。
   (B) キャラクターとは物語中の人物および読者が感じるその人の特徴である。
   (C) キャラクターとは主役を意味する別の語に過ぎない。
   (D) キャラクターは人間である必要はなく、動物でも物でもあり得る。

4. 第2パラグラフから推測できるのは以下のどれであるか。

   (A) レオポルド・ブルームは健全な道徳原理を体現している
   (B) E.M.フォースターの小説『インドへの道』におけるキャラクターはみなラウンド・キャラクターであった。
   (C) 読者にとってキャラクターが生き生きとしたものになるのは、著者が選ぶ詳細においてである。
   (D) 本文の著者はフラット・キャラクターよりラウンド・キャラクターを好んでいる。

5. 第2パラグラフにおける下線語 **encompass** は意味上 _____ に最も近い。

   (A) comprise（包含する）
   (B) accept（受け入れる）
   (C) discover（発見する）
   (D) seek（捜す）

6. 第3パラグラフにおいて著者がプロットについて主張する最も重要な点は以下のどれか。

   (A) 出来事の連続のことである。
   (B) フィクションの重要要素のもう1つである。
   (C) 筋の盛り上がりを伴うことである。
   (D) 問題と衝突を含んでいる。

7. 第3パラグラフにおける下線語 **which** は _____ を指している。

   (A) プロットそれ自体
   (B) 感情の高潮点
   (C) （出来事の）連続の中間段階
   (D) もともとの問題あるいは衝突

8. 第3パラグラフにおける下線語 **plausible** は意味上 _____ に最も近い。

   (A) unexpected and surprising（予期せぬ驚くべき）
   (B) positive and forward-looking（ポジティブで前向きな）
   (C) natural and believable（自然で信じられる）
   (D) deep and significant（深くて重要な）

9. 第4パラグラフ中の下線文をより完成したものにするには、以下のどの節を付け加えればよいか。

   (A) そしてプロットとキャラクターにはほとんど影響しない
   (B) なぜなら話がそれ自体で十分面白いから
   (C) 著者の最良の意図にも関わらず
   (D) そこにおいて出来事が起きる

10. 第6パラグラフの最後の文で下線語 **each** を使うことによって、著者は _____ と示唆している。

    (A) 同じ劇などない
    (B) 劇の上演は毎回異なったものになる
    (C) 役者と監督が上演の前にプロットを変えることがよくある
    (D) 演技は観客の反応に左右される

11. 著者は、_____ を除いた以下のすべてをフィクションの基本要素として紹介している。

    (A) 物語の全般的なテーマ
    (B) 物語が辿る話の展開
    (C) 物語が起こる時と場所
    (D) 著者の声と語調

Lesson 7

12. 以下の選択肢を下の適切なカテゴリーとマッチさせよ。選択肢のアルファベットをカッコ内に示せ。選択肢のうち 2 つは使わないものとする。

    演劇とフィクションに共通する特質
    (　　)
    (　　)

    フィクションのみに見られる特質
    (　　)
    (　　)

    演劇のみに見られる特質
    (　　)
    (　　)

    (A) 物語の要素の中で最も目立つ
    (B) 直接的だが、一時的でもある
    (C) 単独で働く 1 人の人物による創作品
    (D) 「生きた」キャラクター
    (E) ある時と場所に設定される
    (F) 1 つの資質やアイディアを基に構成される
    (G) 1 人称あるいは 3 人称のナレーター
    (H) 設定された視点、固定した視点がない

Lesson 8

ホウクス

リーディング： 以下の文章を注意深く読め。

① ホウクスとは、人を騙してインチキな偽物を本物だと信じ込ませることを意図した行為のことである。この単語は、hocus-pocus という表現にその語源を持つと言われているが、これは手品師が行う巧妙な早業のことであり、hocus-pocus 自体は、カトリックのミサにおける聖餐の間に使われる hoc est corpus（これは私の肉体だ）というラテン用語が転訛したものだと思われている。しかしこの説明は、怪しいもの —— いわゆる語源ホウクス —— なのかもしれない。なぜなら、それを実証する証拠がまだ見つかっていないからだ。

② ホウクスは、多くの理由で行われる。悪意や害心に誘導されたり、単に悪ふざけとしてなされるものもあれば、復讐心からや、傷つけて困らせようとしてなされるものもある。多くのホウクスが、まじめな意図を持っていて、メディアによる誇大宣伝のうそをあばいたり、大衆の騙されやすさを明らかにしたり、人気のトレンドや考えのばかばかしさを暴露したりすることを目的としている。政治家と政府の指導者たちも、政敵の評判を悪くするため、また、不人気 —— あるいは不法な —— 決議および政策を正当化するために、しばしばホウクスを始めるのである。たとえば、イラクで戦争を始めることについてのブッシュとブレアによる原理的説明 —— つまりイラクの大量破壊兵器を見つけ出して破壊し、サダム・フセインにかくまわれているアル・カイダのテロリストたちを根絶するということ —— を金もかかるし人命をも危うくするホウクスであり、しかも弾劾されるべきものでさえあるとした批評家もいる。というのも、そのような兵器やテロリストなどまったく見つからなかったからだ。

(A)

③ 歴史はホウクスに満ちている。最も悪名高きホウクスの1つに、ピルトダウン人がある。1912年に、チャールズ・ドーソンというアマチュアのイギリス人考古学者が、大英博物館の古生物学部門に頭蓋骨と顎骨の化石破片をいくつか提供したのである。**1.** ドーソンは、化石は南イングランドのピルトダウン村の近くの砂利採取場で掘り出されたと主張した。**2.** 破片はただちに本物だと宣言され、大きな人類学上の進展だと絶賛された。かつて知られていなかったヒトの姿 —— ヒトとサルの間の100万年もの失われた環 —— がついに発掘されたのである！ **3.** この発見はセンセーションを巻き起こしたが、少なからず物議をかもし、懐疑的な意見も出た。**4.** し

かしながら、真実が明るみに出るにはその後40年もかかることになる。1953年に、エックス線分析によって分かったのは、骨は捏造されたものであり、ヒトの頭蓋骨にオランウータンの顎骨を貼り付け、チンパンジーの歯を点在させたものから作られた合成物に人工経年変化を加えたものであったということだった。

(B)

4　芸術品の偽造も別のタイプのホウクスであり、金儲けのためだけに行われることが最も多い。が、例外もある。第2次世界大戦中、ナチの指導者たちがヨーロッパの貴重な芸術品を多く略奪するさなか、偽造者たちは疑いを持たない客たちに欲しがるものをせっせと与えていた。そんな偽造者の1人がハン・ファン・メーヘレンで、彼はオランダの芸術家ヤン・フェルメールの作品の偽造を専門としていた。ヒトラーの右腕であったヘルマン・ゲーリングは、ファン・メーヘレンを正当なフェルメールのコレクターだと信じ、ある特定の傑作を買おうと彼のもとを訪れた際、本物であるかどうかを鑑定するために専門家集団を連れてきたのだが、彼らは実際に本物であるとの鑑定を下したのだった。その後何年ものちに、ナチに協力したかどで刑務所に服役中だったファン・メーヘレンはついに白状した。例の絵（および似たようなその他の多く）は彼が偽造した偽物だが、金のためではなく、自分のオリジナルの絵画を芸術評論家が繰り返しさげすんだことが恨みとなって残っていたからやったのだと。偽の芸術品で専門家をだますことは、復讐の手段であったのだ。

(C)

5　2006年、イギリスの作家A.N.ウィルソンは、特に屈辱的と思えたに違いない文学ホウクスの犠牲者になった。ウィルソンは詩人ジョン・ベチェマンの伝記を書いているときに、ベチェマンによって書かれたと称される手紙を郵便で受け取ったのだが、これはそれまで知られていなかった情事を明かすものであった。この新しい文学ゴシップの一片との遭遇に興奮し、その出所の正しさを確かめようともしないで、ウィルソンはすぐにこの手紙を自分の原稿に追加した。しかし、ウィルソンの伝記が2006年に出版されると、真実も同時に明るみに出た。ウィルソンの古いライバルで、自身もベチェマンの伝記をじきに出版することになっていたベヴィス・ヒリアーがあるロンドンの主要新聞社にコンタクトし、例の手紙は彼が偽造したもので、悪意のあるいたずらとしてウィルソンに送ったものだと認めたのだった。

エクササイズ： 正しい選択肢をもってして、以下の文を完成させるか、質問に答えよ。あるいは、指示に従え。

1. 第1パラグラフにおける下線語 **which** は、＿＿＿＿ を指す。

    (A) sleight-of-hand（巧妙な早業）
    (B) *hoc est corpus*（これは私の肉体だ）
    (C) a magician（手品師）
    (D) "hocus-pocus"（ホーカス・ポーカス）

2. 第1パラグラフにおいて、著者は聖餐を ＿＿＿＿ の例として引用している。

    (A) 宗教儀式
    (B) カトリックのミサ
    (C) ラテン語の表現
    (D) 語源説明

3. 第1パラグラフにおける下線語 **apocryphal** は意味上 ＿＿＿＿ に最も近い。

    (A) authentic（真正の）
    (B) verifiable（証明できる）
    (C) unacceptable（受け入れられない）
    (D) fallacious（当てにならない、虚偽の）

4. 第2パラグラフにおいて、＿＿＿＿ を除く以下のすべてがホウクスを犯す動機として言及されている。

    (A) 人がいかに簡単にだまされ得るかを示すこと
    (B) 社会現象を馬鹿にすること
    (C) 他人によい印象を与えること
    (D) 政敵である候補者にスキャンダルをもたらすこと

Lesson 8

5. 第2パラグラフの最後の文は _____ と示唆している。

    (A) イラクで戦争を行う理由は正当ではないということに著者は同意している
    (B) イラクにはアルカイダのテロリストはいない
    (C) サダム・フセインは見つかる前に大量破壊兵器をすべて破壊した
    (D) イラクでの戦争は正当化されると著者は信じている

6. 第3パラグラフに以下の文を追加し得る場所を示す4つの番号を見よ。

    多くの科学者が怪しいと思い、遺骨の信憑性に疑問を投げかけた。

    この文はどこに最もふさわしいか。

    (1)　　(2)　　(3)　　(4)

7. 第3パラグラフにおいて、著者が化石破片について指摘するポイントは何か。

    (A) 主要な人類学的発見であった。
    (B) 少なくとも100万年前のものだと思われた。
    (C) 大英博物館の古生物学者チャールズ・ドーソンによって発掘された。
    (D) 進化の「失われた環」を提供した。

8. 第3パラグラフにおける下線語 amalgam は意味上 _____ に最も近い。

    (A) forgery（偽造）
    (B) fossil（化石）
    (C) composite（混合、合成）
    (D) fragment（破片）

9. 第4パラグラフにおいて、著者はヘルマン・ゲーリングを ＿＿＿＿＿＿ の例として挙げている。

   (A) 貴重な芸術品を買い上げるナチの指導者
   (B) ファン・メーヘレン作品の正当なコレクター
   (C) オランダの芸術偽造者
   (D) フェルメールの専門家

10. 第4パラグラフにおける下線のフレーズ **rankled on** は意味上 ＿＿＿＿＿＿ に最も近い。

    (A) infuriated（激怒させた）
    (B) embarrassed（恥ずかしい思いをさせた）
    (C) confounded（困惑させた）
    (D) amused（面白がらせた）

11. 第5パラグラフから ＿＿＿＿＿＿ と推測できる。

    (A) ベヴィス・ヒリアーによるジョン・ベチェマンの伝記はA.N.ウィルソンによるものより学術的である。
    (B) ウィルソンの出版された伝記には偽の手紙が含まれていた。
    (C) 自分がしたことによってヒリアーは大きな満足感を得た。
    (D) ベチェマンが秘密の情事を行っていたというニュースのおかげでウィルソンの本はベストセラーになった。

12. 以下のパラグラフが加えられ得る場所を示す(A)、(B)、(C)の3箇所を見よ。

    文学にもホウクスがあり得る。1983年に、第三帝国が始まり衰退するまでアドルフ・ヒトラーがつけた60巻以上の日記を発見したとドイツの雑誌シュテルンが発表した。ヒトラーの専門家として名高いヒュー・トレヴァーローパーを含む何人かの歴史家たちが、この日記にお墨付きを与えた。しかし、日記が書かれた紙は最近のものであるということがテストによって明らかにされた。日記は、実のところ、筆跡偽造家による仕業だったのである。

    このパラグラフが最もふさわしいのはどこか。

    (A)　　(B)　　(C)

Lesson 9

哲学と良い人生

リーディング： 以下の文章を注意深く読め。

1　実にふさわしいことなのだが、英単語 philosophy つまり「愛智」は、古代ギリシャの言語に由来するものである。哲学は、たいてい宇宙の究極的な真実、原因および法則の研究と定義される。西洋哲学の起源は紀元前 600 年、ギリシャの思想家たちが神学の考えからは独立した探究の方法を確立したときに遡ることができよう。それゆえ、神学の題目が信仰と教義であるのに対し、哲学はこれらを否定し、真実を客観的あるいは論理的に求めるのである。また、哲学は科学とも異なる。科学は経験的証拠をもとに理論を構築するが、哲学は不確実性とそのような証拠が存在しない問題を扱う。

2　イギリスの哲学者バートランド・ラッセルがその傑作『哲学入門』の中で言ったように、「哲学の不確実性というのは、事実というよりそのように見えるだけというのがほとんどのところである。すでに決定的な答えを出せる質問というものは科学分野に属するものであるのに対し、今のところ、何の確定的な答えを与えられないもののみが残って哲学と呼ばれる残留物を構成しているのである。」

3　使用あるいは目的の点から言うと、哲学の研究は一般に、智、徳、または幸福 ── より良く豊かで意義のある人生 ── へと導いてくれるものだと思われている。ラッセルによると、哲学的熟考が私たちを「世界の市民」たらしめると言う。この市民権の中において、人は真に自由であり、制限された希望と恐れへの奴隷状態から解放されるのだと彼は信じている。

4　西洋哲学は、伝統的にいくつかの異なった部門に分けられ、それぞれ異なった領域の探究に関する質問への答えを追及している。形而上学は、宇宙の性質と意義および究極的には存在そのものについて思いを凝らすものである。認識論は、知識の本質、および個々の人間によって知識がどう獲得され、所有されるのかについての探究を行う。認識論はまた、知覚（見かけと幻想からどう現実を見分けるのか）、記憶（心の中でどう知識が処理され保持されるのか）、そして信念と想像というような関連概念をも研究する。

5　倫理学は、我々がどう生きるべきかを調べる哲学部門である。何が行動の正（道徳）・誤（不道徳）を決めるのかについての質問に答えようとするのだ。倫理の

原理は、個々の人間内に内在する行為の基準および社会がそのメンバーに強要する一連の道徳規則と義務という2つの異なった形を持つ。今日、道徳哲学者はたいてい倫理学を2つの一般的な分野に分類する。メタ倫理学は、倫理学そのものを調査するものである。我々の倫理原理の起源 —— 道徳性は人間から独立した形で存在するのか、それとも完全に人間による創作物なのか —— を確立するのが目的であり、「良い」、「〜すべき」、「正義」というような言葉の意味について考えるのである。

⑥ 対照的に、規範倫理学は人々の行動を統制することを目的とした一連の基準、または規範、の創造を扱う。規範倫理学の中には、どのようにこれがなされるのかに関する3つの理論が存在する。**1.**「義務理論」は人間の道徳性を、義務と責任に関する特定の基本原理の上に成り立つものだとする。**2.** これらの原理には宗教的な性質のものもあり、これは至上者への義務を含んでいる。**3.** 自分自身への義務に関するものもある。たとえば、規律と勉学によって個人の徳と知性を伸ばすというようなものだ。また、他人への責任に関するものもあり、たとえば、約束を守る義務や他人の生活状態を改善する義務、人間の不幸全般を和らげる努力をする義務などである。**4.**

⑦ 「徳理論」が強調するのは、寛大さ、忍耐力、そして勇気というような良い性格習慣を発達させることと、短気および虚栄のような悪い習慣を避けることである。ギリシャの哲学者アリストテレスは人間が育むべき11の具体的な徳を見出したが、我々は「徳のバランス」を発達させる必要があるとも主張した。たとえば、逆境の中で勇気の欠落を示すのは臆病の悪徳に負けることを意味するが、その一方で、勇気を過剰に示すのもやはり軽率という悪徳を容易に生み出しかねないと彼は指摘したのだった。

⑧ 規範倫理学の第3の部門は、「結果主義」である。結果主義者は、長いリストのルールや義務に従ったり、特定の徳を発達させろとは言わない。むしろ、行動を起こす前に、その最終的な結果について考えるように忠告するのである。経験と証拠を頼りに、我々は計画した行動の悪い結果と良い結果をまず検討しなければならない。もし我々個人および他人にとっても、「良い」が「悪い」を凌ぐのであれば、その行動は道徳的に適切なものと考えられる。

エクササイズ：正しい選択肢をもってして、以下の文を完成させるか、質問に答えよ。あるいは、指示に従え。

1. ＿＿＿＿＿のために、著者はこのエッセイの始めのところで **Fittingly**「ふさわしいことに」という単語を使っている。

   (A) なぜ哲学が愛智であるのかを示す
   (B) philosophy という単語がどのようにして英語に入ってきたかを説明する
   (C) philosophy という単語がギリシャ語に由来することがいかに適切なことであるかを強調する
   (D) philosophy という単語の誤解を確実に避ける

2. 第1パラグラフにおける下線語 **theological** は意味上＿＿＿＿＿に最も近い。

   (A) religious（宗教の）
   (B) purposeful（目的のある）
   (C) theoretical（理論的な）
   (D) absolute（絶対的な）

3. 第1パラグラフにおける下線語 **these** は＿＿＿＿＿を指す。

   (A) causes and principles（原因と原理）
   (B) philosophers and theologians（哲学者と神学専門家）
   (C) ideas and subjects（考えと主題）
   (D) faith and dogma（信仰と教義）

4. バートランド・ラッセルについて推測できるのは以下のどれか。

   (A) 彼は、現実の本質に関する全疑問に哲学がいずれ答えを出すだろうと信じている。
   (B) 哲学のほうが科学より優れていると彼は感じている。
   (C) 哲学は世界の市民権のための必修科目になるべきだと彼は思っている。
   (D) 哲学は決定的な答えを見つけられないが、それを研究することは価値あることだと彼は信じている。

Lesson 9

5. 第3パラグラフにおける下線語 **thralldom** は意味上 ＿＿＿＿ に最も近い。

    (A) fascination（魅惑）
    (B) slavery（奴隷の境遇）
    (C) significance（重要性）
    (D) effects（効果）

6. 第4パラグラフにおいて、＿＿＿＿ を除く以下のすべてが認識論的探究の題目として言及されている。

    (A) virtue（徳）
    (B) imagination（想像）
    (C) memory（記憶）
    (D) perception（知覚）

7. 第5パラグラフで、著者は倫理的原理について何と言っているか。

    (A) 倫理学という学問部門それ自身を調べる。
    (B) 人間とは独立して存在している。
    (C) 社会内と同様に個人内にその起源を持つ。
    (D) 道徳に関連する言葉を定義する。

8. 第6パラグラフに以下の文を追加し得る場所を示す4つの番号を見よ。

    良い例が見つかるのは、キリスト教の聖書中の出エジプト記であり、そこでは十戒が神から預言者モーゼに手渡されるのである。

    この文が最もふさわしい場所はどこか。

    (1)　　(2)　　(3)　　(4)

9. 以下のどのステートメントが「規範倫理学」の最も良い描写になっているか。

   (A) 人間の行いを改善することを狙った一連の基準あるいは原理
   (B) 義務と責任の客観的な研究
   (C) 倫理的原理の出自の調査
   (D) 人間の苦痛を和らげる試み

10. 第 7 パラグラフにおける下線語 **vanity** は意味上 ＿＿＿＿ に最も近い。

    (A) pride（自尊心、高慢）
    (B) uselessness（無用、無益）
    (C) confidence（自信）
    (D) appearance（見かけ）

11. 第 7 パラグラフにおける下線文の主要な情報を最もよく表しているのは以下のどの文であるか。誤った選択肢は、重要な点で意味が違うか、大事な情報を欠いている。

    (A) 危険に直面した際に憶病になることはすべての悪徳の中で最悪のものであるが、もちろん軽率さはそこに含まれない。
    (B) 臆病な人たちは、問題が起こると、軽率さを含むあらゆる種類の悪徳にあまりにも早く屈する傾向がある。
    (C) 危険に直面した際に勇気をほとんど発揮できないことは悪いことであり臆病なことであるが、発揮しすぎるのも同様に悪いことであると言える。というのは、それが性急で誤った行動につながりかねないからである。
    (D) 一度悪徳に屈すると、強い道徳心を築くのはほとんど不可能である。

Lesson 9

12. 以下の選択肢を、それらが描写する倫理理論のタイプにマッチさせよ。答えのアルファベットをカッコ内に記せ。使わない選択肢が2つ含まれている。

    義務・徳理論
    (   )
    (   )
    (   )
    結果主義
    (   )
    (   )

    (A) 怒ることや性急な決定を下すことのような悪徳と悪い性格の習慣を避けること
    (B) 自らの行動の結果を見越して、道徳的決断を下すこと
    (C) 悪影響だと思う人々を避けること
    (D) 過去の経験と観察に基づき、個人的な選択をする際にその証拠をよく考えること
    (E) 自分より恵まれない生活状況にある他人を助ける願望を育てること
    (F) 宇宙全般の本質と意義について思いを凝らすこと
    (G) 神とその道徳的案内への信心

Lesson 10

未知の力

リーディング：以下の文章を注意深く読め。

1. 宇宙は存在するすべての物質とエネルギーの総体である。宇宙の構造の包括的な理論を作ろうとする科学の一分野である宇宙論、つまり天体物理学は、宇宙の構成、進化、そしてその最終的な運命に関する基本的な質問を研究する。すなわち、宇宙はどのように生まれたのか。何によって構成されているのか。どこへ向かっているのか。

2. 人間の歴史中ほとんどいつも、これらの疑問に対する答えは単なる推測に過ぎなかった。天体物理学ではなく形而上学の、また科学ではなく神学の研究対象だったのである。しかし20世紀に入ると、強力な新しい望遠鏡、コンピュータ、またその他の科学技術の進歩のおかげで、科学者は様々な理論を構築し、ゆっくりとだが着実に、宇宙とその中における我々の位置について我々が真の理解に近づくのを助けてくれる多くの発見をした。

3. では、宇宙はどのように始まったのだろうか。ある説明によると、宇宙はいつも存在していたし、これからもそうである。最初もなければ予知できる終わりもない。つまり真に無限なのだという。未だにこの説明に固執する信奉者もいるのだが、この「定常宇宙」論は、全般的に見て、歴史書の中に追いやられてしまったものである。

4. 今日、宇宙創成の説明で大勢を占めるものはビッグ・バン理論である。ある特定の「時間ゼロ地点」——80億年前から150億年前の間のどこかの地点——において、すべてのエネルギーと物質がある密集した一点に凝縮され、それが突然爆発し——これがビッグ・バン——宇宙を始動させたのである。ほんの3分ほどしか続かなかったと思われるその爆発の結果、宇宙は急速に拡大した。ビッグ・バンの間に発生した非常な高温の中で起こった物質とエネルギー間の相互作用が、水素やヘリウムといった一般に知られる元素を作り出したのである。新しい宇宙の拡張は続き、その後の数十億年を通して、恒星、銀河、惑星、衛星、命——つまりすべて——を生み出すことになる。

5. ビッグ・バン理論の根底にある仮定は、宇宙は最初の爆発以来拡張し続けているということであり、これは最初にアメリカの天文学者エドウィン・ハッブルが遠方の銀河の移動を観察したのち提唱した考えである。ハッブルが発見したのは、他の銀河は我々の銀河、すなわち天の川、から遠ければ遠いほど速く動いており、宇宙内の

Lesson 10

銀河はどれもどこにあるかに関わらず、中央の出発点から現在の位置に到達するまでに同じ時間を費やしたことを示しているということであった。ビッグ・バン理論をサポートする別の証拠の基盤になっているのは宇宙線という概念であり、これは宇宙の最も遠方から、そしてすべての方角から等しく地球に届く、最初の爆発の名残りのノイズのことである。

⑥ しかし、もし宇宙が常に拡張しているのなら、なぜこんなに長い時間が経っても膨張しすぎて破裂していないのか。ごく最近まで、宇宙内の目に見えるすべての物質（つまり、我々が肉眼とあらゆる科学的な道具を使って見てきたすべてのものを作り上げている一般的な物質のこと）が持っている相互に引き合う力である重力が、拡張のスピードを抑え、すべてが飛び去ってしまうのを防ぐ唯一の力である、というのが標準的な見解であった。しかし1970年代に入ると、「暗黒物質」もまた拡張を減速させるのに一役買っているのかもしれないと提案する科学者が出てきた。これは、すべての銀河を取り巻き、どうもその動きを決定しているらしい、その組成はまだわからない目に見えない微粒子のことである。科学者は今や宇宙の全構成の75%までもが暗黒物質であると推測しているのである。

⑦ その後1998年に、天文物理学者が驚くべき発見をし、これまでの仮定のすべてが怪しいものになってしまった。**1.** 遠方の超新星 —— 爆発している恒星 —— の観察により、超新星はこれまで標準となっていた計算が示すよりもずっと暗く、つまり地球からもっと離れているということが分かったのだ。**2.** これは、超新星と我々の間の空間は、思っていたよりずっと拡張されていたことしか意味し得なかった。**3.** 何がこのような現象を説明できるのか。**4.** 何か未知の力が働いているに違いないのだが、それは一体何であろうか。

⑧ 最新の仮説は、ある種の「暗黒エネルギー」が重力をはねつけて反発し、それによって宇宙の膨張速度がさらに促進されているというものである。この暗黒の力については事実上何もわかっていないのだが、それが存在するという、まさにその可能性が、これまで全然理解できなかった多様な情報を科学者が判読するのに役立っている。またこの未知のエネルギー形態の概念を持つこと、宇宙の特質とその運命について我々がより適切な質問を思いつくのにも役立っているのである。

エクササイズ： 正しい選択肢をもってして、以下の文を完成させるか、質問に答えよ。あるいは、指示に従え。

1. 第1パラグラフにおいて _____ を除く以下のすべてが宇宙の本質に関する基礎的な質問の例として挙げられている。

    (A) 宇宙の起源が何であるか。
    (B) 宇宙の構造とはどんなものか。
    (C) 宇宙の目的とは何か。
    (D) 宇宙にはこれから何が起こるだろうか。

2. 第2パラグラフにおける下線語 **conjecture** は意味上 _____ に最も近い。

    (A) speculation（推測）
    (B) faith（新年）
    (C) miscalculation（計算違い）
    (D) anticipation（予期）

3. 宇宙の本質の真の理解のために科学が成し遂げている進歩を最もよく描写する語は以下のどれであるか。

    (A) hypothetical（仮説的である）
    (B) inevitable（必然的な）
    (C) irrefutable（反駁できない）
    (D) gradual（少しずつの）

4. 著者は定常宇宙論を正当ではないと信じている。第3パラグラフにおける下線文中のどの語あるいはフレーズが、その気持ちを最もよく示しているか。

    (A) still（未だに）
    (B) stubborn（頑固な）
    (C) relegated to（追いやられた）
    (D) history books（歴史書）

Lesson 10

5. 第4パラグラフの情報より、ビッグ・バン理論について無理なく推論できることは何であるか。

    (A) おそらく誤りだと立証されることはないということ
    (B) ほとんどの科学者に受け入れられているということ
    (C) 未解答の質問も憶測もほとんどなくなるということ
    (D) 対抗馬となるような宇宙の起源に関する新しい理論は現れないということ

6. 第4パラグラフにおいて、ビッグ・バンはどのように引き起こされたと著者は言っているか。

    (A) 一度始動させられると、宇宙は素早く拡張したと言っている。
    (B) 何が爆発を起こしたかに関して著者はそもそも説明など提供していない。
    (C) ある密集した一点から始まったのだと指摘している。
    (D) 物質とエネルギーの相互作用から始まったと説明している。

7. 第5パラグラフの著者の主たる目的は ＿＿＿＿ ことである。

    (A) 宇宙は未だに拡張しているということを強調する
    (B) ビッグ・バンの考えを最初に思いついたのはアメリカ人のエドウィン・ハッブルであったことを指摘する
    (C) ビッグ・バン理論に信憑性を与える証拠を提供する
    (D) すべての銀河が同じ速さで地球から遠ざかっていることを示す

8. 第5パラグラフにおける下線文の主要な情報を最もよく表しているのは以下のどの文であるか。誤った選択肢は、重要な点で意味が違うか、大事な情報を欠いている。

   (A) 宇宙線とは、ビッグ・バンそのものが起こった際に最初に発生したノイズのことである。

   (B) ビッグ・バンは宇宙線として知られるノイズを放ったのだが、その痕跡は今でも宇宙中で聞くことができる。

   (C) ビッグ・バンそのものが起こったときに発せられたノイズである宇宙線は、未だに宇宙の最も遠いところでも存在が確認され、地球上ではどの方向から来たノイズも同じ強さで聞くことができる。

   (D) ノイズは宇宙を長距離旅する間に宇宙線に変換されて、地球にむらなく届く。

9. 第6パラグラフで著者が「暗黒物質」に関して指摘する最も重要な点は以下のどれであるか。

   (A) それが何でできているか誰にもわからない。
   (B) 1970年代に数人の科学者によって考え出された。
   (C) 宇宙の拡大を減速させるのに一役買っていると思われてきた。
   (D) ほとんど未知の目に見えない力である。

10. 第7パラグラフに以下の文を追加し得る場所を示す4つの番号を見よ。

    すなわち、宇宙の膨張は実際には加速しているのであり、減速しているのではないというのだ。

    この文はどこに最もふさわしいか。

    (1)　　(2)　　(3)　　(4)

Lesson 10

11. 第8パラグラフにおける下線語 **repelling** は意味上 _____ に最も近い。

   (A) offending（傷つける）
   (B) repulsing（はねつける）
   (C) eliminating（消去する）
   (D) adhering（付着する）

12. この文章の簡潔なサマリーのための最初の1文が以下に与えられている。文章中の最も重要な考えを表す3つの選択肢を選び、サマリーを完成させよ。文章中に出てこない考えを表したり、文章中ではさほど重要でない考えであるためサマリーには属さない文も存在する。

   宇宙の起源に関する他の理論も発表されているが、今日広く受け入れられている科学理論は、宇宙は数十億年前の激しい爆発によって始まったというものである。

   (A) 100年以上前、アルバート・アインシュタインは「暗黒エネルギー」という概念 ── 彼はそれを「宇宙定数」と名付けた ── を提案したのだが、後に自らの「最大のへま」と呼んでその考えに反対した。
   (B) 定常宇宙論が主張するのは、宇宙は事実上無限であり、始まりも終わりもないということである。
   (C) ビッグ・バンとして知られるこの理論は、宇宙はある1つの密集点として始まり、そこからすべてのものが噴出したのだとしている。
   (D) 宇宙はふつう、すべての物質とエネルギーの総合体およびすべての出来事が起こる空間であると定義される。
   (E) 宇宙は「暗黒エネルギー」と呼ばれる隠れた力のせいで加速度的に拡張しているという理論が、我々の宇宙の理解を深め、また新しい疑問も提示してくれた。
   (F) ビッグ・バン以来宇宙はどんどん広がっているが、その速度は重力と、恐らく「暗黒物質」によって抑えられていると最近まで考えられてきた。

Lesson 11

嘘とその発見

リーディング： 以下の文章を注意深く読め。

① 嘘とは、騙そうという意図を持って、真実としてわざと提示する誤ったステートメントと定義される。嘘をつくことは人間の出現と同時に始まり、万人共通のもののようである。確かに嘘をつく性向は我々の遺伝子に組み込まれてさえいるのかもしれないのだ。家族内で受け継がれる性格的特徴に関するある研究で研究者が発見したのは、嘘をつく傾向において、家族構成員が最も密接に類似点を示すということだったのである。

② 嘘に卓越する者もいれば、ダニエル・マクニールが人相学の研究書「顔」の中で表現したように、「本当のピノキオ」（イタリアの児童文学の傑作における、嘘をつくたびに鼻が伸びる少年にちなんで）である者もいる。天性の嘘つきはその才能に気付いており、それを活かすことに恐れも罪の意識も感じないのだが、ピノキオたちには、「ばれることに対する心配そのもの」が顔に出てしまい、心の内をさらしてしまうのである。

③ 嘘をつくことが文明と同時に始まったように、それを発見しようとする試みも同時に始まったのである。容疑者は熱湯の入ったかめに手を突っ込まされたり、真っ赤に焼けた石が敷き詰められたところを歩かされたりすることがあった。もし、手や足が火傷にならなければ、真実を言っているとされた。古代中国のやり方は、ずっと人道的ではあったが、同等に恣意的なものであり、米を嘘発見器として使っていた。自分に対する起訴事実を聴いている間、容疑者は乾いた未調理の米を口に入れておく。感情が乱れると唾液の分泌が止まると信じられていたので、もし米が乾いたままだと、容疑者は有罪とされたのである。無実の者は何と哀れであったことか！

④ 1895年になってようやく、イタリアの犯罪学者チェザーレ・ロンブローゾが科学的な嘘発見法に取り組み、嘘のしるしと思われていた血圧の変化を記録する装置を開発したのだった。1917年、アメリカの心理学者ウィリアム・マーストンは、最初の本当のポリグラフ、つまり有罪の証拠となるような質問をされると、嘘をついている者は目に見える生理反応を伴った強い感情反応を示すという古い仮説に基づいた嘘発見器を発明したのである。

⑤ **1.** テストの前に、被験者は一連のワイヤー、チューブ、センサーにつながれ、

それらが呼吸回数、血圧、皮膚電気活動（発汗）を測定する。**2.** テスト実施中にプロのポリグラフ試験官が、被験者に出来事や事件に関する簡単なイエス・ノー・クエスチョンをする。**3.** ポリグラフ機が被験者の反応を巻紙に、今日ではコンピュータ・モニターの上に記録する。**4.** それから、これらの反応が試験官によって分析され解釈を与えられるのである。

6　ポリグラフは実際に嘘を発見するのではない。被験者が人を騙すような行動を示しているかどうかを探知できるだけである。事実、ポリグラフが嘘を言い当てるのに当てになるという科学的証拠はほとんどなく、その精度予測には大きな幅がある。またテストの裏をかくことだってあり得る。たとえば、瞑想やヨガといった簡単なリラックス法を知っている人なら誰でも表示度数をゆがめることができるのである。よって、何千もの人が毎年ポリグラフテストを受けるが、その証拠が裁判所で認められることはめったにない。

7　近年、信頼のおける嘘発見器の探究は科学技術の進歩、特に脳映像法に助けられてきた。最も興味深い進歩は、容疑者の脳に犯罪や出来事に関連する特定の情報が保存されているかどうかを決定するのに「脳波指紋」を使うというやり方だ。この新技術は、精巧な感知装置を備えたヘッド・バンドを使って、電気脳反応を測るというもの。認識できる情報を受け取ると、脳はMERMER（いわゆる脳波指紋）と呼ばれる脳波反応を発し、それを感知装置が探知・測定するのである。脳波指紋を測る面接の間、犯罪容疑者はヘッド・バンドをした状態で、真犯人しか知り得ない犯罪の詳細を提示される。もし脳が特定の詳細に刺激されMERMERを出すと、その容疑者の有罪が立証されるのである。無実の人ならそんな詳細は何の意味も持たないので、脳がそのような脳波を出すことはない。

8　一方米国国防省は、人々の皮膚に反射されるという目に見えないマイクロ波やレーザー・ビームを使い、その生理的状態を判断してごまかしを探知するという嘘発見器に取り組んでいる。この機器は、テロとの戦いにおける武器として主に飛行場で活用されることになるだろう。しかし、このような探知機がもし完成すれば、必ず公民権およびプライバシー問題を引き起こすはずである。というのも、それは遠隔で秘密裏に、被験者に知らせることも許可を取ることもなく使用できるからである。

エクササイズ： 正しい選択肢をもってして、以下の文を完成させるか、質問に答えよ。あるいは、指示に従え。

1. 第1パラグラフにおいて著者は _____ 、嘘の定義の中で **deliberately** という語を使用している。

    (A) 自分がどれほど嘘をつくことに賛成しないかを示すために
    (B) 嘘が嘘として分類されるには、故意でなくてはならないことを強調するために
    (C) 自分のライティング・スタイルをもっと説得力のあるものにする手段として
    (D) 嘘つきがどれほど動機づけられているかを示すために

2. 第1パラグラフにおける下線文の主要な情報を最もよく表しているのは以下のどの文であるか。誤った選択肢は、重要な点で意味が違うか、大事な情報を欠いている。

    (A) 家族構成員が最もよく共有する性格的特徴は、嘘をつく傾向である、とある研究が示した。
    (B) その研究は、どの性格的特徴がどの家族に受け継がれているのかを発見しようとした。
    (C) 嘘をつく家族メンバーは家族の他のメンバーにもっとよく似る傾向にある。
    (D) 性格的特徴が似ている家族において、嘘つきが引き継がれやすいことが研究者によって明らかにされた。

3. 第2パラグラフにおける下線語 **physiognomy** は _____ に関連する。

    (A) psychological problems（心理的問題）
    (B) body shape（体型）
    (C) facial features（顔の特徴）
    (D) lying（嘘をつくこと）

Lesson 11

4. 第2パラグラフにおいて、「ピノキオたち」がそんなに簡単に内面をさらけ出してしまう主要な理由として何が与えられているか。

   (A) 嘘をつくことに関する罪の感情
   (B) 内面をさらけ出してしまうことに対する心配
   (C) 探知されやすい傾向
   (D) 嘘をつく才能の欠如

5. 第3パラグラフにおける下線語 **arbitrary** は意味上 ＿＿＿＿ に最も近い。

   (A) cruel（残酷な）
   (B) fortunate（幸運な）
   (C) capricious（気まぐれな）
   (D) inessential（本質的でない）

6. 第4パラグラフにおいて、＿＿＿＿ を除く以下のすべてがチェーザレ・ロンブローゾについて言及されている。

   (A) 実際に彼の装置がどのように身体の変化を記録したか
   (B) 彼が嘘の探知をどう見ていたか
   (C) 彼の嘘発見器が何をしたか
   (D) 彼の仕事が何であったか

7. 第4パラグラフで著者はウィリアム・マーストンのポリグラフに関してどのような点を指摘しているか。

   (A) 人々による、犯罪を認めることになるような質問に答えた。
   (B) チェーザレ・ロンブローゾによる発見に基づいたものだった。
   (C) 真の罪を正確に探知した。
   (D) 有罪である人々は感情的、肉体的に反応するという信念に基づいていた。

8. 第5パラグラフに以下の文を追加し得る場所を示す4つの番号を見よ。

　マーストンの時代以来、ポリグラフ・マシーンそのものとそれを中心とした嘘発見テストは着実な精錬と改良を施されてきた。

　この文はどこに最もふさわしいか。

　(1)　　(2)　　(3)　　(4)

9. 第6パラグラフにおける下線のフレーズ **The readings** は＿＿＿＿を指す。

　(A) 予想
　(B) 簡単なイエス・ノー・クエスチョン
　(C) 紙あるいはコンピュータ・モニタに示された反応
　(D) 当てになる表示

10. 第7パラグラフにおける脳波指紋の説明は＿＿＿＿の例である。

　(A) 因果関係分析
　(B) 過程分析
　(C) ナレーション
　(D) 比較対照

11. 第8パラグラフにおいて、新しい嘘発見器が＿＿＿＿かもしれないことを示すために著者は公民権およびプライバシー問題に言及している。

　(A) 将来物議を醸す
　(B) 裁判所で証拠として使われる
　(C) 米国国防省によって完成される
　(D) 密かに最新のマイクロ波とレーザー・ビーム技術を使用する

Lesson 11

12. この文章の簡潔なサマリーのための最初の1文が以下に与えられている。文章中の最も重要な考えを表す3つの選択肢を選び、サマリーを完成させよ。文章中に出てこない考えを表したり、文章中ではさほど重要でない考えであるためサマリーには属さない文も存在する。

    人間の歴史を通して、嘘をつくこととそれを発見することは密接な関係の下でともに行われてきた。

    (A) 今日、科学の進歩、特に脳スキャンのテクニックのおかげで、絶対に間違えない嘘発見器の追及が熱を帯びている。

    (B) 子供もほんの小さなころから嘘をつく。もっともそれが正しい行為なのか誤ったものなのかについての感覚は、もう少し後にならないと発達してこないのだが。

    (C) 古代の嘘探知の方法は、科学的な証拠ではなく、特定の信念と迷信に基づいていた。

    (D) 他人を騙そうとするときに人が見せるかすかなサインを見つけることのできる嘘発見能力を持ち合わせている人もいる。

    (E) ダニエル・マクニールによる本「顔」の中では、ピノキオが嘘の下手な人の例として使われている。

    (F) 20世紀の発明であるポリグラフは、科学の知見を使って人を騙す行動を探知することが可能なのだが、特定の質問に対する人の答えが本当か誤っているかをきちんと言い当てることはできない。

Lesson 12

社会学と宗教

リーディング： 以下の文章を注意深く読め。

[1] 社会学とは、事実と統計的証拠に裏付けられた社会行動の抽象的な説明理論を作ろうとする人間社会の科学的な研究のことである。社会科学の中で最も歴史の浅い分野であり、19世紀の半ば、フランスの実証哲学者オーギュスト・コントが、社会生活の統合的原理を発見し社会調和を促進しようとして、人間の社会生活のすべての具現体 ── 文化、経済および政治といった ── の調査を始めたときに初めて独立した学問分野として出現したに過ぎない。

[2] 19世紀を通して、他の主要な人物がこの分野のさらなる発展・洗練に寄与した。エミール・デュルケーム (1858-1917) は、経験的、統計的証拠を初めて採用し、社会学者に真の科学者たれと促して社会を彼らが理想とする姿ではなく、ありのままの姿で捉えるようにと喚起した。マックス・ヴェーバー (1864-1920) は比較のための固定した基盤を提供することによって社会的な力を理解するための道具として機能する実用的概念モデルである「理念型」という概念を考案した。哲学者カール・マルクス (1818-1883) は歴史的アプローチを取り、社会がどのように進化・発展するかについての理論を立て、社会変化は主に経済システム中の矛盾と衝突の結果としてもたらされるものだと結論付けた。

[3] 今日、社会学の範囲は非常に、ときに当惑するほど、広く、2人の人間による偶然な社会的遭遇から犯罪と離婚の社会的原因・影響、また村落での生活からグローバル化と異文化間の衝突というように、すべての分析をカバーしている。社会学は社会のあらゆる局面を対象とするが、おそらく最も基本的には、個人の行動と関係に強く影響を与える社会現実の先在パターンともいうべき社会構造に目を向けるものである。社会学者はまた全般的な社会構造における個人の相対的な位置を示す社会階級および社会的グループと社会的相互作用の力学をも調査する。社会学者に肝要なのは、アメリカの社会理論家C・ライト・ミルズが言うところの「社会学的想像」を発達させる能力である。これは、偏狭な個人的状況と信念に打ち克ち、世界を新しくより広い観点から見る方法を涵養する能力のことである。

[4] 社会学は、特に社会機構の表裏までを探究することに傾斜していて、広範囲の下位分野に分割され、それらはそれぞれの社会機構 ── 家族、経済、学校と教育、

政治と政府、そして宗教 —— がどう構成され、機能し、そしてどのように個人の生活と行動に影響するかに特化している。

⑤ これらの中で、宗教は社会学的想像に独特な課題を投げかけるものである。宗教は、社会科学者が自らの宗教的信念 —— あるいはその欠如 —— を一時的に抑え、冷静に、また信者のニーズと感情に特に敏感になって宗教機構を見つめることを要求する。よって、社会学者にとって宗教とは、ある特定集団の人々、信念、価値が共有する信念、価値そして基準からなる文化システムに過ぎないものと定義される必要があり、これらが、神聖かつ儀式的で、とりわけ超自然的な存在のビジョンを作り出すことによって、彼らに目的と意味の感覚を与え、また基本的な質問に答えたり、生死に関する基本的な恐れを和らげてくれたりするのだ。

⑥ このように、社会学者は特定の宗教信念が本当であるか誤っているか、あるいは宗教慣行が良いものか悪いものかなどにこだわってはいない。社会学者は、宗教をその神的な、あるいは超自然的な局面からではなく、人間的側面から調べるのである。社会学者は、どのように宗教集団あるいはカルトが構成され、その最も顕著な特徴と主要な信念が何であるか、それをサブ・グループとして含む社会といかなる関係を持ち、どのような影響を与えるのか、それが実際にはどのように機能し、生き残っていくのかというような質問をする。社会学は宗教の主要な魅力が何であるか、どういう方法で信者を募るのか —— またどうやって金を集めるのかさえ —— を発見することを目的としている。なぜ宗教的信念がときに社会調和に貢献し、ときに社会衝突と宗派間暴力を引き起こすのかを問う。言い換えると、社会学は、心理学者兼哲学者であるウィリアム・ジェイムズがその傑作「宗教的経験の諸相」において行ったように、改宗、神秘主義的信仰そして聖人のような振舞いといった個人的宗教現象を純粋に心理学的観点から見る代わりに、そのような経験に対してより世俗的な説明を求め、それらを引き起こす社会構造中の要素に焦点を当てるのである。

エクササイズ：正しい選択肢をもってして、以下の文を完成させるか、質問に答えよ。あるいは、指示に従え。

1. 第1パラグラフから、19世紀までは _____ と推測できる。

    (A) 社会学は他の研究分野の一部分を構成していた
    (B) 社会生活はそれ以前に研究されたことがなかった
    (C) 社会生活の全理論が事実ではなく憶測に基づいていた
    (D) 固定した統合的な社会原理は存在しなかった

2. このエッセイは _____ を除く以下のすべてを社会学の分野の開拓者として言及している。

    (A) カール・マルクス
    (B) ウィリアム・ジェイムズ
    (C) エミール・デュルケーム
    (D) オーギュスト・コント

3. 第2パラグラフにおいて、_____ という理由から著者はマックス・ヴェーバーの「理念型」が便利であると言っている。

    (A) 社会的な力を理解している
    (B) 真の社会状況を理想的モデルに対照させるための道具である
    (C) 経験的、統計的証拠に基づいている
    (D) 社会変化の過程を説明する

4. 第3パラグラフにおける下線語 **bafflingly** というは意味上 _____ に最も近い。

    (A) amazingly（驚いたことに）
    (B) confusingly（困惑したことに）
    (C) critically（批判的に）
    (D) intentionally（故意に）

Lesson 12

5. 第3パラグラフにおいて著者は社会構造を _____ と定義している。

   (A) 社会生活の基礎をなすパターン
   (B) 社会学者にとって基本的に必要なもの
   (C) 社会学の広い範囲
   (D) 個人の振舞いに深く影響される

6. 第3パラグラフにおける下線文の主要な情報を最もよく表しているのは以下のどの文であるか。誤った選択肢は、重要な点で意味が違うか、大事な情報を欠いている。

   (A) 社会階級とは、人が社会において、その社会の他のメンバーと比べてどこに位置しているかを示すものである。
   (B) 社会学の興味は集団のメンバーがお互いとどうコミュニケーションを取り、お互いをどう見ているかというところにある。
   (C) 社会学はいかにそしてどこで人々が社会全般に溶け込むのか、グループがどのように構成され、機能するのか、また人々がどのようにお互いとコミュニケーションを取り、どううまくやっていくのかもまたその研究対象とする。
   (D) 社会階級という概念がいかに社会機構、集団の構成、個人間の関係をむしばんでいるかを示すことによって、社会学は社会階級という概念を廃止しようとしている。

7. なぜ著者は第3パラグラフにおいてC.ライト・ミルズに言及しているのか。

   (A) 社会学がヨーロッパにおいてのみの学問分野でないことを示すため
   (B) 社会学が広い範囲の目的と興味を包括しているという事実を強調するため
   (C) 「社会学的想像」を例証する社会学者の例を読者に提供するため
   (D) 社会学者は社会的ではあるが主観的でない真実の見方を発達させなければならないことを繰り返し言うため

8. 第 4 パラグラフにおける下線のフレーズ **ins and outs** は意味上 ＿＿＿＿＿ に最も近い。

   (A) 様々な部門
   (B) 構造と機能
   (C) より深い意味
   (D) 問題

9. 第 4 パラグラフにおける下線語 **each** は ＿＿＿＿＿ を指す。

   (A) sociology（社会学）
   (B) social institution（社会機構）
   (C) sub-study（下位研究部門）
   (D) individual（個人）

10. 第 5 パラグラフにおいて著者は ＿＿＿＿＿ ために下線語 **necessarily** を使っている。

    (A) 社会学者は宗教が、自分たちにではなく、信者にとって何を意味するのかを調べることに自らを制限するべきだと強調する
    (B) 宗教が社会にとっていかに重要な機構であるかを強調する
    (C) 社会学が与える宗教の定義をすべての社会学者が受け入れなければならないと暗示する
    (D) その定義を真の信者のニーズにリンクさせる

11. 特定の宗教あるいはカルトが提供する人生のビジョンについて最も重要な点は _____ ことだと著者はおそらく感じている。

    (A) その儀式の起源は社会的なものであり、文化的なものではない
    (B) 信者は実際にそれを真実として受け入れる
    (C) それが超自然的存在という考えをも含む
    (D) それがそのメンバーに他の宗教集団のメンバーよりも優れていると感じさせる

12. 最終パラグラフに表されている主要な考えを最もよくまとめる文を以下から4つ選べ。

    (A) 客観性を保つため、社会学者はどの特定の宗教にも従わないほうがずっと良い。
    (B) 社会学者は特定の宗教についての価値判断を下すことを慎まなければならない。
    (C) 社会学者は何が宗教機構を1つにまとめ上げ、何がそれを動かすのかを解明しようとしなければならない。
    (D) 宗教信念はときに衝突と暴力を引き起こす。
    (E) 改宗や神秘主義的信仰のようなことは、いかに社会的原因および要素に関係するかという点においてのみ社会学者の関与するところである。
    (F) 社会学者は、宗教が社会に及ぼし得るポジティブな影響とネガティブな影響の両方を調べなければならない。

Lesson 13

靴墨工場

リーディング：以下の文章を注意深く読め。

[1] 12歳の誕生日のちょうど2日後、ロンドン中心部のテムズ川近くにある、荒れ果ててネズミがチョロチョロする倉庫内の靴墨工場で、『オリバー・トゥイスト』、『大いなる遺産』そして他に15ほどの英文学の傑作を書くことになるチャールズ・ディケンズ（1812-1870）は働き始めた。毎晩仕事の後、疲れ切った若いディケンズは、家族と離れ、たった1人で自活していたちっぽけな部屋へ3マイルも歩いて帰り、どうして「こんなに幼いうちにこうも簡単に見捨てられたのだろうか」と考えるのだった。

[2] 靴墨工場での苦役の時期は「機敏で熱心かつ繊細な、身体的に、また精神的にすぐに傷つくまれな能力を持つ子供」にはとても屈辱的なものだったとディケンズは後に自らを描写した。週に6日、1日10時間、チャールズは靴墨の瓶にラベルを貼り付け、貧しい労働者階級の子供たち（「品のない同胞」と彼は呼んだ）と並んで労苦に耐えるのだった。博学で気品のある紳士になるという大いなる期待は永久に潰されてしまったと確信しながら。

[3] しかしながら、ほんの数か月前、チャールズはその若い生涯の中でこれ以上になく幸せだったのである。彼は、両親と7人の兄弟姉妹とともに、大きくて心地の良い中流階級の家に住んでいた。オックスフォードの学者が家庭教師として勉強を見てくれていたし、チャールズは劇場に通ったり西洋文学の傑作をむさぼり読んで余暇を過ごしていた。チャールズの父、ジョン・ディケンズは、海軍の会計課職員であり、高給がもらえるそれなりの役職にあった。しかし気立ての良い男ジョンは、しばしば贅沢なパーティーと夕食会を開いて多くの友達をもてなし、結局自分の収入内では暮らせず、家族の借金は着実に増えていった。この借金返済の足しにしようと、ディケンズ一家はワンルームのアパートに引っ越し、所有物をすべて質に出した ── そして若いチャールズは仕事に出されたのである。しかしそれでも不十分で、また時すでに遅し。最終的にジョン・ディケンズは借金のため投獄されたのである。

[4] この瓶詰め工場での外傷的エピソードが、人としてのディケンズと彼の小説を理解するのに非常に重要なのである。ディケンズの伝記作家ピーター・アクロイドによると、それはディケンズの生涯を決定づける人格形成の経験であり、多くの意味で

Lesson 13

彼が小説家になること —— そしてどんなタイプの小説家になるかということ —— に影響を与えたのだと言う。**1.** まず、この経験がディケンズの生来の勤勉さと良心を引き出すことになった。**2.** 仕事自体は嫌悪したが、チャールズは早くから工場の他のどの少年よりも熟練しようと決心し、実際にそうなった。その後の生涯において、ディケンズは不屈の仕事人になり、目の前の仕事はどんなものでも全霊を傾けて専心したのだった。**3.** こうして、靴墨工場がこの将来の小説家の比類なきエネルギーと野心の源になったのである。**4.**

⑤ 同時に、両親と家族から離れて生きることによって、チャールズはいやおうなく時間のやりくりと物事のコントロールの仕方を学び、おかげで秩序立てと注意深く計画を立てる癖が育ち、最終的にあれほどまでに多作な小説家およびジャーナリストになったのである。

⑥ 陰鬱な川岸の工場はまた物語作家としてのディケンズを生み出した場所でもあるとアクロイドは言う。ディケンズの詳細への注目と不気味なほどの描写力の才能が初めて現れたのがここだったのである。仲間を楽しませ、自分を慰めるために、チャールズはぎょっとするような自分の家庭生活とロンドンの通りを歩いている最中に観察したり経験したことをもとにして、念入りな笑い話を作り上げるのだった。これらのおとぎ話のような話の中で、チャールズは自分が住んでいる世界の「書き直し」を行った。不正と残酷さに打ち勝ってついには社会の中心人物になる、野心あふれる若い少年として自分を想像しなおして話の展開の中心に置くのだった。物を語りたいというこの初期の衝動が、フィクション作家になるというディケンズの決心を確実に導くことになる。ちょうど靴墨工場での一件が、なぜディケンズ作品の最も顕著な登場人物が孤児や見捨てられた子供たちだったりするのか、また彼がなぜ貧しくて虐げられた者たちの大義を擁護するのに自分の小説を使ったのかについての確かな説明になるのと同じように。

⑦ しかしながら、ディケンズの靴墨工場でのエピソードにあまりいい顔をしない読者も存在する。ディケンズはこのことについて、いつまでも自分を憐れむのをやめない子供のようだと彼らは主張するのだ。この成長を拒む態度は、いくつかのディケンズ小説の感傷的特徴を説明するだけでなく、作品中に行きわたっている深い自己憐憫の雰囲気をも説明する、と彼らは言う。

エクササイズ： 正しい選択肢をもってして、以下の文を完成させるか、質問に答えよ。あるいは、指示に従え。

1. 第1パラグラフにおいて、著者は _____ ためにチャールズ・ディケンズの引用を用いている。

    (A) ディケンズのライティング・スタイルの例を挙げる
    (B) ディケンズの親に責任を押し付ける
    (C) 当時の若いディケンズの心の有様を示す
    (D) 若いディケンズがそのときどうであったかを強調する

2. 第1パラグラフにおける下線のフレーズ **cast away** は意味上 _____ に最も近い。

    (A) overlooked（見逃された）
    (B) taken advantage of（利用された）
    (C) manipulated（操作された）
    (D) abandoned（見捨てられた）

3. 第2パラグラフにおける下線文の主要な情報を最もよく表しているのは以下のどの文であるか。誤った選択肢は、重要な点で意味が違うか、大事な情報を欠いている。

    (A) ディケンズは残りの生涯ずっと靴墨工場で働くことになるだろうと確信していた。
    (B) ディケンズは、良い教育さえ受ければ社会の重要なメンバーになれると信じていた。
    (C) 博学な人間になることのみが少年の望んでいたことであり、この野心が叶わなければ、負け犬になるだろうと信じていた。
    (D) いつも夢見ていた、大きくなったら教養がある重要人物になるというチャンスは決して来ないだろうと彼は感じていた。

Lesson 13

4. 第2パラグラフの情報から判断して、＿＿＿＿を除く以下のすべてが、靴墨工場におけるディケンズの労働条件に触れている。

    (A) 自分より地位が下だと思っていた人々と肩を並べて働くこと
    (B) 簡単に傷ついてしまうこと
    (C) 退屈で繰り返しだけの仕事をすること
    (D) たった1日の休日だけで、長時間労働をすること

5. 第3パラグラフにおいて、著者は＿＿＿＿を除く以下のすべてをディケンズの最も幸福な時代に関して言及している。

    (A) 彼の家がどこにあったか
    (B) どのような家に彼が住んでいたか
    (C) 彼がどのように教育を受けていたか
    (D) 彼の読書習慣がどのようなものであったか

6. 第3パラグラフの情報から判断して、以下のどれがジョン・ディケンズについて推測できないものか。

    (A) 彼はしばしば借金をしなければならなかった。
    (B) 彼は息子の将来の幸福に関心がなかった。
    (C) 彼の給料は家計を賄うのには十分でなかった。
    (D) 彼は人気がありよく好かれていた。

7. 第4パラグラフにおける下線語 **crucial** は意味上＿＿＿＿に最も近い。

    (A) chronic（長期にわたる）
    (B) critical（重大な）
    (C) relative（相対的な）
    (D) recognized（認められた）

8. 第4パラグラフにおける下線語 **it** は _____ を指す。

   (A) 靴墨工場自体
   (B) 工場での外傷的エピソード
   (C) 仕事に対するディケンズの嫌悪感
   (D) 男と彼の小説

9. 第4パラグラフにおける下線語 **indefatigable** は意味上 _____ に最も近い。

   (A) dedicated（専心した）
   (B) adept（熟達した）
   (C) willing（快くやる）
   (D) tireless（疲れを知らない）

10. 第4パラグラフの情報から判断して、工場で働き始めてからのディケンズの態度を最もよく描写するステートメントは以下のどれか。

    (A) 彼は悪い状況を何とか乗り切ろうと思った。
    (B) 彼は他の少年たちには決してかなわないだろうと信じていた。
    (C) みんなに自分がいかに賢いのかを見せつける良いチャンスだと彼は思った。
    (D) 仕事は思ったほど悪くはないと決めつけた。

11. 第4パラグラフに以下の文を追加し得る場所を示す4つの番号を見よ。

    （「することは何でもせよ」、ディケンズは後に向上心に燃える若い小説家に彼らしく語った。「あたかも世界には他に何もすることがないかのように。」）

    この文が最もふさわしい場所はどこか。

    (1)   (2)   (3)   (4)

Lesson 13

12. 以下は、ディケンズの人生および仕事に対する靴墨工場でのエピソードの重要性を簡潔にまとめたサマリーの第1文である。このエピソードがもたらした最も重要な結果を表す選択肢を3つ選んで、サマリーを完成させよ。

   1824年、チャールズ・ディケンズは陰鬱な靴墨工場で働かされることになったが、これは多くの意味でディケンズの大人としての性格ならびに彼の著作の性格とスタイルを形作る経験となった。

   (A) ディケンズは、あんなに小さなうちから働かせたことに対して、両親を決して許さなかった。
   (B) ディケンズはまた家族の所有物を質屋に持っていくようにも強要された。
   (C) 仕事は少年の生来の勤勉さを引き出し、ロンドン周辺を長々と1人寂しく歩くことで、彼の観察力の発達も助けられた。
   (D) しかしながら、ディケンズはこのエピソードからの影響を受け過ぎたのかもしれない。それが彼の小説の弱点になったと言う人もいるのだ。
   (E) 当時は工場での貧しい同僚を見下したものだが、ディケンズは後に恵まれない人たちの苦境に同情し、自分の著作において彼らのために立ち上がったのだった。
   (F) ディケンズは恥ずかしくて、彼の酷い家庭生活のことを誰にも話さなかった。

Lesson 14

手遅れになる前に

リーディング： 以下の文章を注意深く読め。

　1　レイチェル・カーソンが激しく環境問題を悲嘆し不平を述べた『沈黙の春』が1962年に出版された後、1970年4月22日には最初のアース・デイが世界的に祝された。これらが引き金となり現代の環境運動が始まって、空気、水、騒音公害、（カーソンの批判の焦点ともなった）農薬による汚染、減少し続ける自然資源、廃棄物投棄、そして絶滅危惧種といった問題に対する意識が高まってきた。**1.** その結果、これらの問題の多くが直視されるようになり、公序における変化によって縮小を見るケースも現れた。**2.** しかし地球上のすべての生命に対して深刻な脅威となる1つの環境問題に対しては、未だに効果的な対処がなされていない。**3.** この問題とは地球温暖化である。**4.** これに対処するために試験的な手段もとられてきたが、この問題を取り巻く論争によって、より決定的な行動は妨げられてきた。

　2　地球の大気と海の平均気温が上昇していること自体が問題になっているのではない。上昇しているという証拠には動かしがたいものがあるのだ。NASAのゴダード宇宙研究所が行ったリサーチによると、2005年度の世界の平均気温は14.6℃で、記録をつけ始めた1800年代半ば以来、最も暑い年となった。その上、温暖化の傾向は加速しているのである。記録上最も暑かった年のベスト5はどれも1998年以降に起こっている。よって疑いの余地はほとんどあり得ない。地球は暑くなってきているのだ。

　3　専門家の同意を見ないのは、この気候変動の原因である。変数的要素および未知の要素が多すぎて、現在および将来の気候傾向を正確に予想することはできないと言う気候学者もいる（おそらく企業と政治家からの圧力に揺さぶられたのだろう）。彼らが言うには、温暖化はたぶん地球に届く太陽光の量における変動が引き起こす表面温度の通常変化に過ぎない。または、おそらく地球が前回の寒い時期 —— いわゆる小氷河期 —— から抜け出しているだけなのかもしれないと推測する。

　4　しかし、このような言い分はもはや通用しない。大勢を占める科学的見解によると、地球温暖化の大部分は人間の営みにはっきり起因するものであるという。特に化石燃料 —— 産業と交通のために使う石炭と石油製品 —— の燃焼および二酸化炭素、メタン、亜酸化窒素のような気体の空気中への排出に起因するというのだ。

⑤　ふつう地球の表面温度は、温室効果として知られるプロセスによって維持されている。太陽からやってくる波長の短い光は、水蒸気、二酸化炭素、オゾン、その他のいわゆる温室効果ガスから成る大気の保温膜のフィルターを通って地表に届く。それから、この光は地球上で跳ね返り、宇宙に戻っていくのだ。しかし、そうするまでにこの光と熱は幾分弱まっており、容易には気体の保護膜を通り抜けて戻っていくことができずに中に閉じ込められてしまうことになる。理想的な状態下では —— ちょうど温室がそうであるように —— このプロセスは生命を維持するのに最適な地表気温を保ってくれる。しかし、今や大気中には温室効果ガスの集中したところが増えており、この保温膜はより厚く、重たくなって、熱をどんどん地表近くに閉じ込めている。従って、地球温暖化ということになるのだ。

⑥　なぜ大気温の上昇がそんなに危険なのか。科学者が今予想するところによると、もし熱を出す傾向が続き、温室効果ガスの排出を徹底的に減らしてその傾向を抑え、そしてひっくり返すという行動を即時に世界の指導者たちがとらなければ、その影響は —— 全世界を巻き込む戦争や恐慌に匹敵する規模の社会および経済上の崩壊を引き起こして —— 破局的なものになるという。（どういうことになり得るかについての恐ろしい予告が見たい人は、アル・ゴアによる『不都合な真実』を参照のこと。）

⑦　すでに、これらの影響には我々の知るところとなっているものがある。気候変化により山脈の氷河が溶け、極地域の氷冠が小さくなって海の水位を上げ、太平洋のいくつかの島国が年ごとにどんどん海に沈んでいくということを引き起こしている。ほどなくして、海抜の低い大陸の海岸地域も同様に危うくなるであろう。先例のない熱波がすでに世界中の天気パターンを変え、山火事、それに引き続いて起きる豪雨とひどい洪水の件数も増えている。一方、生き残るために居住者全員が他地方への移住を強いられているコミュニティーもある。ワールドウォッチ研究所によると、拡大するゴビ砂漠の近くに住む中国人農家および北アメリカ亜極圏のイヌイットの住民たちが特にひどい影響を受けている。多くの動物種もまた地球温暖化によって自然の生息地を失い、結果として絶滅しかけている。さらに気温が上がれば、これらとその他の傾向は、悪化の一途をたどるだけであろう。

エクササイズ：正しい選択肢をもってして、以下の文を完成させるか、質問に答えよ。あるいは、指示に従え。

1. 第1パラグラフにおける下線語 **jeremiad** は意味上 ＿＿＿＿ に最も近い。

    (A) quarrel（けんか）
    (B) diatribe（非難の文章）
    (C) bestseller（ベストセラー）
    (D) non-fiction book（ノンフィクションの本）

2. 第1パラグラフにおいて、農薬汚染（中毒）は ＿＿＿＿ と著者は指摘している。

    (A) 『沈黙の春』の主題である
    (B) 効果的に対処された問題である
    (C) 現代の環境運動をもたらすのに一役買った
    (D) 空気公害の一種である

3. 第1パラグラフに以下の文を追加し得る場所を示す4つの番号を見よ。

    リサイクルは資源を保存し、廃棄物を減らすのに大いに貢献し、車と工場に対する義務的な排出ガス規制の基準は、空の浄化に役立った。

    この文が最もふさわしい場所はどこか。

    (1)　　(2)　　(3)　　(4)

4. 第2パラグラフにおける下線文の主要な情報を最もよく表しているのは以下のどの文であるか。誤った選択肢は、重要な点で意味が違うか、大事な情報を欠いている。

    (A) 世界中で気温が上昇していることは、本当に問題だとは言えない。
    (B) 地球の平均気温は確かに以前より高い。
    (C) 誰も地球の気温が上がっていないと主張したり論じたりしてはいない。
    (D) 本当の問題は、地球が実際に暖かくなってきているかだ。

5. 第2パラグラフで著者は _____ ために、NASAのゴダード宇宙研究所を引用している。

    (A) 自分がアメリカに特有の問題について話していることを示す
    (B) 自分の主張の裏付けとして権威による統計を紹介する
    (C) エッセイ中の情報を最新のものにする
    (D) 記録をつけることがまだ行われていることを証明する

6. 第3パラグラフにおいて、_____ を除く以下のすべてが地球温暖化の説明案として言及されている。

    (A) 通常の地表温度の上下動
    (B) 地球温暖化についての情報のほとんどが、大都市で測られた気温表示にのみ基づいている。
    (C) 太陽から地球へ届く光量における変化
    (D) 地球は、より寒い時期から抜け出そうとしている。

7. 第3パラグラフにおいて、_____ 、著者は企業と政治家からの圧力に言及している。

    (A) 気候学者がみんな完全には公明正大ではないとほのめかすために
    (B) 経済学が環境と同等に重要であると信じているので
    (C) 政府の指導者たちに行動を起こすことを促すために
    (D) 公正さと客観性の理由から

8. 第4パラグラフの情報から、著者は _____ と推測できる。

   (A) 大勢を占める科学的意見をサポートしている
   (B) 大勢を占める科学的意見に懐疑的である
   (C) 地球温暖化は人工のものだとは限らないと信じている
   (D) 何を信じてよいのかわからない

9. 第5パラグラフにおいて、オゾンは _____ の例として言及されている。

   (A) 太陽からの赤外線
   (B) 普通の大気の状態
   (C) 大気の保温膜の構成要素
   (D) 温室効果

10. 第7パラグラフの情報を基にすると、以下のどのステートメントが最もあり得ることであるか。

    (A) ますます乾いてきて、もはや農業には適さなくなった中国人農家の土地もある。
    (B) 豪雨によってエスキモーの人たちが移動を強いられている。
    (C) 太平洋の島々の多くがすでに消滅してしまった。
    (D) 動物はもはや極地域の氷冠上では生き残れない。

11. 第7パラグラフにおける下線語 **exacerbated** は意味上 _____ に最も近い。

    (A) relieved（救われる）
    (B) worsened（悪化させられる）
    (C) misunderstood（誤解される）
    (D) concerned（心配される）

Lesson 14

12. 問題文を簡潔にまとめたサマリーの第1文が以下に与えられている。問題文の最も重要な考えを表す選択肢を3つ選んで、サマリーを完成させよ。文章中に出てこない考えを表したり、文章中ではさほど重要でない考えであるためサマリーには属さない文も存在する。

   地球温暖化はますますひどくなってきており、すでに地球上の生命に悪影響を与えている。何かすぐになされないと、さらに深刻な影響が将来必ず現れるはずである。

   (A) 化石燃料燃焼による排ガスが、この現象の主要な —— そして人為的な —— 原因であるとの動かしがたい証拠がある。
   (B) 地球の大気中に温室効果ガスを最も多く吐き出しているのはアメリカである。
   (C) 極地域の氷冠上のオゾン層がどんどん薄くなってきていると今科学者たちは信じている。
   (D) 自国から締め出される人々もいるし、無数の動物が生息地を失ってその絶滅が危惧されている。
   (E) 温暖化のスピードもヒートアップしており、記録上最も暑かった年のトップ5が1998年以降に起きている。おかげで、熱波と洪水が起こり、海の水位も上昇した。
   (F) 効果的に対処され、減少さえした環境問題もある。

Lesson 15

PTSD

リーディング： 以下の文章を注意深く読め。

⬜1 今日の生活はあらゆる種類の危険に満ちており、多分歴史上最悪ではないかと思われる。戦争とテロ行為からジャンボ機の墜落と自然災害、また正体不明のウィルスから恐ろしい暴力犯罪まで —— 災害（あるいはテレビと新聞によってそう思い込まされているもの）はどこにでも潜んでいる。生活が以前より実際に危険なのかどうかには議論の余地があるが、統計によると、心的外傷後ストレス障害 (PTSD) は確実に増えている。おそらくこれ以上の証拠は要らないだろう。

⬜2 心的外傷後ストレス障害は極度の精神的ストレスを伴う経験から個人に発症する精神の病である。ストレスのたまる出来事の後には、たいてい感情的麻痺状態、逃避、否定の期間が長く続く。PTSD 患者は、不眠症、記憶喪失、ひどい鬱病、慢性的なイラつきに陥りやすくなる。彼らはまた幻覚症状、悪夢およびフラッシュバックを通して、最初にトラウマを引き起こした出来事を持続的に再経験する。アル中、薬物乱用も珍しくない。

⬜3 PTSD を引き起こす出来事は、たいてい実際の死あるいは死の危険、または大怪我に関係するものである。**1.** これらに含まれるものには、子供時代の肉体的、情緒的、または性的虐待、自動車事故や他の事故に巻き込まれること、地震、津波、大嵐のような自然災害を経験すること、そしてレイプがある。（拷問の被害者と捕虜の場合のように）個人の尊厳と心理的高潔感を失うことも原因の一要素になることがある。**2.** 被災地における救助員もまた PTSD にとても無防備である。**3.** 9 月 11 日の世界貿易センターへの攻撃をテレビで観た人にさえ、症状を訴える者があった。**4.** 今や医者による概算では、アメリカ人の 10 パーセント近くがその一生中に PTSD を被るのだと言う。

⬜4 しかし、当然かもしれないが、最もよく見られる PTSD の直接原因は戦争に送り出されることである。第一次世界大戦後、この症候群は「シェル・ショック」と呼ばれていた。（イギリス人作家パット・バーカーによる『再生三部作』の小説では、当時あまり知られていなかったこの病の被害者に初めて治療を施した心理学者の努力が生々しく描かれている。）第二次世界大戦後、「戦争神経症」という用語がこの疾病を描写するものとして作られた。しかし、ベトナム戦争の復員軍人に対する大規模な

調査の直後、心的外傷後ストレス障害という用語とその診断が広く使われるようになったころには、もう 1980 年代になっていた。これらの調査によると、ベトナムで奉仕したアメリカ人男女の 30 パーセント近くが PTSD の症状を訴えたという。湾岸戦争とイラクとアフガニスタンでの現在の戦争から帰った兵士も同じような発症率を示している。

⑤　男も女も同様に外傷的な出来事を経験するものだが、女のほうが 2 倍心的外傷後ストレス障害を発症しやすく、子供時代のトラウマがその最も一般的な原因となっている。シャイというような特定の性格、および鬱病・心配症の病歴があると、この病にかかるリスクが大きくなることもわかってきた。また、通常よりひどく外傷的ストレスを被る遺伝体質の人もいるのかもしれない。

⑥　しかしながら、外傷的出来事を経験する人のすべてが PTSD の症状を発症するわけではない。なぜ他人よりリスクの高い人がいるのかを突き止めるために、研究者は fMRI のような神経画像法のテクニックを用い、PTSD にかかる人とそうでないトラウマ経験者では脳活動に —— 特に恐怖に対処し、記憶と感情の処理を司る脳領域において —— 目立った違いがあると今では主張している。たとえば、知覚保持に関わる脳領域である海馬が、PTSD 患者においては普通より小さいことがわかった。事実、突然の外傷的ストレスが実際に脳の構成を物理的に変えてしまい、それによって脳自体が障害を起こすということを示す証拠が次々に見つかっているのだ。

⑦　PTSD は、心理療法と抗不安薬・抗鬱薬のような向精神性薬を組み合わせることで、今では一般的に、そしてかなりの割合で完全に治療されている。グループ・セラピー —— 似たような外傷的経験をした人と話すこと —— が患者の教育および彼らを自らの問題に立ち向かわせるのに特に役立っている。しかしながら、回復へのカギは早期の介入にあるようだ。外傷的事件後、被害者に救いの手が差し伸べられ、緊急事態ストレス管理マネージメント (CISM) のセラピーに入れられるのが早ければ早いほど、PTSD の深刻な徴候を避けられる可能性が高くなるのである

エクササイズ： 正しい選択肢をもってして、以下の文を完成させるか、質問に答えよ。あるいは、指示に従え。

1. 第1パラグラフにおいて、著者は _____ と主張している。

    (A) 飛行機事故が最悪の自然災害である。
    (B) どこにでも危険が潜んでいる。
    (C) メディアは現代生活の危険を誇張するかもしれない。
    (D) 心的外傷後ストレス障害はテレビの観すぎによって引き起こされる。

2. 第2パラグラフにおける下線文の主要な情報を最もよく表しているのは以下のどの文であるか。誤った選択肢は、重要な点で意味が違うか、大事な情報を欠いている。

    (A) 外傷的な出来事により人々は自分の中に閉じこもり、他人に対する感情を失い、自分に問題があることすら認めようとしない。
    (B) 外傷的な出来事を経験したことによる症状は、ふつうその後長い間表には出てこない。
    (C) 外傷的な出来事の被害者にはほとんど友達がおらず、彼らはめったに外出しない。
    (D) 外傷的な出来事について忘れるのが早ければ早いほど、それから回復するのに時間がかかる。

3. 第2パラグラフにおいて _____ を除く以下のすべてが心的外傷後ストレス障害の症状として言及されている。

    (A) 不眠症
    (B) 悪夢
    (C) 夫婦間の問題
    (D) 自暴自棄および絶望の感情

Lesson 15

4. 第3パラグラフにおける下線語 **trigger** は意味上 ＿＿＿＿＿＿ に最も近い。

    (A) discharge（放つ）
    (B) precipitate（突然引き起こす）
    (C) undergo（経験する）
    (D) release（放す）

5. 第3パラグラフに以下の文を追加し得る場所を示す4つの番号を見よ。

    PTSD を発症するのに、必ずしも自らが外傷的出来事を経験する必要はない。他人が被害に遭うのを目撃することでも、症状が発症し得るのである。

    この文が最もふさわしい場所はどこか。

    (1)　　(2)　　(3)　　(4)

6. 第4パラグラフにおいて著者は ＿＿＿＿＿＿ ため、下線語 **pioneering** という語を用いている。

    (A) 心理学者の努力がいかに成功に終わったかを示す
    (B) 「シェル・ショック」が何なのか医者にはさっぱりわからなかったことを強調するため
    (C) 議論の対象が第一次世界大戦であることを読者に思い起こさせる
    (D) トラウマを被っている退役軍人を最初に診ようとしたのは心理学者だったことを指摘する

7. 第4パラグラフにおける下線語 **these** は ＿＿＿＿＿＿ を指す。

    (A) ベトナムの男と女
    (B) 調査
    (C) PTSD の症状
    (D) PTSD という用語とその診断

8. 第5パラグラフにおいて、＿＿＿＿＿＿＿を除く以下のすべてがPTSDにかかりやすくなる要因として言及されている。

   (A) 女であること
   (B) PTSDを持って生まれてくること
   (C) 生まれつき内気であること
   (D) 酷い子供時代を被ったこと

9. 第6パラグラフで使われている **perception retention** という下線用語は＿＿＿＿＿＿＿を指す。

   (A) 感情
   (B) 記憶
   (C) 脳内における物理的な変化
   (D) PTSDの原因

10. 第7パラグラフにおいて、抗鬱薬は＿＿＿＿＿＿＿の例として言及されている。

    (A) 向精神薬
    (B) 精神療法
    (C) 組み合わされた治療法
    (D) 心配を処置する薬

Lesson 15

11. 第 7 パラグラフにおいて、著者はグループ・セラピーのどのような重要点を指摘しているか。

    (A) 精神療法との組み合わせによってのみ効果を発揮する
    (B) 外傷的出来事の直後に始められない限り、効き目はない。
    (C) 患者が自分の問題を理解し直面することの手助けになる。
    (D) 完全な回復へのカギである。

12. この文章の簡潔なサマリーのための最初の 1 文が以下に与えられている。文章中の最も重要な考えを表す 3 つの選択肢を選び、サマリーを完成させよ。文章中に出てこない考えを表したり、文章中ではさほど重要でない考えであるためサマリーには属さない文も存在する。

    心的外傷後ストレス障害は、10 人に 1 人に近いアメリカ人を悩ます心理的な問題である。

    (A) ストレス・マネージメントのカウンセリングにかかるのが早ければ早いほど、患者の回復の確率が高くなる。
    (B) かつて「戦争神経症」として知られたこの病について、小説が書かれている。
    (C) この病の症状には、幻覚、悪夢、感情の損失、深刻な鬱などがある。
    (D) 症状を引き起こす出来事は深刻な感情的および／あるいは肉体的ダメージを伴う、ほとんど致命的なものであるのが普通である。
    (E) PTSD はアメリカのみにおける問題ではなく、世界中の人がかかっている。
    (F) 子供時代にトラウマを被った男が PTSD を経験することはほとんどない。

Lesson 16

動物園：賛成と反対

リーディング： 以下の文章を注意深く読め。

1. 動物園は、紀元前 15 世紀のエジプトの女王ハトシェプストがふさわしい求婚者を惹きつけるため、また訪問して来る高官に好印象を与えるために、猿、ライオン、豹、そしてその他のアフリカの動物を集めて個人動物園を作って以来、少なくとも 3,500 年は続いている。千年後、マケドニアのアレクサンドロス大王が 300 以上の動物個体を集めたのだが、ギリシャの哲学者アリストテレスはこれらの動物を詳しく観察し、最初の科学的な動物学論文「動物誌」の題材にしたのだった。

2. しかし、最も熱心なコレクターはローマ帝国の市民で、彼らは広範囲に渡る軍事征服に従事する間に捕らえたり、降参した支配者からの貢物として受け取ったりした何万もの動物たちを連れ帰った。しかし、これらの動物の多くは一時的に公開されただけで、中でも獰猛な動物はじきに檻から「スポーツ」アリーナへ移され、血に飢えた観客の前でグラディエーターと死の戦いを行ったのである。

3. 帝政時代（15 世紀から 18 世紀）を通して、ヨーロッパの王や女王たちは世界中からの珍しい動物の大きな個人コレクションを持っていたが、これは植民地支配による富、力、そして威信を見せびらかすためのものであった。しかし、大衆的な娯楽の場としての動物園が生まれたのは 19 世紀になってからのことである。動物園は主要な大都市圏のほとんどに作られるようになり、ロンドン動物学会の例にならって、娯楽と同時に科学的で教育的な目的を持つところだと主張されるようになった。

4. **1.** 今日でも動物園はまだまだ人気があり、毎年何百万もの人が訪れている。**2.** 動物が鉄製の小さな檻や冷たいコンクリートの囲いに閉じ込められていたのは、ありがたいことに、今では昔のことである。**3.** そういう粗野で残酷な動物園はずっと進んだ考えを持つ園に取って代わられ、そこでは動物の自然な居住環境をできるだけ念入りに再現する努力が払われており、小さな沼地、人工の川、特別な気候状態が作られ、複数種共生展示が見られるのだ。今日の一流動物園はまた野生動物の疾病と生殖について研究したり、新しい動物外科手術のテクニックの開発および他の真剣なリサーチ・プロジェクトに積極的に従事している。**4.**

5. これらの歓迎すべき改善点にも関わらず、動物園は未だに大きな議論の対象で、多くの動物権利活動家たちが動物園の完全廃止を主張しているのだ。動物園は本質的に非倫理的で残酷なものだと彼らは言う。監禁するということは野生動物をさげすむ

だけでなく、我々の品位までをも落とすものである。飼育下にある動物は、凝視、行ったり来たり、ぐるぐる歩き、檻へのかみつきといった「狂った」行動 ── みな自由の欠如から来る退屈心、欲求不満、および混乱によって引き起こされるもの ── を示す。動物園側がどんなに声をあげて存在の権利を言い張っても、この基礎事実は否定できないと活動家たちは言う。動物園の主張は何であろうか。そしてそれに対する活動家の反論は何であろうか。

6 今日のより進んだ動物園は、園が野生動物の生活、習性および問題について一般人を教育するのに重要な役割を果たしていると主張する。動物園反対者は、このようにはとらえていない。彼らにとっては、動物園が教育に努力するというのは、ある意味で賞賛に値するものの、心得違いで、自己を欺くものであり、せいぜいうわべだけのものに過ぎない。飼育下の動物はすぐに本来の特徴を失い、もはや自らの種を代表するものとは言えなくなる。そんな飼い慣らされ野生味を消された動物から何が学べるのかと動物福祉グループは問う。もし動物園が本当に動物について人々を教育し、動物の苦痛に対する同情心を呼び起こしたいのなら、たとえば、人間がいかに動物という同胞を食い物にし、彼らの生来の生活環境を破壊してきたかを示すドキュメンタリー映画の一般鑑賞会を持ったほうがましなのではないか。

7 動物園はまた野生動物の行動や病気などに関する科学リサーチのセンターでもあると主張する。そうではないと動物権利グループは言うのだが、それは上に引いたのものと同じ理由でである。動物園の動物は野生動物ではない。彼らに対して行われるリサーチは真に科学的でも役に立つものでもない。なぜなら、それは動物園の動物にしか当てはまらないからだ。

8 しかしながら、動物園が提供する、存在のための最も重要な口実というのは、動物園は動物の保護と維持のためにあるというものである。飼育下繁殖プログラムを通して、多くの絶滅危惧種を絶滅から救っているのだと動物園は主張する。これらの動物はそのあと野生に戻され、そこでまた種を増やし、生物多様性維持の手助けになり得ることが期待されているのだ。

9 動物支援者たちは同意しない。こういう再生プログラムはほとんど成功した試しがないと彼らは言う。事実、動物園が野生に戻す動物よりも、そこから連れ去り続ける動物の数のほうが多いのだ。飼育下繁殖という考えは別の意味でも心得違いである。ほとんどの場合、動物の居住環境は破壊されているので、たとえ「救われた」としても、動物が帰るべき「野生」はもうないのである。このように、動物は飼育下で生きることを運命付けられているのだ。動物が死に絶えるのを防ぐ唯一の正当な方法は、彼らの本来のすみかを保護し復元することであると活動家たちは言う。

エクササイズ： 正しい選択肢をもってして、以下の文を完成させるか、質問に答えよ。あるいは、指示に従え。

1. 第1パラグラフにおいて著者はアリストテレスを _____ の例として言及している。

    (A) 有名なギリシャの哲学者
    (B) 動物研究の開拓者
    (C) アレクサンドロス大王の家庭教師
    (D) 何百もの動物個体の収集家

2. 第2パラグラフにおける下線語 **assiduous** は意味上 _____ に最も近い。

    (A) enthusiastic（熱心な）
    (B) cruel（残酷な）
    (C) notorious（悪名高い）
    (D) systematic（体系的な）

3. 第2パラグラフにおける下線語 **subjugated** は意味上 _____ に最も近い。

    (A) distant（遠く離れた）
    (B) deceased（死んだ）
    (C) conquered（征服された）
    (D) captured（とらえられた）

4. 第1-3パラグラフにおいて _____ を除く以下のすべてが歴史上の動物園について言及されている。

    (A) 富と力の誇示であった。
    (B) 武器を持った戦士によって動物が殺されたところである。
    (C) 動物は軍事遠征中に集められた。
    (D) 主に個人のコレクションであった。

Lesson 16

5. 第3パラグラフの情報から ＿＿＿＿＿＿ と推測できる。

    (A) 1800年代には、大都市の外に動物園は存在しなかった。
    (B) 最初の19世紀の動物園はヨーロッパの王や女王たちから動物を譲り受けた。
    (C) ロンドン動物学会が世界で最初の一般用動物園を設立した。
    (D) 19世紀まで一般大衆は野生動物を見る機会が多くなかった。

6. 第4パラグラフに以下の文を追加し得る場所を示す4つの番号を見よ。

    しかしながら**現代の動物園**は、大方のところ、**過去の動物園**とはまったく違う。

    この文が最もふさわしい場所はどこか。

    (1)   (2)   (3)   (4)

7. 4パラグラフにおいて、著者は ＿＿＿＿＿＿ の例として複数種共生展示に言及している。

    (A) 特別な気候状態
    (B) 動物園が行わなくなってからだいぶ時間のたつ慣例
    (C) 自然の居住環境を再現しようとする試み
    (D) まじめなリサーチ・プロジェクト

8. 第5パラグラフにおける下線文の主要な情報を最もよく表しているのは以下のどの文であるか。誤った選択肢は、重要な点で意味が違うか、大事な情報を欠いている。

   (A) 動物を檻に閉じ込めることによって、我々は彼らを虐待すると同時に我々自身にも恥をもたらすことになる。
   (B) 管理下にある動物が可哀そうだと感じると多くの動物園職員が告白している。
   (C) 動物は恥や当惑を感じないので、彼らの自由を奪うことはそれほど彼らを困らせるわけではない。
   (D) 飼育下の動物を凝視することは人間ができる最も下劣なことの1つである。

9. 第5パラグラフにおける下線のフレーズ **this basic fact** は _____ を指す。

   (A) 動物園の廃止
   (B) 退屈と欲求不満が原因の動物による「狂った」行動
   (C) 動物園の存在する権利
   (D) 動物を飼育下に置き続けるという不道徳

10. 第6パラグラフにおける下線語 **laudatory** は意味上 _____ に最も近い。

    (A) unintentional（故意でない）
    (B) praiseworthy（賞賛に値する）
    (C) explicable（説明可能な）
    (D) unforgivable（許せない）

11. 第8パラグラフにおいて、_____ を除く以下のすべてを、飼育下繁殖の目的として動物園が挙げている。

    (A) 動物の生殖習慣を観察すること
    (B) 絶滅危惧種を自然に戻すこと
    (C) 種を絶滅から救うこと
    (D) 生物多様性の維持の手助けになること

Lesson 16

12. 動物権利活動家による動物園廃止要求の簡潔なサマリーにおける最初の1文が以下に与えられている。彼らの主要な主張を表す3つの選択肢を選んでサマリーを完成させよ。問題文中にはなかったり、あってもマイナーなアイディアに過ぎないため、サマリーには適さない選択肢も存在する。

動物園による正反対の見解にも関わらず、動物を飼育下に置くことは本来的に道徳に反することである。

(A) 動物園は、絶滅危惧種の個体を持ってくる動物ハンターに高い金額を支払う。
(B) 動物園の動物の間には、とても高い死亡率と病気発生率が存在する。
(C) 動物園の動物が事実上家畜化されているのなら、動物園が真に教育的になることも、本物の科学リサーチを行うこともあり得ない。
(D) 多くの動物の本来の居住環境は破壊されてからかなりたつので、彼らを「野生」に戻すという計画は無駄であり偽善である。
(E) 飼育下の動物を研究することが、動物が自然の中でいかに行動するかについて学ぶために我々が持つ唯一の方法である。
(F) 飼育下の動物は自然のままの特徴を失うだけでなく、その過程において頭もおかしくなる。

Lesson 17

パナマ運河

リーディング：以下の文章を注意深く読め。

1. 土木工学はビジネス、産業、そして日常生活のニーズに応えるため、景観地理を変えることに専心する職業である。土木工学者は、オフィス、工場、橋、トンネル、鉄道、ダム、高速道路、灌漑・給水システムといったあらゆる種類の構造物の設計、建設、維持を行う。

2. 20世紀の初期、パナマ共和国からリースされた土地にアメリカが建設したパナマ運河は、これまでに行われた土木工学プロジェクトの中でも最も壮大なものの1つである。50マイルに及ぶこの運河は、17の人工湖、入り組んだシステムの人工水路、水位を上げ下げする3セットの水圧式閘門から構成されている。また、西半球をきちんと二分する位置にあり、太平洋と大西洋を結ぶので、船は危険の潜む南アメリカ先端のホーン岬の水域を通る必要がなくなり、航行時間、距離、費用の大幅な縮小を可能にしている。

3. パナマ地峡に運河を通すことが最初に提案されたのは16世紀初期の頃で、スペインが、新たに確立したアメリカの植民地の豊かな資源を積極的に搾取し、東洋との貿易を増加させている時代であった。スペインの役人はそのようなプロジェクトの予備計画を確かに立案したのだが、ヨーロッパにおける戦争がその実現を阻んでいた。太平洋と大西洋をつなぐという計画が本格的に復活したのは、1848年にカリフォルニアで金が発見され、次いで起こったゴールド・ラッシュの後の19世紀半ばになってからのことである。1881年にフランスの土木工学会社が運河の仕事を開始したが、不十分な計画、資金および機材の問題、そして労働者の間で猛威をふるった病気のためにこの計画は失敗の運命をたどってしまった。

4. その後、1903年にアメリカがパナマの租借権を獲得し、その翌年に工事を本格的に開始した。アメリカのエンジニアたちはフランス人がやり残したところから仕事を再開する格好になった。役人たちは最初の3年をこの場所に最も適した運河の種類の決定（最終的には高架の水門システムを選んだ）、土地の調査、そしてプロジェクト全般の計画のために費やした。特に重要なことは病気の制圧であった。致命的なフランスの経験から、プロジェクトが成功するには労働者の食・住環境を良いものにし、彼らが病気にかからないようにする必要があった。彼らのためにパナマのジャ

ングルに完全な街が作られ、店、教会、学校、病院までが完備された。淀んだ沼地は排出され、排水溝が作られ、配管と下水設備も設置された。マラリアと黄熱病予防に関する新しい知見を武器に、保健担当官が工事現場に殺虫剤と殺菌剤を休みなくスプレーして回った。

5 にもかかわらず、状況は厳しかった。ダイナマイト、ぎこちない蒸気シャベル、そして馬、牛に引かれるワゴンを使って、労働者たちは炎熱のなかで骨を折って働き、あらゆる種類の虫と蛇を追い払いながら、1億平方ヤード以上の土と石を掘り起こして運び出さねばならなかった。集中豪雨が頻繁に —— しばしば命取りになる —— 土石流と地すべりを引き起こした。運河の水門、ダム、擁壁を作るのに、労働者は粉砕した岩から作った何百万トンものコンクリートを混ぜて注いだのだった。

6 最終的に、運河の建設には20万以上の人足と9年の歳月がかかり、そのコストは3億4千万ドルの費用と6千人近くの人命となった。最初の船 — 商貨物船アンコン —— が運河を通り抜けたのは、1914年8月15日であった。

7 今日、パナマ運河は未だに国際貿易と輸送の肝心な水路になっている。**1.** 毎年、1万4千ほどの船がおよそ2億5千万トンもの荷物を積んでパナマ運河を通り抜けているのだ。**2.** しかしながら、運河の建築に際してもともと想定していた船のほとんどはすでに過去のもの。**3.** 現代の輸送量に対応して船のサイズは大幅にアップし、30万トンもの積荷を運べるものさえ出現している。**4.** これらの巨大な貨物船と定期船は2010年までには世界の輸送量の丸々3分の1も運ぶと予想されていて、運河の将来に深刻な疑問を投げかけている。メキシコ、ニカラグア、あるいはコロンビアを通る他の場所が、もっと大きくて優れた運河の候補地として提案されたところだ。それに対し、経済と福祉を運河がもたらす収入に完全に頼っているパナマは、大胆にも、拡大・最新化計画を進めているのである。

エクササイズ： 正しい選択肢をもってして、以下の文を完成させるか、質問に答えよ。あるいは、指示に従え。

1. 第1パラグラフにおいて、_____ を除く以下のすべてが土木工学者が行うプロジェクトとして言及されている。

    (A) 産業工場
    (B) 一般住居
    (C) ビジネス施設
    (D) 交通施設

2. 第2パラグラフにおける下線語 **intricate** は意味上 _____ に最も近い。

    (A) elaborate（精巧な）
    (B) complete（完全な）
    (C) practical（実用的な）
    (D) efficient（能率的な）

3. 第2パラグラフで著者が描写する最も重要な考えは _____ ことである。

    (A) パナマ運河が50マイルである
    (B) パナマ運河の閘門が水位の上げ下げをする
    (C) パナマ運河は壮大な土木工学プロジェクトである
    (D) パナマ運河は船積会社の時間と金を大幅に節約する

4. 第3パラグラフにおける下線語 **them** は _____ を指す。

    (A) スペインの役人
    (B) 運河の計画
    (C) ヨーロッパでの戦争
    (D) 資源の搾取

Lesson 17

5. 第3パラグラフにおいて、19世紀半ばに運河プロジェクトに対する興味が復活したことの理由は何だとされているか。

   (A) 新世界における植民地設立
   (B) カリフォルニアでの金の発見。
   (C) スペインとの競争
   (D) アジアとの増加する貿易

6. 第3パラグラフにおける下線文の主要な情報を最もよく表しているのは以下のどの文であるか。誤った選択肢は、重要な点で意味が違うか、あるいは大事な情報を欠いている。

   (A) 1881年にプロジェクトに従事したフランスの会社は、計画にもっと時間と金をかけるべきだった。
   (B) 1881年のフランスのプロジェクトは、運河建設をきちんと仕上げる前に資金が底をついてしまった。
   (C) 1881年に運河を作り始めたフランスの建設会社は、より効果的な病気対策、よりすぐれた機材、そして資金と先見の明をもっと持っていたら、仕事を成し遂げられたかもしれない。
   (D) 1881年のプロジェクトで使われた機材は、労働者と医療職員と同じく、その状況には不適切なものだった。

7. 第4パラグラフから _____ と推測できる。

   (A) アメリカ人はフランス人が行った仕事も利用し、彼らの過ちからも学んだ
   (B) アメリカは、軍事、外交手段を通して租借権を手に入れた
   (C) 運河は外国人労働者によって建てられた
   (D) 病気は労働者にとって完全に問題ではなくなった

8. 第5パラグラフにおける下線語 **toiling** は意味上 ＿＿＿＿ に最も近い。

    (A) working（働く）
    (B) sweating（汗をかく）
    (C) suffering（苦しむ）
    (D) living（生きる）

9. ＿＿＿＿ を除いた以下のすべてが、運河建設プロジェクト遂行中の労働状況の例として言及されている。

    (A) 高温
    (B) 悪天候
    (C) 害虫
    (D) 粉砕した岩からコンクリートを作ること

10. 第7パラグラフに以下の文を追加し得る場所を示す4つの番号を見よ。

    パナマ運河は小さなヨットから最大積載量6万5千トンの商貨物船までに及ぶサイズの船を受け入れることができる。

    この文が最もふさわしい場所はどこか。

    (1)　　(2)　　(3)　　(4)

11. 第7パラグラフによると、これからの数年で何が起こるというのだろうか。

    (A) パナマ運河が過去のものとなる。
    (B) より大きく、より優れた運河がメキシコを横切って建てられる。
    (C) 巨大船が世界の輸送船団の大きな割合を占めることになる。
    (D) パナマが運河の通航料を引き上げてその収入を維持する。

Lesson 17

12. 問題文の主要なアイディアの簡潔なサマリーの第 1 文として最もふさわしいのは以下のどの文か。

    (A) 毎年 1 万 4 千ほどの船がパナマ運河を航行するが、この運河は今やアメリカではなくパナマ共和国によって所有され、運営されている。

    (B) パナマ運河の建設は 2 つの段階を踏んで行われた。最初はフランスの会社が請け負って 1881 年に始まり、その次は 1904 年にアメリカ政府が始めたのだった。

    (C) 工学技術および人間の労働と犠牲からなる偉業であり、国際輸送ビジネスに革命をもたらしたパナマ運河であるが、その未来は今やはっきりしない。

    (D) 今日では多くの船が大きくなり過ぎたため、パナマ運河を迂回し、ホーン岬の危険な海域を通って南アメリカを回るという、長距離でコストのかかる旅をしなければならない。

Lesson 18

ジョン・デューイの実験学校

リーディング：以下の文章を注意深く読め。

1　ジョン・デューイ (1859-1952) は、南北戦争 (1861-1865) 後の数十年の間に発達したアメリカの思想学派、実用主義の創始者のひとりであった。あのぞっとするほど血なまぐさい戦争の後、アメリカ人たちは、戦争によって否定された古い信念と時代遅れのアイディアの代わりになる新しい考え方 —— 増加する人口・移民、進む産業化、そして迅速な科学上の発見といった、19世紀末の生活を取り巻く激変する状況に対処する手助けとなる一連の新しい考え —— を必要としていた。実用主義が、これらのニーズへの答えだとされたのである。

2　デューイとウィリアム・ジェイムズのような他の実用主義者たちは、考えとは、独自に存在する絶対的で永久的なものではなく、特定の状況に対しての、常に変化し暫定的である人間の反応であるとした。考えの真実は、より良い生活のための道具としてのその利便性にあり、経験と観察を通してのみ決定され得るのである。

3　実用主義者たちはまた、仮定と信念が退廃して凝り固まったドグマやイデオロギーに変化するのを決して許すべきではないと教えた。仮定と信念は、常に誤りがないか見直し、変化する状況に合うように修正するべきなのである。デューイと仲間の実用主義者は、この新しい考え方が人種と文化間の相違に対する寛容性を育む手助けになり、古くて凝り固まった考えが憎しみと暴力の言い訳に使われることがより難しくなることを望んだ。

4　仕事を始めてすぐのころ、ジョン・デューイは、自分の実用主義の信念を反映した教育の本をいくつか出版した。1896年には、自分の理論と信念をテストするために、実験学校として知られることになる実験的な小中学校をイリノイ州のシカゴに開いたのだった。

5　従来の机仕事的な教育へのアプローチは、効果がなく無駄なものだとデューイは確信していた。彼は、一人一人の個人勉強を通して宿題を完成させることに重きを置く伝統的な教授法は、「教科内容において変化がなく、やり方において独裁的であり、主に受動的で受容的な」ものであると信じていたのである。当時の教員は、教育メソッドや理論における訓練をほとんど、あるいはまったく受けておらず、主に考えを押し付け、特定の思考と規律の習慣を植え付けるために学校にいたのだった。カリ

Lesson 18

キュラムは定められた科目から成り立っており、また科目は決まったレッスンに分けられ、さらにレッスンは決まった定則と事実に分類されていた。デューイの目には、こういう教室環境における子どもは、こまごまとした情報を受け取る単なる「導きやすく従順な」入れ物のように映った。伝統的な教室は、「幾何学的に配置された醜い机の列が、可能な限り動き回るスペースがなくなるようにぎゅうぎゅう詰めにされており」、学習へのこの丸暗記的、受身的なアプローチを反映するように作られていた。このような教室における教育はまた、社会全般の必要不可欠な部分およびその延長を成すのではなく、そこから切り離されていたのである。

6 デューイはこのすべてを変えたかった。彼が信じたのは、教育とは単なる「将来の生活のための準備」ではなく、「生きる過程」であるべきだということだった。よって、実験学校では子どもが教育の中心に置かれた。**1.** 単なる知識と情報の蓄積ではなく、自己実現がその目的であった。**2.** 学業に優れることも重要ではあるが、創造的に問題を解決することには遠く及ばない。この学校は2つの点においてまさに実験室だった。まず新しい教育の理論と考えが生み出され、試される場所であった。**3.** そこはまた、生徒が自分の学習の責任を持ち、個人のニーズおよびグループのニーズに合ったアプローチを開発する場所でもあったのだ。**4.**

7 おそらくデューイの最も偉大な洞察は、学習と知識はすることと行動に始まるということだった。実験学校における学習の多くが、実地のプロジェクトを通して行われた。読書において自然を知るのではなく、自然をじかに探索する。地図に熱中するのではなく、旅行する。歴史的事実を暗記する代わりに歴史的な演劇を鑑賞するのである。デューイの生徒たちはまた、自分の服を縫い、大工課題に取り組み、自らの弁当を作った。たとえば料理は、学習者にとって算数（材料の重さと分量を量る）、生物学（栄養と消化について議論する）、そして地理（植物と動物の自然における生息地について学ぶ）のレッスンにもなった。また、みんなのために協力することも関係していた。

8 ジョン・デューイがシカゴからニューヨーク・シティに移ったのを機に、実験学校は数年でたたまれた。ローレル・タナーは、実験学校についての彼女の素晴らしい研究書において以下のように指摘している。「当時は影響力を持ったものだが、ジョン・デューイの作った学校はほとんど忘れ去られている。1世紀経って、その考えと慣行はまだほとんど無視されたままだ。デューイの考えと慣行は、我々に深く関わる物事についてまだ学ばれていないレッスンとして、この学校の記録の中で、我々を待っているのだ。

エクササイズ：正しい選択肢をもってして、以下の文を完成させるか、質問に答えよ。あるいは、指示に従え。

1. 第 1 パラグラフにおける下線語 **discredited** は意味上 ＿＿＿＿ に最も近い。

    (A) less well known（より知られていない）
    (B) less trusted（より信頼されていない）
    (C) less clearly understood（より理解が怪しい）
    (D) less doubted（より疑わしくない）

2. 第 1 パラグラフにおいて、＿＿＿＿ を除く以下のすべてが、アメリカで 19 世紀の終わりに起きていた社会変化として言及されている。

    (A) 南北戦争の暴力
    (B) 人口の増加
    (C) 外国人の流入
    (D) 科学における進歩

3. 第 2 パラグラフにおける下線語 **provisional** は意味上 ＿＿＿＿ に最も近い。

    (A) temporary（一時の、仮の）
    (B) long-lasting（長く続く）
    (C) absolute（絶対的な）
    (D) generous（寛容な）

4. 第 3 パラグラフにおける下線語 **They** は ＿＿＿＿ を指す。

    (A) ドグマとイデオロギー
    (B) 実用主義者たち
    (C) 変化する状況
    (D) 仮定と信念

Lesson 18

5. 著者によると、第3パラグラフにおいて、実用主義者たちは自らの新しい考え方が何をもたらすかもしれないと期待していたのか。

    (A) 憎しみと暴力の言い訳として使われる
    (B) 常に見直される
    (C) 他の文化について人々を教育する
    (D) 心の広さを促進する

6. 第4パラグラフから、_____ と推測できる。

    (A) ジョン・デューイが実験学校において最初の先生になった
    (B) 教育についてのデューイの本はとても影響力がある
    (C) 実験学校は、異なる文化の人々が互いを知ることができる場所だった
    (D) デューイは、生徒たちに実生活の問題・状況に対処するのに役立つ考えと道具を、彼の学校をもってして与えたかった。

7. 第5パラグラフにおける下線語 **docile** は意味上 _____ に最も近い。

    (A) friendly（有効的な）
    (B) passive（受け身の）
    (C) rote（丸暗記的な）
    (D) attentive（注意深い）

8. 第6パラグラフにおける下線文の主要な情報を最もよく表しているのは以下のどの文であるか。誤った選択肢は、重要な点で意味が違うか、大事な情報を欠いている。

   (A) デューイは、教育は将来のための下地を築く方法としてではなく、人生そのものとともに進行するものとみなされるべきだと信じていた。
   (B) デューイによると、学校は生徒の選んだ職業において彼らが成功する手助けをするべきだという。
   (C) デューイは教育をもっと過程を重視するものにしたかった。
   (D) デューイは、彼の生徒たちに将来のことを悩むのを止め、目の前の勉強に集中してほしかった。

9. 第6パラグラフに以下の文を追加し得る場所を示す4つの番号を見よ。

   教室内でも、学校周辺でも、子どもたちは自由に互いと混ざり合って交流し、それによって「合同体の協力的な一員として行動すること」と「自らの行動と感情の狭さから抜け出す」ことが育まれたのである。

   この文が最もふさわしい場所はどこか。

   (1)　　(2)　　(3)　　(4)

10. ＿＿＿＿＿＿ を除く以下のすべてが、実験学校の生徒による実地の学習プロジェクトの例として言及されている。

    (A) 自然の中へ旅すること
    (B) 歴史劇を書くこと
    (C) 自分たちの服を作ること
    (D) 自分たちの弁当を作ること

Lesson 18

11. 以下の選択肢を、それらが描写する学校のタイプとマッチさせよ。選択肢のアルファベットをカッコ内も記せ。選択肢中には2つ使われないものがある。

    伝統的な学校
    (　　)
    (　　)

    実験学校
    (　　)
    (　　)
    (　　)

    (A) ひとりで勉強することと特定の宿題を完成させることに重きが置かれていた。
    (B) 実際にすることおよび協力を要するプロジェクトに積極的に参加することに重きが置かれていた。
    (C) 教育心理学における教えを教員が受ける場所だった。
    (D) 学業に秀でることや知識の蓄積にはまったく重きが置かれていなかった。
    (E) 教員が生徒に考えを押し付け、凝り固まった思考習慣を与えた。
    (F) 教育は子ども中心であり自己実現のためのものであった。
    (G) 生徒たちは、自分たちの教育のなされ方をいくらか自分たちで決めることができた。

12. 以下のステートメントのどれが、ローレル・タナーによるジョン・デューイの本における主要な論点について本当である可能性が最も高いか。

    (A) デューイの考えを現代の読者が理解するのに、より難解でなくしようとしている。
    (B) 今日の学校がデューイの考えとメソッドにもっと注意を払うべきだと提案している。
    (C) 長い年月の間に、デューイの考えは関連性も利便性もなくなってきたと主張している。
    (D) 実用主義および人々が実際にどう考え、また学ぶのかに関しての洞察に深く関わっている。

Lesson 19

アパルトヘイトの終焉

リーディング： 以下の文章を注意深く読め。

1　アパルトヘイトは、1948年から1992年まで人種の線で国を厳しく分け隔てていた南アフリカの身分制度である。総人口の75パーセントほどを占める黒人アフリカ人、およびインド人、アジア人、そして「カラード」（混血の人々）は、強制的に白人支配層から分離され、白人たちは全住民のたった13パーセントを構成するに過ぎないのに、事実上南アフリカの富と資源のすべてをコントロールし、主要なビジネスと産業のほとんどを所有・経営して、政府も独占していた。

2　南アフリカの人種分離自体は17世紀の白人による植民地入植の初期にまで遡るのだが、アパルトヘイトが正式な政府の政策として正式に承認されたのは、第二次世界大戦後になってからのことだった。この政策が引き起こした人権侵害は主に白人至上主義からなされるものであったが、アパルトヘイトにはまた経済的な理由も存在した。社会階級の低いところにいた労働者クラスの白人は、より安い黒人労働力の前に、仕事と生計を取られるのではないかと恐れていた。白人農家は穀物の作付けと収穫および家畜の世話のために安い黒人労働力を必要としていたのだ。戦争直後の数年の間、これらおよび他の利益団体が、黒人の自由を厳しく制限するようにロビー活動を行った。

3　その結果、1950年代を通して、南アフリカ政府は白人支配を堅固に守るための一連の法律を制定した。1950年の集団地域法により、異なった地理的区域に人種が割り当てられた。都会の黒人は強制退去させられ、町からずっと離れた「居住区」と「ホームランド」に移されて、事実上田舎での貧困生活を運命づけられたのだった。「パス法」と夜間外出禁止令によって、黒人の国内での移動は厳しく制限された。黒人はみな、身分証明用の通行許可手帳をいつも携帯せねばならず、特別許可証を持っている者のみが白人地域で働くことを許された。黒人は選挙権を否定され、教育権も実質的に切り詰められていた。いかなる類の政治活動への参加もできず、土地所有も労働組合への加入も許されなかった。規制によりあらゆる種類の人種間交流が禁止され、すべての公共交通施設、娯楽施設、医療施設が厳密に分離された。

4　南アフリカ政府は、これらの法律を容赦なく施行するためにあらゆる手段を使って弾圧を行った。警察と軍隊は逮捕と拘留の絶大な力を有していた。にもかかわら

ず、白人以外による、よってそのほとんどが当然地下組織的な、アパルトヘイト反対運動が 1950 年代と 1960 年代を通して大きくなっていった。国の中で最も力を持っていた黒人組織、アフリカ民族会議（ANC）は、様々な作戦 —— ストライキ、デモ、サボタージュ、通行許可手帳を燃やす —— による抵抗を奨励したが、これらの戦略には政府がしばしば迅速かつ暴力的な報復を行った。

5　**1.** 70 人ほどの無防備な黒人抗議者が警察に背中から撃たれた 1961 年のシャープビル大虐殺、そして ANC のリーダーであるネルソン・マンデラと他の黒人反対者の投獄事件によって、黒人たち（と彼らに同情的な白人の支援者たち）による反対運動の盛り上がりに拍車がかかった。さらなる抵抗はさらなる報復をもたらすことになる。1976 年のソウェト居住区での暴動では、数百人の黒人犠牲者が出ることになった。**2.** ローデシア、アンゴラ、そして他のアフリカ植民地における人種差別的白人体制への南アフリカによる軍事支援は、国際コミュニティーの間に反アパルトヘイトの感情を掻き立てた。**3.** 黒人解放のための財政的、精神的援助が世界中から集まってきた。**4.** 南アフリカは急に世界ののけ者になってしまったのだった。重要な貿易相手は関係を打ち切った挙句に制裁措置を取り、旅行者はボイコット、投資家は逃げ出す始末だった。

6　南アフリカ政府のさらなる悩みの種になったのが、黒人意識高揚運動の高まりだった。これは、いかなる手段を使っても革命をするんだという若い黒人が次々に増えてきたことを意味する。こうして、1980 年代半ばまでには、国は常に緊急事態にあるという状況に陥り、テロ行為と暴動がほとんど日常茶飯事になってしまったのだ。誰かが妥協せねばならなかったが、実際にそうなった。

7　1986 年、国内外からの圧力によって、指導者たちはパス法の破棄と黒人の意見を政治にもっと反映させることを許さざるを得なくなった。3 年後、南アフリカ大統領ピーター・ボタは監獄でネルソン・マンデラに会い、それにより翌年マンデラが解放されるに至る。1991 年、ボタの後継者である F.W. デクラークと南アフリカ国会は政治犯を解放し、病院、学校、そして他の公共施設の差別を撤廃して、少しずつアパルトヘイトの廃止を始めた。アパルトヘイトはその翌年に正式に終りを迎えることになる。1 年のうちに、全員の選挙権と黒人の政府への完全参加を許す新憲法が提案され、認可された。そしてその翌年、国は最初の民主選挙を行ったのである。国の投票者は圧倒的多数でネルソン・マンデラを彼らの最初の黒人大統領に選出したのであった。

エクササイズ： 正しい選択肢をもってして、以下の文を完成させるか、質問に答えよ。あるいは、指示に従え。

1. 第1パラグラフによると、_____ を除く以下のステートメントのすべてが本当である。
   (A) 白人は人種を別々にしておくために威圧行為を行った。
   (B) アジア人とインド人は「カラード」ではなく、別の人種グループとして分類された。
   (C) この国では、白人が最多の人種グループであった。
   (D) 政治において、白人以外にはほとんど、あるいはまったく果たす役割がなかった。

2. 第2パラグラフにおける下線語 **engendered** は意味上 _____ に最も近い。
   (A) gave rise to（引き起こした）
   (B) set up（設立した）
   (C) did away with（廃止した）
   (D) was known for（知られていた）

3. 第2パラグラフから _____ を除く以下のすべてが推測できる。
   (A) 南アフリカの農業は黒人労働力に頼っていた。
   (B) 南アフリカの白人のすべてが等しいステータスの恩恵にあやかっていたわけではない。
   (C) 人種差別主義は、ほとんどの人が思うほどアパルトヘイトに関して重要な役割を果たしはしなかった。
   (D) 白人農家と労働者は南アフリカの政府に大きな影響を及ぼした。

Lesson 19

4. 第3パラグラフにおける下線語 **entrenching** は意味上 _____ に最も近い。

   (A) improving（改善する）
   (B) strengthening（強化する）
   (C) defining（定義する）
   (D) generating（生成する）

5. 第3パラグラフにおいて著者は通行許可手帳を _____ として言及している。

   (A) 集団地域法による直接の結果
   (B) 様々な人種間交流に対する制限の例
   (C) 仕事を見つけるのに黒人が必要とした書類
   (D) 黒人の移動を制限する政策

6. 第3パラグラフにおける下線文の主要な情報を最もよく表しているのは以下のどの文であるか。誤った選択肢は、重要な点で意味が違うか、大事な情報を欠いている。

   (A) 黒人は投票できず、学校へ行く機会のある者もほとんどいなかった。
   (B) 黒人に対する学校教育は改善の余地を多く残していた。
   (C) 投票権も教養もないので、黒人には発揮できる政治力がほとんどなかった。
   (D) 無教養なので、黒人は投票を許されなかった。

7. 第4パラグラフにおいて、政府による報復の主要な原因として何が挙げられているか。

   (A) 逮捕・拘束の絶対的な力
   (B) アフリカ民族会議
   (C) 白人以外の者が密かに開いた会合
   (D) ストライキ、デモ、およびサボタージュ

8. 第5パラグラフに以下の文を追加し得る場所を示す4つの番号を見よ。

   一方、国外での進展がこの危機状態を悪化させた。

   この文が最もふさわしい場所はどこか。

   (1)　　(2)　　(3)　　(4)

9. 第5パラグラフにおける下線語 **pariah** は意味上 ＿＿＿＿ に最も近い。

   (A) victim（犠牲者）
   (B) suspect（容疑者）
   (C) defendant（被告）
   (D) outcast（のけ者）

10. 第3パラグラフにおける下線語 **sanctions** は意味上 ＿＿＿＿ に最も近い。

    (A) tacit approval（無言の許可）
    (B) embargoes（通商停止）
    (C) limited conditions（制限された状況）
    (D) urgent requests（緊急の要求）

Lesson 19

11. 第6パラグラフにおいて、著者は _____ ために下線の表現 **by any means** を使っている。

    (A) 若い黒人たちが自分たちの要求を通すために益々暴力に訴えるようになったことをほのめかす
    (B) 革命が成功に向かっていたことを示す
    (C) 黒人意識高揚運動を批判する
    (D) 若い黒人たちの努力に対する同情を示す

12. 第7パラグラフにおける情報に基づいて、以下の出来事をそれぞれ起こった年と一致させよ。適切なアルファベットを線上に書け。

    1. _____ 新憲法が提案され認可される。
    2. _____ ネルソン・マンデラがボータに会う。
    3. _____ 通行許可手帳がもはや要求されなくなる。
    4. _____ 初めて、黒人が投票する。
    5. _____ 正式な政策としてのアパルトヘイトが廃止される。
    6. _____ 政治犯が解放され、学校が人種差別をやめる。

    (A) 1986   (B) 1989   (C) 1991   (D) 1992   (E) 1993   (F) 1994

Lesson 20

ビジネスの転換

リーディング：以下の文章を注意深く読め。

1　世界の現状、特に社会正義と環境問題について大衆が次々と気が付き関心を寄せているという状況において、企業の社会的責任に対するビジネス上の必要性はかつてないほど強いものになっている。益々明らかになってきたのは、企業がこの新しい一連の状況にビジネス慣行を適合させなければならない —— さもなければ大変なことになる —— ということである。最近の研究によると、文明と社会の拠り所である生態系が悪化の一途をたどり、「今しかない」ところにまで来ているという。地球の自然作用に対するこの圧力と負担は、人間生活の質とその未来を危うくしているだけでなく、ビジネスの最も痛いところ —— 帳尻の上 —— に深刻な影響を与えているのだ。

2　同等の価格と品質を持つ2つの製品から選ぶ際に、今日の賢い買物客は社会のニーズと環境に対してより敏感である会社が作ったものを買うことが増えている。自らが活動拠点とするコミュニティーに対して責任感を持って活動する会社とそうでない会社で働くという選択を提示された場合、個人的利益より個人的満足感に価値を見出す労働者であれば、前者のほうを喜んで受け入れている。同様に、手軽な儲けだけでなく意義ある貢献を望む投資家は、資金の運用先を探すにあたり、すべての利害関係者 —— 従業員、消費者、地域の隣人、ビジネス・パートナー、そして投資家 —— を公平に、思いやりを持って扱う会社を選ぶことが増えてきている。こういうことを気にかけている消費者、労働者、そして株主は、自らと強い利害関係にある会社が児童労働を使って海外の搾取工場を運営したり、密かに有毒廃棄物を捨てたり、不良品を市場で売ったりするのがわかると、良心から、その会社との関係を断つ時が来たと思うのである。

3　このような傾向から、会社は自らの行動を潔白なものにせざるを得なくなった。もはや、真実をないがしろにする余裕などない。環境を維持し社会のためになるように振舞うか、競争力の低下と減益に直面するかのどちらかである。

4　もちろん、これは従来の会社と資本家が思っていた真実とはまったく逆である。伝統的に、企業は利益 —— つまり、欲深く要求の厳しい株主に彼らの投資に対する最大限の短期利益を与えること —— が第一という認識のもとで営業活動をしてきた

のだ。伝統的な会社の活動はどれもこの目的のためのもの。すべて —— 倫理、社会福祉、環境 —— が二の次に回されるのである。このように、ビジネスをするのにより望ましく環境に優しいシステムを作る代わり、また社会全体の恩恵のために働く代わりに、企業は私己的な権益 —— たとえば、環境法の緩和や税制上の優遇措置の増加 —— を促進するために努力してきたのである。しかし、これはもはや許されることではない。

⑤ **1.** 多少の犠牲は避けられないが、より社会的に責任を持ち維持しやすいタイプの営業にスイッチすることが、長い目で見れば、財政上のパフォーマンスを大幅に改善し、利益を増やすのだということを、企業は認識させられねばならないし、多くが既に認識している。**2.** 世界規模の研究が示すように、今日の就職希望者は、就職面接の席で手当と給料についての質問をするのと同じくらいに社会問題に関する会社の対応記録についても質問をする傾向にある。**3.** リサーチ、そして一般常識からもわかることだが、会社のコミュニティー・パフォーマンスに誇りを感じることが、労働者の職務上の満足感を高め、実際に労働生産性も向上させるのだ。**4.** たとえば、慈善事業の寄付金集めやボランティア活動を通して従業員によるコミュニティー活動への参加を企業文化の一部にすると、その会社は良い職場として知られるようになるし、より能率的で忠誠心の篤い正社員を生み出すのに役に立つ。一方、「環境的に考え」、電力消費を減らし、無駄を省き、リサイクルを通してさらなる資源の有効活用を推し進めるといった責任のある政策手段を始めることによって、会社はコストを削減し、競争力を高めることができるのである。

⑥ 一度会社が「エコ・フレンドリー」、「従業員フレンドリー」、また「社会フレンドリー」だという評判を得れば、その恩恵はすぐに表れ始める。倫理観の強い消費者はその会社の製品を競って買う。投資家と銀行は融資提供のために列をなす。社会活動家と政府監査員はもう後を追いかけてこない。また、株主も望みのものを手にするのである。

エクササイズ: 正しい選択肢をもってして、以下の文を完成させるか、質問に答えよ。あるいは、指示に従え。

1. 第1パラグラフにおける下線文の主要な情報を最もよく表しているのは以下のどの文であるか。誤った選択肢は、重要な点で意味が違うか、大事な情報を欠いている。

    (A) ますますはっきりしてきたのは、変化する社会状況により、会社は新しいビジネスの仕方を見つける必要があるということだ。さもなくば、倒産のリスクを背負わねばならない。
    (B) 言うまでもなく、企業は時代とともに変わるものではない。
    (C) ビジネス・パフォーマンスを改善したい会社は世界を自らの利己的なニーズと利益に合うように変えなければならない。
    (D) 言うまでもなく、現在の状況を変えるために世界はビジネスを必要としている。

2. 第1パラグラフにおける下線語 **jeopardizing** は意味上 ＿＿＿＿ に最も近い。

    (A) underestimating（過小評価する）
    (B) threatening（脅威をつきつける）
    (C) ameliorating（改良する）
    (D) complicating（複雑にする）

3. 第1パラグラフにおいて、著者は悪化する生態系によってどのようにビジネスが最も影響を受けると言っているか。

    (A) 現在のビジネス慣行を守ることを余儀なくされる。
    (B) 利益を上げるのが難しくなる。
    (C) 益々社会に頼るようになる。
    (D) 良い労働者を雇うのが不可能になる。

Lesson 20

4. 第2パラグラフにおいて、著者はいかに今日の消費者が買う製品を選ぶかということについてどのような点を指摘しているか。

    (A) 彼らは質と価格にはもはや関心がない。
    (B) 彼らは2つの同じような会社の製品から選択したいのである。
    (C) 彼らは製品の値段および品質と同様に会社のポリシーに興味を持っている。
    (D) 品質が同等なら、彼らはより高い製品を買う。

5. 著者は第2パラグラフにおいて _____ の例として搾取工場に言及している。

    (A) 責任感を示している会社
    (B) 不当で非人道的なビジネス慣行
    (C) 欠陥製品
    (D) 秘かな廃棄活動

6. 第2パラグラフにおける下線語 **sever** は意味上 _____ に最も近い。

    (A) renew（更新する）
    (B) discuss（議論する）
    (C) strengthen（強化する）
    (D) discontinue（停止する）

7. 第3パラグラフにおける下線のフレーズ **These trends** は _____ を指す。

    (A) 次第に大きくなる企業の社会的責任
    (B) 労働者、消費者、投資家の間に見られる新しい態度
    (C) 地球の悪化する自然作用
    (D) 児童労働を使い、有毒廃棄物を投棄し、欠陥製品を売ること

8. 第4パラグラフにおいて、著者は _____ 、伝統的な企業のビジネス慣行について語っている。

   (A) 真の状況の例として
   (B) 従来のビジネスマンにとって現在の状況がいかに希望のないものに思えるかを強調するため
   (C) 会社がもっと責任感を持つのに、どのようなニーズが克服されねばならないのかを強調するため
   (D) 企業システムがいかに邪悪なものかを証明するため

9. 第5パラグラフに以下の文を追加し得る場所を示す4つの番号を見よ。

   社会に対してもっと目に見えるように説明責任を果たすことで、会社はより教養があり、質も高く、献身的な労働者を獲得し保持することができる。

   この文が最もふさわしい場所はどこか。

   (1)   (2)   (3)   (4)

10. 第5パラグラフにおいて、著者は社会的にもっと責任を持つことが会社の財政的パフォーマンスを改善し得る方法として、_____ を除く以下のすべてに言及している。

    (A) 公害に関する法令の緩和と減税のためにロビー活動すること
    (B) 資源をもっと効率よく使うこと
    (C) 企業文化を改善すること
    (D) 無駄を減らすこと

Lesson 20

11. 第 6 パラグラフにおける下線語 **accrue** は意味上 _____ に最も近い。

    (A) fall off（減少する）
    (B) mount up（増えてくる）
    (C) move forward（前進する）
    (D) bear out（証明する）

12. 問題文の簡潔なサマリーの第 1 文が以下に与えられている。本文中の最も重要な考えを表す 3 つの選択肢を選んでサマリーを完成させよ。本文中にない、あるいは本文中のマイナーな考えに過ぎないためサマリーには適さない文もある。

    近年、環境的・倫理的配慮が企業社会責任の概念にスポットライトを当てるようになった。

    (A) 社会的に責任を持つことは会社に多少の犠牲を強いるかもしれないが、最終的には増益として報われるだろう。
    (B) 海外の搾取工場で働く子供たちは、ほんの僅かの賃金で奴隷のように働いている。
    (C) 社会的に説明責任を果たすことには、すべての利害関係者およびコミュニティー全般が会社のビジネス慣行から確実に恩恵を被るようにすることも含まれる。
    (D) 毒性廃棄物を投棄することは会社の評判に大きなダメージを与えかねない。
    (E) 買い物客は社会に献身する会社の製品を買い、銀行はそういう会社に融資をする傾向にあり、そんな会社の従業員はより熱心に働き、より長く勤めてくれるものである。
    (F) リサーチによると、多くの従業員が外でのボランティア活動に関わること、また給料のいくらかを慈善事業に寄付することを楽しんでいるという。

アンサー・キー

1. イングリッシュ 101　批判的思考と読書

1. **C**　第1パラグラフの以下の個所がポイント。reams of information by the mass media—print, broadcast, and now the World Wide Web— ... a growing number of "blogs"—websites that profess to be the new, alternative journalism ... *print*（印刷物）は新聞、雑誌を含む。*broadcast*（放送）はラジオとテレビのこと。*blog* は *Web log* の短縮形。*university lectures* には言及されていない。

2. **D**　単語の問題。このコンテキストにおける persuasion は「説得」ではなく「信条」という意味。

3. **A**　ポイントは第1パラグラフの以下の個所。Advertisements and commercials plug every product under the sun. Can they all be as beneficial and necessary to our lives as the advertisers say they are?（広告とコマーシャルはこの世の全ての製品を推奨する。それらは本当に広告主の言う通り私たちの生活に有益で必要なものなのか。）第2文には3つの they があるが、最初と最後の they は every product を指し、2番目は advertisements and commercials を指す。as the advertisers say they are は、「広告主が、すべての製品がそうだと言う通り」ということ。

4. **A**　このパラグラフでは反語的表現（e.g. Who are we to believe?）が多用されている。ここから読み取れるのは「提供される情報に懐疑的になるべきだ」ということで、A 以外の選択肢にあるようなことは断言されていない。

5. **2**　この文は、第2パラグラフの第1文にある「より批判的に考える」ということを説明するものである。よって 2 が最もふさわしい場所である。

6. **D**　ポイントになる個所は以下のとおり。... instill in us a narrow or slanted way of seeing the world ... In other words, we think uncritically.（偏狭な、あるいは歪んだ世界の見方を我々にしみ込ませる…つまり、我々は反批判的に考える。）A のような考えはどこにも書かれておらず、B は著者の主張の正反対である。C は、このパラグラフ以降にあるように、批判的に考える人がすることである。

7. **A**　ポイントは第3パラグラフの以下の個所。a set of assumptions, beliefs, and prejudices that we are loath to part with（我々が手放したくない一連の仮説、信念、偏見）。このことから人々の信念を描写するのに precious「大事な、貴重な」という形容詞が用いられていることがわかる。

8. **B** 単語の問題。discern は find out, recognize（見つける、認める）という意味。

9. **C** ポイントは第5パラグラフの以下の個所。[Critical thinkers] have a sense of curiosity about the world and remain open to new and different interpretations of it.（批判的に考える人たちは、好奇心を持って世界を見つめ、世界の新しい解釈や異なった解釈にもオープンであり続ける。）つまり、世界に対する好奇心は、オープンな心から来るものだということ。

10. **C** 下線部の意味は「(批判的に考える人は) 感情よりも道理を頼りにし、かたくなに自らの正しさを証明しようとするよりも、物事に対する最良の説明を見つけようと努力する」。批判的に考える人が何をどう思考するのかがポイント。A は批判的に考える人の特性として正しいのかもしれないが、彼らの思考パターンを描写するものではない。B および D は批判的に考える人についての描写ではない。よって答えは C。pig-headedness = stubbornness

11. **C** 第5パラグラフの以下の個所がポイント。... critical thinking doesn't come overnight; it is a skill that is acquired gradually through trial and error（批判的思考は一夜にして成るものではない。試行錯誤を経て徐々に獲得される技術なのである）。A は著者の主張とは正反対。B は「いつも」というのが問題。critical thinkers の考えと情報は、いつも間違っているわけではない。D における自己欺瞞と自己認識は反対語である。よって、これはナンセンスな選択肢になっている。

12. **4** 第6パラグラフでは、批判的読書家の読書法が紹介されている。まず、テキストにざっと目を通してその大まかな構成および強調点を探る。次に精読してキー・ポイント等に下線を施したり、丸をつける。そして最後に自分の疑念と反応を注釈として余白に書き込む。この順番が最も妥当なものと思えるので、「自分の疑念と反応を注釈として余白に書き込む」という追加文の入るべき位置は 4 となる。

2. イングリッシュ 102：エッセイのタイプとストラテジー

1. **D** 「38歳で引退したフランス貴族」という描写から、彼が裕福であったことは想像に難くない。A に関しては、モンテーニュが宗教的反目にうんざりしていたという描写こそあれ、彼が定期的に教会へ行っていたことをうかがわせる描写はない。B は、実際にそうなのかも知れないが、このパラグラフでは「短い散文体の文章」と定義されている。C に関しては、モンテーニュがフランス人であ

ることはわかるが、彼の作品が最初にフランスで出版されたということを示唆する記述はどこにもない。

2. **A** 単語の問題。repulsed は、文脈によって turned away（追い払われた）になり得るが（e.g. The army attack was repulsed by stubborn rebels）、ここの文脈では「うんざりして」という意味が適当である。

3. **B** 「現代のエッセイは、ミシェル・ド・モンテーニュによって築かれた基盤をもとにして、あらゆる文芸形式の中でも最も柔軟なものに進化し…」とあるので、A はアウト。C は「重々しい内容もエッセイになり得る」という主張、D は「エッセイは娯楽にもなり得る」という主張にそれぞれ矛盾する。よって、答えは B。

4. **C** 第 3 パラグラフの以下がポイントの個所。There are many different types of essay, each with a specific writing strategy adopted to carry out its overall purpose.（多くの異なるタイプのエッセイが存在し、各々が、その全般的な目的遂行のために使われる特定のライティング・ストラテジーを持って）。「その」は「（多くの多様なエッセイ・タイプの）各々」を指していることがわかる。

5. **C** 動詞 subordinate が意味するのは、「あるものの重要性を他のそれより低くする」ということ。描写エッセイが、著者の意見より、物事の客観的描写に重きを置くことを言っているのである。

6. **A** 第 3 パラグラフにおいて「印象に基づいた描写」、「個人的な反応はさておき、可能な限り事実に忠実な叙述」、「ものを言葉で描くこと」、「五感の捉えるものを伝えること」には言及されているが、描写エッセイのスタイルに関する描写はない。よって答えは A。

7. **4** 例証エッセイのストラテジーは、「印象的な逸話などの紹介」、「具体的な数字（統計）の提供」、「論点を読者に馴染みのあるものにする努力」であるが、これらの具体的なまとめとなっているのが、この追加文である。よって、第 4 パラグラフの最後がその適切な位置となる。

8. **D** 網掛け部の意味は「著者は、たとえば、ある国における少子化現象の現下の原因を超えたところにある、さほど明確ではないかもしれないが等しく重要な遠因に目を向けねばならないのである」。つまり、「現下の原因を超えたところにあるさほど明確ではないかもしれないが、等しく重要な遠因」を見落としてしまうと、エッセイとしては失敗作になるということ。よって D が答え。

9. **A** 次のパラグラフは、process analysis essay に関してであり、それが先のパラグラフの主題である cause and effect essay に似ているというのが、その最初の1文になっている。よって、次のパラグラフへのスムーズな移行というのが答えである。

10. **C** 「過程の順序を逆にする」というのは、第6パラグラフの最後にある arranged in its proper order と矛盾する。よってCが答え。

11. **A** 第7パラグラフの以下がポイントとなる個所である。Such essays are also more memorable and effective when they avoid the obvious ... influence or persuade the reader more effectively. 「そのようなエッセイはまた、当たり前を避けて、ふつう似ていないと思われるものを比べたり、通常ほとんど同じと思われるものを対比させることによって、より記憶に残り、効果的なものにもなる」。BとCは言及されていない。Dは正反対のことを言っている。

12. **C, E, F** A、Bは主題からするとマイナーなポイント。Dは言及されていない情報である。以下がそれぞれポイントとなる個所。
C: coined from the French verb for "to attempt" 「フランス語の動詞「試みる」からの造られた」（第1パラグラフ）。Built up on the foundation laid by Montaigne, the essay today ... almost any authorial aim or intention「現代のエッセイは、ミシェル・ド・モンテーニュによって築かれた基盤をもとにして、あらゆる文芸形式の中でも最も柔軟なものに進化し、著者の目的や意図のほとんどに適応できるものになった」（第2パラグラフ）。
E: Although there are many different kinds of essay, most are a blend of various types and utilize a variety of strategies to get their point across and fulfill their purpose 「エッセイには多くの様式があるが、そのほとんどが様々なタイプの混合であり、主張を伝え、目的を達成するために多様なストラテジーを利用するのである」（第8パラグラフ）。
F: 第7パラグラフの内容。

3. 色

1. **D** 単語の問題。adjacent は「隣接した」という意味。よって答えはDである。

2. **C** A、B、Dに関してもこのパラグラフで触れられてはいるが、どれも著者の目的ではない。ここでの目的は、光の正体を読者に伝え、それによって色の説

明をする次のパラグラフの理解を助けることなのである。

3. **B** 第2パラグラフにAのような結論を導ける記述は存在しない。Cであるが、偉大な科学者ニュートンは「平均的観察者」ではないであろう。誰が分散プリズムを発明したかについての記述もないのでDもアウト。よって答えはB。

4. **C** Aは事実とは正反対の記述である。Bはまとめにはなっておらず、専門的に聞こえる用語を用いた不必要に冗長な言い換えに過ぎない。光は波長という概念で描写できるので、Dも事実と異なる。よって答えはC。

5. **D** 我々が何を色として知覚するかを考えれば答えられる問題であろう。Aの網膜、Bの脳はすぐ候補から消える。itのすぐ前にthe information encapsulated in the light があるのでCを選びがちだが、脳がこの情報を処理することによって光そのものを色として知覚するというのが著者の主張。よって答えはDである。

6. **A** これも単語の問題である。opaqueが「不透明な、光を通さない」という意味だと知っていれば、簡単にAを選ぶことができよう。

7. **C** この選択肢のみが事実とは正反対のことを言っている。カギとなる個所は第3パラグラフのBlack and white, however, are not normally considered true colors「しかし、黒と白は普通本当の色とはみなされない」。

8. **A** 単語の問題。impetusは「(物事を引き起こす) 刺激」という意味。よってcolor itself is the impetus behind much of our symbolic thoughtを直訳すると、「色そのものが我々の象徴的な考えの多くの背後にある刺激である」となるが、これは「色が、我々が象徴的な考えを持つ際の引き金になっている」ということである。

9. **C** 色に関する更なる科学的描写であるこの選択肢は、もともと色を化学的に解説する第2パラグラフに追加されるべきであろう。色の持つ象徴的な意味がトピックである第4パラグラフには適さないものである。

10. **4** 4以下には英語における「黒」という単語を用いたネガティブな慣用表現が列挙されている。よって「英語にはそのようなフレーズや比喩表現がある」とするこの追加文は、この場所でそれらのイントロとして機能するのが最も適切であろう。

11. 黒：**A、C、E、I**
    白：**B、F、H、J**

カギとなる個所
　　黒：まず第5パラグラフに注目。A の evil and suffering は wickedness, anguish、C の grief は death, mourning、I の failure and shame は ruin および opprobrium の言い換えと言える。E の sophistication and influence は第7パラグラフにある tuxedo … elegance and prestige に近い。influence には「威光」という意味もあるので注意。
　　白：第6パラグラフに注目。F の knowledge and wisdom は enlightenment … intellectual awakening、H の future prosperity は rich with potential や the promise of plenty、J の virginity は、purity and innocence と同義である。B の defeat に関しては第7パラグラフに白旗に関して submit and surrender という同義の表現が出てくる。
　　D は赤に関するもの。G は黄色に象徴されるものであるので除外される。

12. **B**　問題文のメインポイントは以下の2つ。色とは何か。そして色が持つ、人および社会との関係である。この両方を簡潔にまとめているのが B。A はマイナーな情報に過ぎない。C の情報もマイナーであるが、さらに黒と白を逆の順で言っている。D は色の認識に関する簡潔な紹介文であるが、色の持つ象徴的意味というポイントを欠いている。

4. コウモリ

1. **D**　第1パラグラフによると、コウモリは都会や郊外でも見られるというので、A はアウト。またその世界中での分布に関して「極域は除く」とあるので、B も候補から外れる。さらに、コウモリの数は齧歯類に次いで2番目に多いとあるので C も正しくない。D の事実は第1パラグラフの最後に書かれている。

2. **A**　第2パラグラフにおける以下の個所がポイント。doing their hunting and feeding at night「獲物を捕らえて食べるのは夜であり…」。

3. **C**　第2パラグラフにおける以下の個所がポイント。grouping together in colonies for warmth and security「コロニーを形成し、暖を取り、安全を確保する」。メッセージを送りあうのはコロニー生活をしているからで、メッセージのためにコロニーを作るのではない。よって A はアウト。群居しないコウモリも存在するが、問われているのは群居する種類。よって B も適切でない。D に関

する記述は、このパラグラフ中にない。

4. **C** 単語の問題だが、直後に helping feed and protect ill or injured fellows「病気や傷ついた仲間が餌を食べるのを助け、保護してやる」とあるので、文脈からも見当がつくであろう。

5. **A** 下線文の意味は、「哺乳類の寿命は一般に体の大きさに比例するので、コウモリは、驚くほど長生きということになる」であるから、意味がきちんと取れればAを選ぶのは簡単であろう。

6. **D** このパラグラフでは、microbats（オオコウモリに対するコウモリ）に関して either insectivores or carnivores（食虫動物か肉食動物のどちらか）とあり、その直後に Of the latter, three known "vampire bat" species「後者のほうでは、知られている3種の吸血コウモリが…」とあるので、「肉食コウモリ＝吸血コウモリ」であるとわかる。

7. **C** A、B、Dについてはすべて言及されているが、Cに関しては書かれていない。第5パラグラフの最後に「物体がどれくらいの大きさであるか、それが右側に位置するのか左側なのか、そしてどの方向に進んでいるかを知ることができる」とあるので、自らが物体の方向へ向かうのではなく、エコロケーションによって物体が進んでいる方向を知ることができるというのである。

8. **A** 単語の問題。これは「滋養・栄養」という意味の単語である。よってAが最も近い。

9. **C** ポイントとなる個所は以下である。When the mother returns, she immediately picks her own pup out of all the others through scent and sound「母親は戻ると、臭いと音を頼りに、他のすべての子供たちの中から自分の子供を直ちに見つけ出す」。よってCが答えだとわかる。

10. **A** これはもともと「操作・操縦しやすい」という意味の単語。ここではコウモリの飛行について言っているので、「進路・方向を自在に変えることができる」という意味になる。

11. **B** 選択肢の中でコウモリの飛行能力に関する描写はBのみ。他はみなコウモリの肉体的特徴を指摘している。

12. **B** Bが問題文を最も適切にまとめている。Aに関しては以下の問題がある。まず「他のリスとは違い」とあるが、コウモリはリスではない。またコウモリの

食性と飛行能力に言及しているが、このふたつの間には何の関連性も見られず、同一の文で語られるべきものではない。C ではコウモリの文化的・象徴的な重要性が語られているが、このことは問題文中のどこにも書かれていない。D にある「大きなコロニーを形成して場所から場所を移動する」というのも問題文中には見られない。そして、A、D は共通して「コウモリの人間に対する影響」という重要なポイントを欠いている。

5. 絵画と油絵

1. **A**　著者は読者の興味を引くために、この逸話をもってしてヒトの芸術への欲求がはるか昔へ遡ることを指摘しているのである。よって答えは A。B は事実であろうが、問題文とは関係がない。C と D は、問題文のメインテーマ（絵画と油絵）とはかけ離れたものである。

2. **D**　すぐ後にある stumbled across「偶然発見した」からも想像できるように、答えは D。この単語は文脈によっては「不注意に」とも訳せるが、本問題文中の少年たちは不注意であったわけではなく、ただ偶然に壁画を発見したのである。

3. **C**　以下がポイントとなる箇所。either a naturalistic representation of the "real" world or a more abstract manifestation of the artist's personal vision「「本当の」世界を写実的に表現したり、芸術家個人の心象をもっと抽象的に表したりすることである」（第 2 パラグラフ）。ここから、答えは C だとわかる。他の選択肢は絵画の目的を達成するための手段にこそなれ目的そのものではない。

4. **A**　単語の問題。直前に using a sharp rock or shattered bone「鋭い石や砕かれた骨を使って」とあるから、「ひっかく」という言葉が容易に連想できるであろう。専門用語としての etch は、銅板に硝酸をかけて作る腐食銅板の作成を意味する。また比喩的に The scene was etched in my memory「その光景が私の心に永遠に刻み込まれた」などとも言える。

5. **C**　問題の個所の意味は「それ以来、芸術家は自らが望む効果を効果的に再現し、時間と風雨による攻撃にも頑として持ちこたえてくれる材料とテクニックを見つける努力をしてきた」である。A には「芸術家が望む効果を効果的に再現する」という情報がない。B は「時間と風雨による攻撃」の結果により起こり得ることの描写であり、問題の文の主要な情報は伝えてはいない。D は「時間と風雨による攻撃にも頑として持ちこたえてくれる」という情報を欠いている。よって C が最も適切な言い換えである。

6. **C**　第3パラグラフでは「芸術家の絵具は、色を与えてくれる顔料と表面に付着させるための展色剤とを必要とする」と書いた後で「古代エジプトの芸術家は、顔料をアカシアの木から採った樹脂と混ぜた」と続く。よって正答Cが導かれる。アカシアは顔料になるのではないのでAはアウト。BとDは著者の意図する選択肢ではない。

7. **B**　ポイントとなる箇所は still regarded today ... the centerpiece of all the visual arts「今日でもすべての画家にとっての「標準」であり、あらゆる視覚的芸術の中心とみなされる」というところ。「標準」というのは評判が高くなければありえないことである。よってBが答え。

8. **D**　「イタリアの芸術家たちは、高温多湿にもっと強い絵の具を必要としていたが、これがその答えであると歓迎した」とあるので、Dが答え。Aに関しては何の言及もないし、そもそも当時このような旅は無理であっただろう。Bだが、本文にあるのはフレスコ画を描くには北部では難しかったということのみで、ヨーロッパ中でそうであったとは言っていない。またCのようなことも書かれていない。

9. **2**　この文は2以降に書かれている内容の紹介文として機能しているので2が答え。油も展色剤の一種なので、2直後のOther binders「他の展色剤」というのがヒントになるだろう。

10. **C**　単語の問題。「形式的なルールや束縛に less inhibited だった他の芸術家たちが新しいテクニックを用いて実験を始めた」というのだから restrained が「抑制された」という意味だとわかっていれば簡単な問題。

11. **B**　Aのグレージングは、「自分の発明した新絵具をとても薄く、ほとんど透明なくらいに塗り、繊細かつ隠し味的な筆づかいで、絵具の薄層に別の薄層を重ねるのだった（これはグレージングというテクニックとして知られている）」と説明されている。Cは、レンブラントがオランダの芸術家であるファン・エイク（第3パラグラフ）の compatriot「同国人」である、というところからわかる。Dの「ティツィアーノ芸術の主題の種類」も In his religious paintings とあるから説明済み。Bのテンペラ画法だけが、言及こそされてはいるが、説明はされていない。

12. **C**　Aであるが、これは「ウェット・イントゥ・ウェット」の呼び名で、その特徴ではない。Bは「ファット・オーバー・リーン」方式について言えること。Dだが、これはどの芸術技法にも言えることである。よって答えはC。

6. エネルギーとエネルギー源

1. **C** ＊の前後の文の主題はともにエネルギーである。特に＊の後にある「事実エネルギーという英単語の語源は…」というところから、その前文の主題もエネルギーであることがわかる。A は happen、B は work の定義であるからアウト。D はエネルギーのことを言っているが、脈絡のない内容。C にある take this into account「このことを考慮に入れて」の「このこと」とはまさに最初の 2 文の内容を指している。よってエネルギーの教科書における定義についての選択肢 C が答え。

2. **B** エネルギーの大家と言われるファインマンでもエネルギーについて正確には分かっていないということを示すのが著者のここでの目的。B 以外の選択肢ではエネルギーの専門家を指すことにはならない。

3. **B** 単語の問題。elude は、文脈によっては D が適当である場合もあるが、この文脈では B のほうがずっと適切な言い換えである。

4. **A** 下線文の意味は「エネルギーはすべての物質に内在する、物事を起こすあるいは起こす可能性を持つ特性や特徴のことであるということだけは自信を持って言えよう」である。B の「様々な目的で」、C の「物質の様々な形態を通して現れてくる」、D の「特徴がどんなものであれ」というのはこの下線文には含まれていない情報である。

5. **A** B は自然現象のことであり、位置エネルギーの定義ではない。C は崖の上の石についてのこと。D もまた位置エネルギーについての描写ではない。ポイントとなる個所は because of its condition or position relative to other bodies or objects「その状況あるいは他の物体や物質に対するその相対的な位置により」というところである。

6. **C** KE=1/2mv² が示すのは、運動エネルギーは物体の質量の半分に速度の 2 乗をかけたものだということ。よって C の描写は誤りである。

7. **A** 単語の問題。precariously は「不安定に」という意味。これと同じ意味を持つのは A のみである。

8. **C** A はエネルギーの大きな実用性の理由、B はそれゆえ、エネルギーの探究が文明社会の発展および科学の進歩とともに歩んできたということ、D は、新しいエネルギーとより良いエネルギーの探究において人類の実力が発揮され、自

然の理解が深まったということを言っている。このように、このパラグラフではエネルギーと人類の関係についての流れが見て取れるのだが、Cのみエネルギー保存の法則を説明していてこの流れからはずれたものになっている。

9. **B** insatiable は（しばしば食物に関して）「飽くことを知らない、貪欲な」という意味。ここではBがぴったりである。

10. **A** このパラグラフは化石燃料についてのものである。

11. **D** Though challenges still remain to perfect it「完全なものになるまでにはまだ課題が残るものの」というところから、専門家が水素燃料電池のデザインや能率をさらに向上させようとしていることがうかがえる。よって答えはD。Aについてだが、第6パラグラフでは値段について何も触れられていない。Bは逆のことを言っており、「化学エネルギーを電気エネルギーに変える」というのが正しい。Cであるが、水素燃料電池の可能性は確かに高い。しかし、それをもってしてすべてのエネルギー源が取って替えられるというのは妥当性の低い話であろう。

12. **B** サマリーの第1文は、全体のメイン・アイディアをうまくまとめたものであるべき。本文の主要なアイディアは、「エネルギーは便利で測定可能である一方、まだわからないことが多い」ということと「新しく、より良いエネルギー源の探究が、社会および科学の発展と足並みを揃えて進んできた」という歴史的事実である。この2つを含んでいるのはBのみ。Aにはこの歴史的事実の部分が欠けている。CとDは本文全体からするとマイナーな情報である。

7. フィクションと演劇の初歩

1. **3** この追加文は、その内容からして、前文で提供されるキャラクターの意味に肉付けをするものである。よって、3の個所が答え。また専門用語であるprotagonistが次の文に出てくるが、追加文が3にあれば、その説明が事前になされることになるので文の流れがスムーズになろう。

2. **C** 単語の問題。eponymous は「本・映画などのタイトルと同名の」という意味である。

3. **B** 本文ではキャラクターという語の2つの意味が提供されているが、第1パラグラフは「登場人物」という意味、第2パラグラフは登場人物の様々な「特徴・性格」という意味を紹介し説明している。よって答えはB。Aは後者の意味

に言及するのみ。キャラクターは主役を意味する場合もあるが、それだけではないので、Cのように断言することはできない。Dは登場人物がどんなものであり得るかの可能性を語ったもので、キャラクターという語の意味とは関係がない。

4. **C** Aであるが、第2パラグラフ中ではブルームが「どんな道徳原理を体現しているのか」とあるだけで、「健全な道徳原理を体現している」などとは書かれていない。またこのパラグラフは、「インドへの道」のキャラクターがラウンドなのかフラットなのかについても言及していないので、Bもアウトである。さらにラウンド・キャラクター、フラット・キャラクターに関する著者の嗜好も書かれていない。よってDも正しくない。Cにある「著者が選ぶ詳細」には2つ目の意味でのキャラクター描写も当然含まれる。よってCが答えである。

5. **A** 単語の問題。encompassは「取り巻く、包含する」という意味。フラット・キャラクターが1つのアイディアや資質から成るものであるのに対し、ラウンド・キャラクターが「多くの思想と習性を」云々というところからもこの意味は想像できよう。

6. **D** 以下がヒントとなる個所。The exposition phase sets up the conflict or problem that the protagonist must deal with, without which there would be no story「序説的説明段階において、主役が立ち向かわざるを得ない衝突と問題が提示されるが、これらがなければ話が成り立たない」。Aはプロットの定義に含まれることではあるが、著者が伝えたいプロットの重要性ではない。Bも正しいことは正しいが、著者が主張するプロットの重要性とはずれている。Cもふつう本当のことではあるが、著者が第3パラグラフで主張したいことではない。

7. **B** whichの先行詞はan emotional high or turning pointである。よってBが答え。

8. **C** 単語の問題。plausibleは「妥当な、信頼できそうな」という意味。これに一番近いのはCである。

9. **A** 「舞台背景は、単に話の展開のための背景に過ぎないこともある」というのが下線文の意味。「舞台背景は単に背景に過ぎない」のだから「プロットとキャラクターにはほとんど影響しない」というのが一番筋の通る解釈だろう。

10. **B** eachは「各々の」という意味。第6パラグラフで著者が言いたいのは、毎回毎回の劇の上演（each performance）がライブであり、いろいろな人たちによる共同作業であるがゆえ、たとえばそのときの役者の状態や気分、観客の反応

などといった様々な要因により少しずつ異なったものになるということである。

11. **D** 本文中には、作家が使う言葉のスタイルや語調について何の言及もない。

12.
演劇とフィクションに共通する特質
　・D
　・E
以下のところがポイント。Character in this sense is what makes the hero or heroine of a story come alive for the reader or theatergoer「この意味でのキャラクターによって読者や観劇者は物語や劇中のヒーローあるいはヒロインがあたかも実在するかのように思うのである」（第2パラグラフ）。A third attribute shared by drama and fiction is setting「演劇とフィクションが共有する第3の要素は舞台背景」（第4パラグラフ）。

フィクションのみに見られる特質
　・C
　・G
以下がヒントの個所。the writer of fiction is the sole creator of the fixed work of art「フィクション作家は確固たる芸術作品を単独で創作する」（第6パラグラフ）。this most often means a first-person type narrative, ... or third-person narration ...「これが意味するのは、1人称タイプの物語か、あるいは3人称ナレーションであることが最も多い」（第5パラグラフ）。

演劇のみに見られる特質
　・B
　・H
以下のところがポイント。a play always unfolds in the present—right before the audience's very eyes「演劇はいつも現在形で、そして観客の眼前で展開する」（第6パラグラフ）。It is more like a point of reference supplied or taken up by the audience「（演劇における視点は）どちらかというと観客が補ったり選んだりする判断基準のようなものに過ぎない」（第5パラグラフ）。
Aはキャラクターについての情報。Fはフォースターによるフラット・キャラクターの定義である。

8. ホウクス

1. **D** 先行詞はダッシュの前にあるホーカス・ポーカスであることに注意。

2. **A** 答えは消去法で出るだろう。Eucharist「聖餐」はミサのことではない。ラテン語の表現とは hoc est corpus「これは私の肉体だ」を指す。または語源説明というのも hocus pocus が hoc est corpus にその語源を持つことを言っている。よって答えは A。

3. **D** 単語の問題。apocryphal は「出所の怪しい」という意味。よって D が最も近い。

4. **C** 選択肢 A は「大衆の騙されやすさを明らかにする」ことであり、B、D はそれぞれ「人気のトレンドや考えのばかばかしさを暴露する」、「政敵の評判を悪くする」ことを言っている。これらはいずれも第 2 パラグラフに書かれていることであるが、「他人によい印象を与えるためにホウクスを犯す」ということは書かれていない。

5. **A** 最後の文の要点は、「イラクの大量破壊兵器の破壊とフセインがかくまうアルカイダの根絶というのが、イラク戦争の理由だそうだが、結局イラクにはそんな兵器もテロリストも見つからなかったのだから、これは弾劾ものである」というもの。この内容からして、著者がイラク戦争に反対であることは容易に判断できよう。

6. **4** 直前の文は、遺骨の発見が物議をかもしたとしている。追加される文はその物議の説明になっている。

7. **B** A についてだが、化石破片は「主要な人類学的発見」だと思われただけであり、実際はそうではなかったことに注意。チャールズ・ドーソンはアマチュアの古生物学者であったので、C も不正解。D であるが、発見された化石破片はホウクスであり、進化の「失われた環」を提供しなかったということが第 3 パラグラフのポイントである。よってこれも不正解。答えは B。

8. **C** 単語の問題。amalgam は「混合物、合成物」という意味。最も近いのは C である。

9. **A** 第 4 パラグラフでは、ナチの指導者たちがいかに貴重な芸術品を貪り集めていたか、またその 1 人がゲーリングであり、いかにしてフェルメールの作品を手に入れるために偽造者ファン・メーヘレンに近づいたかが書かれている。よ

って答えがAであることは明らかだろう。

10. **A** 単語の問題。rankle on は「(あとあとまで) 腹立たしい気持ちにさせる」と言う意味である。

11. **B** 学術性については、ヒリアーによる伝記に関してもウィルソンによる伝記に関しても何の記載もないのでAはアウト。Cにある「満足感」であるが、第4パラグラフにおけるファン・メーヘレンは、はっきり「復讐」と言っているのだから、彼には当てはまるのだろうが、ヒリアーについては伺い知ることなどできない。Dであるが、まず「秘密の情事」そのものがフィクションであり、またウィルソンの本がどのくらい売れたかに関する記述もないのでこれも不正解である。

12. **C** 付け加えられるパラグラフは、文学ホウクスに関するイントロダクションである。よって、文学ホウクスを描写する第5パラグラフの直前であるCが最適な場所である。

9. 哲学と良い人生

1. **C** 著者の目的は、philosophy という単語と最初に西洋で哲学をしたのがギリシャの思想家たちであったことを結びつけることである。The origins of Western philosophy …以下のところにギリシャの思想家たちが神学から独立した探究法を確立し、それが哲学になったことが書かれている。

2. **A** 単語の問題。theological「神学の」という語はここでは哲学に対する宗教学という意味で使われている。

3. **D** these が指すのは、カンマの前にある faith and dogma であり、神学がこれらを題材にするのに対し、哲学は否定するという対照を示している。

4. **D** 第3パラグラフの According to Russell 以下でラッセルが主張すること、すなわち、「哲学的熟考が私たちを世界の市民たらしめる」、「この市民権の中において、人は真に自由であり、制限された希望と恐れへの奴隷状態から解放される」から判断してDが答えであることがわかる。

5. **B** 単語の問題。thralldom は「奴隷の状態」という意味。直前にある liberation「解放」がわかれば、答えが slavery であるという想像がつくであろう。

6. **A** 第4パラグラフの Epistemology also looks into …以下に、認識論の対象物が紹介されているが、そこには imagination、memory、perception が出てくる。virtue は後に説明されている倫理学が対象とするものである。

7. **C** 第5パラグラフの Ethical principles take two distinct forms …「倫理の原理は、個々の人間内に内在する行為の基準および社会がそのメンバーに強要する一連の道徳規則と義務という2つの異なった形を持つ」の個所がカギである。A はメタ倫理学がすること。B は事実ではなく、メタ倫理学における推測にすぎない。D のような記載はどこにもないし、また事実とも異なっている。

8. **3** 3の直前の描写、すなわち「これらの原理には宗教的な性質のものもあり、これは至上者への義務を含んでいる」の具体例として出エジプト記の描写が出てくるのである。

9. **A** 第6パラグラフの最初の1文「対照的に、規範倫理学は人々の行動を統制することを目的とした一連の基準、または規範、の創造を扱う」がカギである。B は規範倫理学のサブフィールドにすぎない義務理論の目的である。C はメタ倫理学の目指すところ。D も義務理論のみに関連するものである。

10. **A** 単語の問題。ここでの vanity は「虚栄」という意味だが、pride にもその意味がある。

11. **C** 下線文の意味は「逆境の中で勇気の欠落を示すのは臆病の悪徳に負けることを意味するが、その一方で、勇気を過剰に示すのもやはり容易く軽率という悪徳を生み出しかねない」であるから、答えがCであるのは当然であろう。

12. **義務・徳理論：A、E、G；結果主義：B、D**　A が徳理論に含まれるのは、第7パラグラフのアリストテレスに関する記述より明らかである。E は義務理論に関することで、第6パラグラフの最後に記載がある。G も義務理論に当てはまることであり、第6パラグラフの Some of these principles are religious …「これらの原理には宗教的な性質のものもあり、これは至上者への義務を含んでいる」の個所からそうだとわかる。また結果主義であるが、第8パラグラフにある記述「行動を起こす前に、その最終的な結果について考えるように忠告する」、「経験と証拠を頼りに、我々は計画した行動の悪い結果と良い結果をまず検討しなければならない」から B と D が答えだとわかる。

10. 未知の力

1. **C**　宇宙の目的や意味というのは科学というより哲学や神学が研究対象とするものであり、本文中では触れられていない。

2. **A**　単語の問題。conjecture は「推測、憶測」という意味。よって、意味上最も近いのは A である。

3. **D**　gradual が意味するところは「時間をかけてゆっくり、少しずつ」という意味。カギとなる個所は、第 2 パラグラフの slowly but surely bringing us closer to … and our place in it「ゆっくりとだが着実に、宇宙とその中における我々の位置について我々が真の理解に近づくのを助けてくれる」というところ。

4. **B**　stubborn「頑固な」という批判的な言葉を使うことによって、著者が定常宇宙論に賛同していないことがわかる。その他の選択肢は、みなニュートラルなもので、そこから著者の気持ちを測ることはできない。

5. **B**　このパラグラフの第 1 文、Today, the dominant explanation for … the Big Bang Theory「今日、宇宙創成の説明で大勢を占めるものはビッグ・バン理論である」というところから B が答えだとわかる。他の選択肢はみな誤りか無理のあるものばかりである。

6. **B**　著者は何がビッグ・バンを引き起こしたかについては何の説明もしていない。よって答えは B である。A と C はビッグ・バンの原因を指摘するステートメントではないので、聞かれている問題の答えにはなっていない。D は、水素やヘリウムといった一般元素の生成についての記述である。

7. **C**　このパラグラフにおいて著者がしていることは、ハッブルによる他の銀河の観察がビッグ・バン理論の根拠になったということと、この理論には other evidence corroborating the Big Bang Theory「ビッグ・バン理論をサポートする別の証拠」があるということを示すことである。つまり、この理論にはかなりの信憑性があると言いたいのである。

8. **C**　下線文の意味は「…宇宙線という概念であり、これは宇宙の最も遠方から、そして全ての方角から等しく地球に届く、最初の爆発の名残りのノイズのことである」である。これをうまく言い換えているのは C。A と B は下線文にある多くの重要な点を省いており、D に関しては下線文に書かれていないことが記述されている。

9. **C** このパラグラフのメイン・ポイントは、宇宙の拡大がいかに抑えられてきたかという問いについて、「暗黒物質」がその答えだと信じられていたという事実を紹介することである。よってCが正答。他の選択肢はすべて「暗黒物質」に関する事実であるが、どれも「暗黒物質」の主要な機能とは関係がない。

10. **3** 付け加えられる文は、「言い換えると、宇宙の膨張は実際には減速どころか加速していたということである」。これは3の直前にある「これは、超新星と我々の間の空間は、思っていたよりずっと拡張されていたことしか意味し得なかった」ということの言い換え。よって答えは3。

11. **B** 単語の問題。repelling は「はねつける、追い払う」という意味。よって答えはBである。

12. **C、E、F** カギとなる個所は以下の通り。C：all energy and matter were concentrated ... setting the universe in motion「全てのエネルギーと物質がある密集した一点に凝縮され、それが突然爆発し ―これがビッグ・バン― 宇宙を始動させたのである」（第4パラグラフ）；E："dark energy" is repulsing gravity, ... grow faster「『暗黒エネルギー』が重力をはねつけて反発し、それによって宇宙の膨張速度がさらに促進されている」、helping scientists understand ... the nature and fate of the universe「宇宙の特質とその運命について我々がより適切な質問を思いつくのにも役立っているのである」（ともに第8パラグラフ）；F：An underlying assumption of ... expanding ever since that original explosion「ビッグ・バン理論の根底にある仮定は、宇宙は最初の爆発以来拡張し続けているということであり」（第5パラグラフ）、the "dark matter" may also play a role in decelerating the expansion「「暗黒物質」もまた拡張を減速させるのに一役買っているのかもしれない」。アインシュタインに関する記述であるAは本文中には出てこない。BとEはともに本文のサマリーには無関係のものである。

11. 嘘とその発見

1. **B** deliberately は「故意に、わざと」という意味。故意でなければ、ただの間違いであり嘘にはならない。Aに関しては、著者が嘘に賛同するか否かはこの問題に全く関係がない。またCも同様に著者のライティング・スタイルも本問題とは無関係。Dであるが、著者は嘘つきの動機について何も言っていないのである。

2. **A** 下線文の意味は「家族間に受け継がれる性格的特徴に関するある研究で研究者が発見したのは、嘘をつく傾向において、家族構成員が最も密接に類似点を示すということだった」である。よって、この言い換えとなっているのはAであることがわかる。他の選択肢にはいずれも足りない点があるか、誤った情報を含んでいる。

3. **C** 単語の問題。physiognomyは「人相学」のこと。「顔」というタイトルのマクニールによる本から想像がつくであろう。

4. **B** カギになるのはtheir very worry about detection「ばれることに対する心配そのもの」というところ。

5. **C** 単語の問題。arbitraryは「恣意的な、きまぐれな」という意味。よって答えはCである。

6. **A** ロンブローゾは嘘の探知を科学の視点から見つめ (scientifically)、彼の装置は血圧の変化を記録した (recorded changes in a person's blood pressure)。また彼は犯罪学者であった (criminologist)。よって選択肢B－Dに関しては記述があるが、Aに関しては何もない。

7. **D** カギとなるのは以下の個所。the old assumption that ... physiological changes「有罪の証拠となるような質問をされると、嘘をついている者は目に見える生理反応を伴った強い感情的反応を示すという古い仮説」。よって正答Dが導かれる。A、B、Cについての根拠になるようなことは第4パラグラフには見当たらない。

8. **1** 追加される分はその意味からして第4パラグラフと第5パラグラフをつなぐ役目をしている。また、その内容は第5パラグラフの内容の適切な紹介文にもなっているので1が答えとして最も適当である。

9. **C** readingには計器等の「表示度数、示度」という意味もある。ここでのreadings「表示度数」とは、第5パラグラフにある「巻紙、今日ではコンピュータ・モニターの上に記録」された反応のことを指す。よって答えはC。

10. **B** 脳波指紋の説明はThis new technology以下のところであるが、ここではこの技術を使って行う嘘探知の過程が順を追って記されている。

11. **A** controversial「物議を醸す」と問題文にあるが、これは第8パラグラフで紹介されている（完成前の）新しい嘘発見器に関してのことである。この装置は、

被験者の知らないところで何の許可もなく使用できてしまうので、もし完成すれば、is sure to raise civil rights and privacy issues「必ず公民権およびプライバシー問題を引き起こす」ものになるということを言っているのだ。Bに関しては、単にそういう可能性もあるだけで公民権問題等とは関係がない。同様にC、Dに関しても、公民権やプライバシーとの直接的関係が見出せない。

12. **A、C、F** カギとなる箇所はそれぞれ以下の通り。A：the quest for an infallible lie detector ... particularly brain imaging「信頼のおける嘘発見器の探究は科学技術の進歩、特に脳映像法に助けられることになった」(第7パラグラフ)；C：Early lie-detection methods were both crude and cruel「初期の嘘発見メソッドは粗野で残酷なものであった」(第3パラグラフ)および第3パラグラフ全体の内容；F：The polygraph doesn't really detect ... deceptive behavior「ポリグラフは実際に嘘を発見するのではない。被験者が人を騙すような行動を示しているかどうかを探知できるだけである」(第6パラグラフ)、およびポリグラフの前身である装置をロンブローゾが科学に基づいて作ったという第4パラグラフの内容。BとDの内容は問題文中に出てこない。Eはマイナーな情報に過ぎない。

12. 社会学と宗教

1. **A** having emerged as a discipline in its own right only in the middle of the 19th century「19世紀の半ばに独立した学問分野として出現してきたにすぎない」というところがカギである。Bに関してだが、独立した学問分野としてではないが、もちろん社会生活は以前にも研究されていた。Cのようなことは書かれていない。実際のところは逆で、全ての理論が必ず事実の裏付けを必要とする。Dだが、固定した統合的な社会原理があるのかないのかは未だに答えのわからない問題である。

2. **B** 第6パラグラフに明らかなように、ジェイムズは心理学者兼哲学者であり、社会学者ではない。

3. **B** 第2パラグラフにおけるworking conceptual models that ...「比較のための固定した基盤を提供することによって社会的な力を理解するための道具として機能する実用的概念モデル」という理念型の描写から答えがわかる。理念型が社会的な力を理解するのではなく、社会学者がそれを理解する手助けになるのだからAはアウト。Cはデュルケームのことであり、ヴェーバーのことではない。Dはマルクスのことを言っている。

4. **B**　単語の問題。bafflingly は「当惑するほど、困惑するほど」という意味。よって B が答え。

5. **A**　social structure, the preexisting patterns of social reality「社会現実の先在パターンともいうべき社会構造」というところから答えがわかる。

6. **C**　A は社会集団と社会的相互作用の力学という点が抜けている。B には社会階級という情報が足りない。D はまさに社会学がしないことを言っている。C の how and where people fit into society at large「いかにそしてどこで人々が社会全般に溶け込むのか」というのは社会階級の描写である。

7. **D**　D はまさにミルズが呼ぶところの「社会学的想像」の内容である（第 3 パラグラフの最後の文を参照）。つまり、このことを強調するためにミルズに言及しているのである。

8. **B**　ins and outs は調査対象物の詳細を指す。第 4 パラグラフでは社会機構の詳細、すなわちそれがどのように構成され機能するか（how each ... is organized and functions）が描写されている。よって答えは B。

9. **B**　ここでの each は each social institution のこと。社会機構には種類がたくさんあり、その例が each の後に列挙されている（i.e. the family, the economy, schools and education ...）。

10. **A**　カギになるのは necessarily を含む文の直前の文。It demands で始まるこの文が言っているのは、「宗教は、社会科学者が自らの宗教的信念 ─ あるいはその欠如 ─ を一時的に抑え、冷静に、また信者のニーズと感情に特に敏感になって宗教機構を見つめることを要求する」ということ。つまり社会学者に主観的にではなく客観的に世界を見つめることを促しているのである。necessarily はこの点を強調するものである。

11. **C**　第 5 パラグラフの最後に above all, supernatural「とりわけ超自然的な」とあるのがカギ。A は誤ったステートメントである。B は大事なことかもしれないが、本文中にこのような描写はない。D も著者によって触れられてはいない事柄である。

12. **B、C、E、F**　それぞれ以下の個所がカギである。B：sociologists are not concerned ... good or bad「社会学者は特定の宗教信念が本当であるか誤っているか、あるいは宗教慣行が良いものか悪いものかなどにこだわってはいない」；C：Sociologists ask questions like ... manages to survive「社会学者は、どのよう

に宗教集団あるいはカルトが構成され、その最も顕著な特徴と主要な信念が何であるか、それをサブ・グループとして含む社会といかなる関係を持ち、どのような影響を与えるのか、それが実際にはどのように機能し、生き残っていくのかというような質問をする」；E： sociology seeks more ... give rise to them「社会学はそのような経験に対してより世俗的な説明を求め、それらを引き起こす社会構造中の要素に焦点を当てるのである」；F： It wonders how ... sectarian violence「なぜ宗教的信念がときに社会調和に貢献し、ときに社会衝突と宗派間暴力を引き起こすのかを問う」。Aであるが、社会学者も特定の宗教を信仰しても構わない。ただそれによって他人の信仰に関する観察や結論に色がつかないように客観性を保つという条件が付くのではあるが。Dは事実だが、社会学者がそのような事態をどう見るかという情報を欠いているのでアウト。

13. 靴墨工場

1. **C** この引用の内容から、若いディケンズが自分の境遇にどう感じていたのかが容易に読み取れるだろう。

2. **D** 単語の問題。cast away は abandoned「見捨てられた」という意味である。

3. **D** 下線文の意味は「博学で気品のある紳士になるという大いなる期待は永久に潰されてしまったと確信しながら」である。この言い換えとして最も適切なのはDである。

4. **B** A「自分より下だと思っていた労働者階級の子供たちと一緒に働く」、C「靴墨の瓶にラベルを貼り付けるのみという退屈で繰り返しだけの仕事」、D「休日1日のみという長時間労働」は、すべて当時のディケンズが置かれていた労働条件の描写である。Bの「傷つきやすいこと」だけが例外。

5. **A** 第3パラグラフには、ディケンズの家がどこにあったかについての記述はない。

6. **B** the family's debts steadily mounted「家族の借金は着実に増えて行った」、John ... was unable to live within his means「ジョンは自分の収入内で生きることはできなかった」、John, an amiable man who often entertained his many friends「多くの友人をしばしばもてなした愛想の良い男、ジョン」という個所からA、C、Dの内容がそれぞれ推測できる。Bについて確証のある記述はどこにもない。

7. **B**　単語の問題。crucial は critical（重大な）という意味で使われている。

8. **B**　it が指すのは、直前の文の主語である this traumatic episode である。

9. **D**　単語の問題。indefatigable は tireless「疲れを知らない」という意味である。

10. **A**　問題文中の make the most of は「（不満足な事情・条件）を何とかうまく切り抜ける、（不利な機会など）を最大限に利用する」という意味。Despite his hatred for the work itself, … and he did「仕事自体は嫌悪したが、チャールズは早くから工場の他のどの少年よりも熟練しようと決心し、実際にそうなった」というところから彼の前向きな態度がうかがえる。

11. **3**　3 の直前の文 For the rest of his life, … at hand「その後の生涯において、ディケンズは不屈の仕事人になり、目の前の仕事はどんなものでも全霊を傾けて専心したのだった」の内容の具体例が問題の 1 文である。よって 3 が最もふさわしい場所と言える。

12. **C、D、E**　C は以下の個所から正答だとわかる。The experience brought out Dickens's native diligence and conscientiousness「この経験がディケンズの生来の勤勉さと良心を引き出すことになった」、Charles would make up elaborate, humorous tales based on … the streets of London「チャールズはぎょっとするような自分の家庭生活とロンドンの通りを歩いている最中に観察したり経験したことをもとにして、念入りな笑い話を作り上げるのだった」。D は以下の個所に記載がある。Some readers, however, … over it「しかしながら、ディケンズの靴墨工場でのエピソードにあまりいい顔をしない読者も存在する。ディケンズはこのことについて、いつまでも自分を憐れむのをやめない子供のようだと彼らは主張するのだ」。E に関してだが、ディケンズが工場での他の子供たちを最初身分の低い者たちだと思っていたことは問題 4 で見たとおり。common companions の common には、相手を蔑む意味があるので注意。彼が後に彼らのために立ち上がったということは just as the blacking factory incident … the poor and downtrodden「ちょうど靴墨工場での一件が、なぜディケンズ作品の最も顕著な登場人物が孤児や見捨てられた子供たちだったりするのか、また彼がなぜ貧しくて虐げられた者たちの大義を擁護するのに自分の小説を使ったのかについての確かな説明になるのと同じように」というところからわかる。A および B に関する記述はない。F だが、ディケンズは自分の家庭生活を創作のネタにして同僚に話していたのだから、F の描写は事実とは異なっている。

14. 手遅れになる前に

1. **B**　単語の問題。**jeremiad** は「悲嘆、長々とした不平」という意味。選択肢の中では diatribe「痛烈な批判」が最も近い。同パラグラフにある Carson's attack「カーソンによる攻撃」から想像がつくだろう。

2. **A**　カギになるのはやはり the focus of Carson's attack「カーソンの批判の焦点ともなった」という農薬汚染（中毒）に関するかっこ内の描写である。

3. **2**　追加される文は、この位置の直前にある「その結果、これらの問題の多くが直視されるようになり、公序における変化によって縮小を見るケースも現れた」という内容に対する具体例を挙げるものである。

4. **C**　下線文の意味は「地球の大気と海の平均気温が上昇していること自体が問題になっているのではない」である。ここに含意されているのは、次の文からもわかるように温暖化は実際に起こっているのだが、そのこと自体に異議を唱えている者がいるのではないということである。よって答えはC。

5. **B**　NASA のゴダード宇宙研究所に言及することにおける著者の意図は、自分の主張に対する客観的で信頼のおけるサポートを提示することである。

6. **B**　a normal fluctuation in surface temperatures「表面温度の通常変化」、variations in the amount of sunlight reaching the earth「地表に達する日光量の変化」、just emerging from a previous cooling period「地球が前回の寒い時期から抜け出している」ということが指摘されていて、これらがそれぞれ A、C、D の根拠になる。B のような描写はない。

7. **A**　著者の意図は、個人の金銭的な見返りや自身の政治的信条の促進のために公明正大になりきれない科学者の存在をほのめかすことである。よって答えはA。

8. **A**　このパラグラフの最初の文 But these arguments are no longer tenable「しかし、このような言い分はもはや通用しない」から、第2文以降に描写されている「大勢を占める科学的意見」をサポートしていることがわかる。

9. **C**　カギとなる箇所は以下のところである。a thermal blanket composed of water vapor, carbon dioxide, ozone, and other greenhouse gases「水蒸気、二酸化炭素、オゾン、その他のいわゆる温室効果ガスから成る大気の保温膜」。

10. **A**　Chinese farmers near the expanding Gobi Desert「拡大するゴビ砂漠の近くに住む中国人農家」（およびエスキモー）が particularly hard hit「特に打撃を受けている」とある。よって「ますます乾いてきて、もはや農業には適さなくなった中国人農家の土地もある」というのは十分あり得ることであろう。B に関しては、豪雨ではなく、氷が溶け出していることがエスキモーに影響を与えているはずである。C だが、すでに沈んでしまった太平洋の島があるという記述は第7パラグラフにはない。また、動物が自然の居住環境を失っていることは書かれているが、どの地域の動物がそうなのかということは書かれていないので D もアウト。

11. **B**　単語の問題。exacerbated は「悪化する」という意味。よって答えは B である。第 7 パラグラフの内容からしても、「さらに気温が上がれば、これらとその他の傾向は」とくれば「悪化する」という答えが導けるだろう。もちろん worsened もそれを意味する単語だと知っていればの話だが。

12. **A、D、E**　カギになるのはそれぞれ以下の個所。A：prevailing scientific opinion is that ... the burning of fossil fuels「大勢を占める科学的見解によると、地球温暖化の大部分は人間の営み、特に化石燃料の燃焼にはっきり起因するものであるという」（第 4 パラグラフ）；D：to survive, entire communities are ... to other areas「生き残るために居住者全員が他地方への移住を強いられているコミュニティーもある」（第 7 パラグラフ）、animal species are also ... dying out as a result「多くの動物種もまた地球温暖化によって自然の生息地を失い、結果として絶滅しかけている」（第 7 パラグラフ）、E：Furthermore, the warming trend is accelerating. The five warmest years ... since 1998「その上、温暖化の傾向は加速しているのである。記録上最も暑かった年のベスト 5 はどれも 1998 年以降に起こっている」（第 2 パラグラフ）。B、C のよう情報は本文中にはない。F は確かに本文中にある記載だが、本エッセイの主題とは外れたマイナーな点の描写に過ぎない。

15. PTSD

1. **C**　or so television and the papers would have us believe「あるいはテレビと新聞によってそう思い込まされている」というところから答えは C だとわかる。A だが、飛行事故は自然災害ではない。B は、そのようにメディアに思わされることがあるだけである。D のような記述はどこにもない。

2. **A**　下線文の意味は「ストレスのたまる出来事の後には、長く感情的麻痺状

態、逃避、否定の期間が続く」である。A はまさにこの言い換えである。B だが、症状が現れるのにかかる時間に関する記述はない。C および D のような記載も本文中には存在しない。

3. **C**　insomnia、nightmares、depression というのがそれぞれ A、B、D に対応するが、C の夫婦間の問題に関する記載はない。

4. **B**　単語の問題。B の precipitate は「突然引き起こす」という意味で、trigger と同義である。

5. **2**　2 の後には実際にトラウマを引き起こすような経験をしなくても PTSD にかかるケース、すなわち、レスキュー隊員のケースや 9/11 の事件をテレビで見た人たちのケースの説明が続くので、ここがもっともふさわしい場所である。

6. **D**　パイオニアというのは何事でも最初にした人のことを指す。よって「トラウマを被っている退役軍人を最初に診ようとしたのは心理学者だったことを指摘する」ために著者がこの言葉を使ったことがわかる。

7. **B**　問題の These は直前の文にある extensive studies of Vietnam War veterans を指す。よって答えは B。他の選択肢は These の後にある動詞 showed の主語としてふさわしくないものばかりである。

8. **B**　誰も PTSD を持って生まれてくるのではない。PTSD にかかりやすい体質の人はいるが、みな生後の経験によって PTSD を発症することになるのである。

9. **B**　perception retention とは memory「記憶」のことである。

10. **A**　anti-depressants「抗鬱薬」は psychotropic drugs「向精神薬」の一種である。精神療法でも組み合わされた治療法でもないので B と C はアウト。また psychotropic drugs such as anti-anxiety medications and anti-depressants「抗不安薬、抗鬱薬のような向精神薬」という表現から anti-depressants が anti-anxiety medications「抗不安薬（心配を処置する薬）」とは別物だとわかる。

11. **C**　カギになる箇所は especially helpful in educating victims and getting them to come to terms with their problem「患者の教育および彼らを自らの問題に立ち向かわせるのに特に役立っている」。A だが、グループ・セラピー自体が精神療法の一種である。B は緊急事態ストレス管理マネージメント（**CISM**）に関してのこと。

D のようなことは記述されていない。

12. **A、C、D**　B は PTSD に関するマイナーな情報。E、F に関する記述は本文中にはない。A は以下の個所がカギ。The sooner a victim can be reached, ... avoiding a severe onset of PTSD「外傷的事件後、被害者に救いの手が差し伸べられ、緊急事態ストレス管理マネージメント（CISM）のセラピーに入れられるのが早ければ早いほど、PTSD の深刻な徴候を避けられる可能性が高くなるのである」。C は Sufferers are subject to insomnia, ... and flashbacks「PTSD 患者は、不眠症、記憶喪失、ひどい欝病、慢性的なイラつきに陥りやすくなる。彼らはまた幻覚症状、悪夢およびフラッシュバックを通して、最初にトラウマを引き起こした出来事を持続的に再経験する」、D は The events that trigger the disorder ... physical injury「PTSD を引き起こす出来事は、たいてい実際の死あるいは死の危険、および／または大怪我に関係するものである」の個所から答えだとわかる。

16. 動物園：賛成と反対

1. **B**　カギとなるのは the first scientific zoological treatise「最初の科学的な動物学論文」を書いたというところ。

2. **A**　単語の問題。assiduous は「根気強い、勤勉な」という意味。これに最も近いのは enthusiastic「熱心な」である。

3. **C**　単語の問題。subjugated は「征服された、服従させられた」という意味。よって答えは C。

4. **B**　A は exotic animals from around the globe ... wealth, power, and prestige「植民地支配による富、力、そして威信としての世界中からの珍しい動物」というところに記載がある。C は creatures that had been captured during far-flung military conquests「広範囲に渡る軍事征服に従事する間に捕らえた生き物」というところに記述されている。同様に、D は kings and queens of Europe maintained large private collections「ヨーロッパの王と女王は大きな個人コレクションを持っていた」に記載がある。答えの B であるが、実際にグラディエーターが動物と闘ったのはスポーツ・アリーナで、動物園ではない。

5. **D**　A であるが、確かに動物園が作られたのは大都市が多かったのだが、田舎に全く作られなかったという記述はない。また B のような記述も存在しない。C に関しては、ロンドン動物学会が最初にしたのは、自らを科学的・教育的な機

構であると主張したことであり、一般用動物園を設立したことではない。D は It wasn't until the 19th century ... was born「しかし、大衆的な娯楽の場としての動物園が生まれたのは 19 世紀になってからのことである」という個所から推測のできることである。

6. **2** 付け加えられる分は、第 4 パラグラフの最初の文「今日でも動物園はまだまだ人気があり、毎年何百万もの人が訪れている」を受けたものになっているので 2 が答え。またその直後の文「動物が鉄製の小さな檻や冷たいコンクリートの囲いに閉じ込められていたのは、ありがたいことに、今では昔のことである」とのつながりもスムーズである。

7. **C** endeavor to replicate as closely as possible the animals' natural habitats「動物の自然な居住環境をできるだけ念入りに再現する努力」の方法の 1 つが「複数種共生展示」なのである。よって答えは C。

8. **A** 下線文の意味は「監禁するということは野生動物をさげすむだけでなく、我々の品位までをも落とすものである」なので、A の「動物を檻に閉じ込めることによって、我々は彼らを虐待すると同時に我々自身にも恥をもたらすことになる」が基本的に同じことを言ってのがわかるだろう。

9. **D** 「この事実」というのは第 5 パラグラフの主題、つまり Zoos, they say, are inherently unethical and inhumane「動物園は本質的に非倫理的で残酷なものだと彼らは言う」を指している。よって答えは D。

10. **B** 単語の問題。laudatory は「賞賛の、賛美の」という意味。よって B の praiseworthy「賞賛に値する」が答え。

11. **A** 第 8 パラグラフには A に関する記述はない。B、C、D はそれぞれ以下のところに書かれている。B: These animals (= endangered animal species) ... can then be reintroduced into the wild「これらの動物（＝絶滅危惧種）はそのあと野生に戻され」、C: saving many endangered animal species from extinction「多くの絶滅危惧種を絶滅から救っている」、D: help maintain biodiversity「生物多様性の維持の手助けになる」。

12. **C、D、F** これらの選択肢の記述は以下の通り。C: What ... can we learn from such tame, sanitized animals?「そんな飼い慣らされ野生味を消された動物から何が学べるのか」；Any research conducted on them cannot be truly scientific「彼らに対して行われるリサーチは真に科学的でも役に立つものでもない」、D: in most cases, the animals' habitats have been destroyed ... no "wild" for them to

return to「ほとんどの場合、動物の居住環境は破壊されているので、たとえ「救われた」としても、動物が帰るべき「野生」はもうないのである」、F: Animals in captivity soon lose their natural characteristics … display such "mad" behaviors as staring, pacing, circling, and bar-biting「飼育下にある動物は、凝視、行ったり来たり、ぐるぐる歩き、檻へのかみつきといった「狂った」行動を示す」。AとBは本文中に記載がない。Eはまさに動物権利活動家が反対する行為である。

17. パナマ運河

1. **B** 第1パラグラフ中に一般住居に関する記載はない。あるのは「オフィス、工場、橋、トンネル、鉄道、ダム、高速道路、灌漑・給水システム」である。

2. **A** 単語の問題。intricate は「入り組んだ、込み入った」という意味。よってAが最も近い。

3. **D** 第2パラグラフのポイントは、パナマ運河のおかげで航行する船の時間とコストを大幅に節約できることである。A‐Cの情報はどれも正しいが、パナマ運河の特徴に関するマイナーな点ばかりである。

4. **B** them が指し得るものは直前の節にある Spanish officials「スペインの役人」か some preliminary plans for such a project「そのようなプロジェクトの予備計画」のいずれかである。しかしこの them は being realized「実現される」という述語に続くのでBが答えとなる。Cの wars in Europe はこのプロジェクトを阻んだ原因であるから them が指すことはない。Dの resources exploitation は単数なのでそれだけでアウト。

5. **B** following the discovery of gold in California and the ensuing Gold Rush … that plans for connecting the two oceans were seriously revived「太平洋と大西洋をつなぐという計画が本格的に復活したのは、1848年にカリフォルニアで金が発見され、次いで起こったゴールド・ラッシュの後の19世紀半ばになってからのことである」の部分がキー。

6. **C** 下線文の意味は「1881年にフランスの土木工学会社が運河の仕事を開始したが、不十分な計画、資金および機材の問題、そして労働者の間で猛威をふるった病気のためにこの計画は失敗の運命をたどってしまった」であるので、この意味と合致するのはC。

7. **A** カギとなる箇所は以下の通り。with American engineers picking up where the French had left off「アメリカのエンジニアたちはフランス人がやり残したところから仕事を再開する格好になった」、the deadly French experience had shown …「致命的なフランスの経験から」。BとCに関する記述はない。Dに関しては、確かに病気対策が取られたが、それによって病気の恐れが完全になくなったというのは言い過ぎであり、そのような記述も存在しない。

8. **A** 単語の問題。toil は「骨を折って働く」という意味。よってAが最も近い。

9. **D** 「粉砕した岩からコンクリートを作ること」というのは労働状況ではなく、仕事の描写である。

10. **2** 追加される文はパナマ運河が許容できる船のサイズを描写するもの。2の位置に置くことによって、このサイズはもはや現在の輸送量からすると小さすぎるという内容の後続文にうまくつながっていく。

11. **C** このパラグラフから確信を持って言えることは These gargantuan freighters and liners … the world's shipping by 2010「これらの巨大な貨物船と定期船は2010年までには世界の輸送量の丸々3分の1も運ぶと予想されている」ことである。よって答えはC。Aは「今日、パナマ運河は未だに国際貿易と輸送の肝心な水路になっている」というこのパラグラフの第1文に矛盾するし、パナマ運河の拡大・最新化計画もあるのだから、このような断言はできない。Bについても、まだこのような決定はされていない。Dについての記述はない。

12. **C** 問題文のメイン・ポイントは以下の通り。壮大な土木工学プロジェクトとして完成したパナマ運河は、太平洋と大西洋を結ぶことによって我々に多大な恩恵をもたらした。しかし今では世界の輸送量が格段に増加したため、この運河を航行できないほど大きな船が現れるようになった。よってこの運河の時代はもう終わりを迎えているようにも思え、その未来は不確かなものになっている。これをうまくまとめているのはCである。Aには本文に記述がない情報があり、BとDはパナマ運河に関する部分的な情報に過ぎない。

18. ジョン・デューイの実験学校

1. **B** 単語の問題。discredit は「…を信頼できないものとする、…の信用を落とす」という意味。よって答えはB。

2. **A** 南北戦争は 1861 年から 1865 年までの戦争。19 世紀末のおよそ 40 年前の出来事である。B、C、D はそれぞれ a burgeoning population、increasing immigration、rapid scientific discovery に対応する。

3. **A** 単語の問題。provisional は「仮の、暫定的な」という意味。よって答えは A である。

4. **D** They が指すのは、前文の主題となっている assumptions and beliefs であり、They に続く術部「常に誤りがないか見直し、変化する状況に合うように修正するべき」とも意味の上で合致する。よって答えは D。

5. **D** カギとなるのは以下の個所。this new way of thinking would help foster tolerance towards differences among peoples and cultures「この新しい考え方が人種と文化間の相違に対する寛容性を育む手助けになり」。これは心の広さの促進に他ならない。よって答えは D。A であるが、これとは正反対のことが第 3 パラグラフには書かれている。B であるが、これは assumptions and beliefs に関しての描写（設問 4 の解説参照）。C であるが、実用主義者が目指したのは、他の文化について人々を教育することではなく、人々が他の文化にもっと寛容になることである。よってこれもアウト。

6. **D** デューイは「自分の理論と信念をテストするために」実験学校を作ったのであり、その理念と信念は第 2 パラグラフにある An idea's truth lies ... through experience and observation「考えの真実は、より良い生活のための道具としてのその利便性にあり、経験と観察を通してのみ決定され得るのである」などからわかる。よって実験学校でデューイがしたかったのは、まず生活に役立つ考えと道具を生徒に教えてみることであった。よって答えは D。A、B のような記述はない。他文化理解も実験学校のテーマではあったが、多文化から生徒が集まったという記述もないので C もアウト。

7. **B** 単語の問題。docile は「従順な、教えやすい」という意味。第 5 パラグラフの内容は、教師主導型の伝統的な教え方についてであり、これでは生徒は受身の存在でしかないとうことを指摘している。よって、docile がこのコンテキストでは「受け身の」という意味で使われていることは容易に想像できる。

8. **A** 下線文の意味は「彼が信じたのは、教育とは単なる「将来の生活のための準備」ではなく、「生きる過程」であるべきだということだった」。これの言い換えになっているのはもちろん A。

9. **4** 第6パラグラフの最後に developing approaches that fit ... of the group「個人のニーズおよびグループのニーズに合ったアプローチを開発する」とある。この具体的な内容とその発展的内容が追加される文によって与えられている。よって4の位置が最適な場所だとわかる。

10. **B** 第7パラグラフに seeing historical plays instead of memorizing historical facts「歴史的事実を暗記する代わりに歴史的な演劇を鑑賞する」とあるが、どこにも「歴史劇を書く」という描写はない。

11. 伝統的な学校：**A、E**　　実験学校：**B、F、G**
カギとなる箇所は以下の通り。

（伝統的な学校）A：traditional teaching, with its emphasis on completion of assignments through isolated private study「一人一人の個人勉強を通して宿題を完成させることに重きを置く伝統的な教授法」（第5パラグラフ）；E：Teachers of the time ... specific habits of thought and discipline「当時の教員は、教育メソッドや理論における訓練をほとんど、あるいはまったく受けておらず、主に考えを押し付け、特定の思考と規律の習慣を植え付けるために学校にいたのだった」（第5パラグラフ）。

（実験学校）B：learning and knowledge begin in doing and activity「学習と知識はすることと行動に始まる」（第7パラグラフ）、It also involved cooperation for the good of all「また、みんなのために協力することも関係していた」（第7パラグラフ）。F：the Laboratory School put the child at the center of education「実験学校では子どもが教育の中心に置かれた」（第6パラグラフ）、Self-realization, ... was its goal「単なる知識と情報の蓄積ではなく、自己実現がその目的であった」（第6パラグラフ）；G：pupils could take charge of their own learning「生徒が自分の学習の責任を持ち」（第6パラグラフ）。

Cだが、実験学校で教員研修が行われたという記述はない。Dに関しては、実験学校の描写として Academic excellence was important, but not nearly as important as problem-solving「学業に優れることも重要ではあるが、創造的に問題を解決することには遠く及ばない」とある。Dの内容はこれと一致しないし、また伝統的な学校の描写としてもアウトである。

12. **B** 第8パラグラフの最後に They (= Dewey's ideas and practices) are waiting for us, ... deeply concern us「デューイの考えと慣行は、我々に深く関わる物事についてまだ学ばれていないレッスンとして、この学校の記録の中で、我々を待っているのだ」とある。これに最も近いのはB。

19. アパルトヘイトの終焉

1. **C** このパラグラフにははっきりと黒人が75%を占め、白人は13%に過ぎないと記載されている。よってCが明らかに誤りである。

2. **A** 単語の問題。engenderは「発生させる」という意味。これに一番近いのはAである。

3. **C** カギになるのは以下の個所。human rights abuses ... were primarily motivated by white supremacist racism「この政策が引き起こした人権侵害は主に白人至上主義からなされるものであった」。よってCの内容は正しくない。

4. **B** 単語の問題。entrenchは本来「塹壕で囲む」という意味だが、「固定化する、定着させる、確固たるものとする」という意味も持つ。ここでは後者の意味で使われている。よって答えはB。

5. **D** 通行許可手帳に関連する「パス法」に関する記述に severely curtailed black mobility within the country「黒人の国内での移動は厳しく制限された」とある。よってDが答え。集団地域法は人種を異なった地域に割り当てたもので通行許可手帳とは関係がない。よってAはアウト。また通行許可手帳と人種間交流も無関係。よってBも当てはまらない。Cの「仕事を見つけるのに黒人が必要とした書類」というのも通行許可手帳とは別物である。

6. **A** 下線文の意味は「黒人は選挙権を否定され、教育権も実質的に切り詰められていた」である。この趣旨を伝えているのはAである。

7. **D** 第4パラグラフの最後にstrikes, demonstrations, sabotage, ... which often brought swift, violent reprisals from the government「ストライキ、デモ、サボタージュ … これらの戦略には政府がしばしば迅速かつ暴力的な報復を行った」とある。Aは報復のため政府が行使した力。BのANCは抗議行動を奨励はしたものの、その存在自体が報復の原因になったわけではない。Cの「白人以外の者が密かに開いた会合」というのも報復の直接原因ではない。

8. **2** 2以降の描写はすべて国外での出来事についてである。追加される文はまさにそのイントロダクション。よって2が答え。

9. **D** 単語の問題。pariahはもともとタミル語からきた「社会ののけ者」という意味の単語。これに最も近いのはDである。

10. **B** 単語の問題。sanctions は「制裁」という意味。よく trade sanctions「貿易制裁」として用いられる。これに最も近いのは B の embargoes「通商停止」である。

11. **A** by any means は「いかなる手段を使っても」という意味。第6パラグラフではこの後「テロ行為と暴動がほとんど日常茶飯事になってしまった」という記述がある。つまり「いかなる手段を使っても」とは、若い黒人たちが自分たちの要求を通すために暴力も厭わなかったということ言っているのである。

12. **1：E、2：B、3：A、4：F、5：D、6：C**
1. 第7パラグラフにデ・クラークがアパルトヘイトの廃止を1991年に始めたという記述がある。「アパルトヘイトの廃止はその翌年に達成され、それから1年以内に新憲法が提案され認可された」とあるから、これは1993年のことだとわかる。
2. 第7パラグラフの初めに1986年の状況が書かれているが、その直後「3年後」との前置きに続いて、ボータがマンデラに会ったと記されている。よって1989年のことだとわかる。
3. 第7パラグラフの初めに書かれているのは1986年に「パス法」が破棄されたということ。これによって通行許可手帳が要求されなくなったのである。
4. 1で見た新憲法の提案・認可は1993年のことであったが、第7パラグラフには「翌年、初めて民主的選挙が行われた」との記述が続く。よって1994年のことだとわかる。
5. 1で見たとおり、アパルトヘイトの廃止は1991年の翌年のこと。よって1992年が答えである。
6. 第7パラグラフにおけるデ・クラークに関する記述によると、1991年に彼は政治犯を解放し、病院、学校、その他の公共施設での人種差別を撤廃することでアパルトヘイトを徐々に廃止し始めたということがわかる。よって1991年が答え。

20. ビジネスの転換

1. **A** 下線文の意味は「益々明らかになってきたのは、企業がこの新しい状況にビジネス慣行を適合させなければならない ── さもなければ大変なことになる ── ということである」である。これの言い換えとして適切なのはもちろんA。Bは本文の主張と矛盾するもので、このような記載はどこにもない。Cも会社がするべきことの反対を述べている。Dはナンセンスである。

2. **B** 単語の問題。jeopardize は「危険にさらす」という意味。よってこれに最も近いのは B ということになる。

3. **B** 以下がカギとなる個所。where it hurts most—the bottom line「ビジネスの最も痛いところ ― 帳尻の上」。すなわち会社の利益に影響を与えるというのである。bottom line はもともと「企業の収益報告の最下行」のこと。転じて「収益」、「最重要事項」などを意味することが多い。

4. **C** カギとなるのは以下の個所。faced with a choice between two products of comparable price and quality, ... more sensitive to the needs of society and the environment「同等の価格と品質を持つ 2 つの製品から選ぶ際に、社会のニーズと環境に対してより敏感である会社が作ったものを買うことが増えている」。A はまさにこの逆のことを言っている。B、D のような記述はどこにもない。

5. **B** 「子供を不当に働かせる」という意味の上から答えが B であるのは明らか。A だが、搾取工場は責任感のある会社が運営するものではない。また工場は製品ではないので、欠陥製品という C もアウト。D の「秘かな廃棄活動」も、搾取工場の運営と並ぶ悪い慣行であるが、搾取工場の例ではない。

6. **D** 単語の問題。sever は「(関係など)を断つ」という意味。よって D が最も意味の近い単語となる。

7. **B** These trends が指すのは第 2 パラグラフで描写されている労働者、消費者、投資家たちの新しい態度 (=社会的に責任感のある会社に傾倒すること) である。よって答えは B。

8. **C** 第 4 パラグラフのポイントは、会社が伝統的に何を求めてきたのかを示すことによって、社会に責任を持つ存在になるためには何をすればよいのか、つまり今までとは何を変える必要があるのか、を示して次のパラグラフへの話の移行をスムーズにすることである。よって答えは C。

9. **2** 2 以下に出てくる文はどれも第 5 パラグラフの第 1 文および追加される文の説明になっている。すなわち最初にメインのアイディアを示し、その後に解説を加えるというパラグラフ構造になっているのだ。よって答えは 2。

10. **A** 第 4 パラグラフで見たとおり、「公害に関する法令の緩和と減税のためにロビー活動すること」というのは、社会に対しての責任など考えなかった会社がかつてしていたことである。よって A が答え。

11. **B** 単語の問題。accrue は「(利益など) が生ずる、(資本など) が増える」という意味。よってこれに意味上最も近いのは B である。

12. **A、C、E** カギとなる個所は以下の通り。A：while some sacrifices are unavoidable, … improve their financial performance and increase profits「多少の犠牲は避けられないが、より社会的に責任を持ち維持しやすいタイプの営業にスイッチすることが、長い目で見れば、財政上のパフォーマンスを大幅に改善し、利益を増やす」(第 5 パラグラフ)；C：第 2 パラグラフの内容；E：第 2 パラグラフおよび第 6 パラグラフの内容。B はマイナーな情報であるとともに、本文中にはない記述が含まれている。D も真実ではあろうが、本問題文の中ではマイナーなものである。F だが、この選択肢中で触れられているリサーチは問題文中には存在しない。また、内容そのものもサマリーに適したものではない。

GLOSSARY   数字は Lesson ナンバーを示す。

A

abandon (13)	to leave a person, place, or thing behind, often forever; forsake　見捨てる
abolishment (16)	the act of banning or prohibiting something; eradication; annulment　廃止
abound (8)	to be plentiful; teem　いっぱいいる（ある）
absorb (1)	to soak up a liquid; to take in information or ideas　吸収する
abstract (5)	based on images or ideas, not on real things; theoretical　抽象的な
absurdity (8)	the state of being ridiculous or nonsensical; foolishness　ばかばかしさ
abuse (15)	using someone or something in a bad or often cruel way; misuse　濫用、虐待
academic (2)	scholarly; having to do with education　学問的な、アカデミックな
accelerate (14)	to speed up or go faster; expedite　加速する、拍車をかける
accommodate (17)	to provide space or room for someone or something　収容する、収容能力がある
accountable (20)	responsible; answerable for; to be to blame for　説明責任がある
accumulation (18)	a gathering together or piling up of something; buildup; collection　蓄積
accurate (6)	precise; exact; correct　正確な
acquire (1)	to obtain or receive　獲得する
acute (1)	sharp; severe; serious　鋭い、深刻な
adaptability (4)	the capacity to change to fit a new situation; flexibility　適応性
adept (13)	highly skilled; proficient　熟達した、精通した
adhere (9)	to stick to or remain with　くっつく、固守する
adherent (10)	a person who supports a cause or idea; supporter; proponent　支持者、信奉者
adversity (9)	trouble; problems; misfortune; hardship　不運、苦労、災難
affiliation (3)	connection; relationship　関係、加入、所属

affliction (15)	disease or health problem　苦悩をもたらすもの、病気
aftermath (10)	a period of time following an event; result or consequence　（災害・戦争などの）余波、結果
allay (12)	to reduce the seriousness of something; relieve; make less difficult　（苦痛・悲しみなど）を和らげる
alter (17)	to change or make different; adjust; modify　変える、改める
alternative (1)	choice; option　選択すべきもの、代案
amalgam (8)	combination; mixture　混合物、合成物
amass (16)	to gather or collect in great numbers; pile up　集まる、群がる
amiable (13)	friendly and outgoing; amicable; affable　人当たりの良い、愛想の良い
anecdote (2)	a short, interesting, often amusing story about something that has happened to a person　逸話
anguish (3)	severe mental or physical pain; torment; suffering　苦悩
annotate (1)	to add notes or explanations to a text　注釈をつける
anthropological (8)	having to do with the study of the origins and culture of human beings　（文化）人類学に関する
antithesis (3)	direct contrast or opposition　完全な相違、対立
anxiety (15)	a strong feeling of worry or fear　心配、懸念
appalling (13)	causing serious concern or disappointment; shockingly bad　ぞっとさせる、びっくりさせるほどの
apparent (9)	easily seen or understood; very clear; obvious　明白な、明らかな
archeologist (8)	a person who studies the history of the things that human beings have made and built in the distant past　考古学者
arise (15)	to come up or occur　起る、生じる
aristocrat (2)	a member of the ruling class or nobility　貴族、上流階級の人
arouse (16)	to cause someone to have a strong feeling or emotion; excite　刺激する、奮い立たせて…させる
array (6)	a large number or variety of things or objects; an impressive display　…の勢ぞろい
articulate (7)	to express clearly and logically; state　（考え・物事など）をはっきり述べる
artificial (16)	man-made; not real or authentic　人工の、人工的な
aspiring (13)	having an ambition or goal; ambitious　野心に燃える、意欲的な

assert (16)	to state one's opinions or feelings openly or strongly; avow; declare　断言する
assertion (2)	a strong opinion or statement　断言
assess (11)	to estimate the value or worth of something or someone; judge; evaluate　算定する、査定する、評価する
assumption (1)	something believed or taken for granted as true or correct, often without much evidence　想定、推定
astonishment (5)	great surprise or amazement　（大変な）驚き
astronomer (10)	a space scientist　天文学者
astrophysicist (10)	a person who studies the physical properties of the stars and planets　天文物理学者
attribute (7)	to relate or connect a specific cause to something; ascribe; account for　（結果）を…に帰する、…のせいにする
authenticity (8)	the condition of being real or genuine　真正（本物）であること
authoritarian (18)	in favor of absolute obedience to the people in power; not supporting individual freedom　権威（独裁）主義の
avoidance (15)	intentionally staying away from something or someone; shunning; evasion　回避、忌避

B

beneficial (2)	good; positive; advantageous　有益な
bias (1)	a strong preference or prejudice　先入観、偏見
biodiversity (16)	the variety of living things found in a certain region or on the earth as a whole　生物多様性
biopic (1)	a movie based on the life of a famous person　(biographical picture)　伝記映画
blob (6)	a soft, shapeless mass of something　小さな塊、ぼんやりとした形、ぼうっと（丸く）見えるもの
bloodthirsty (16)	eager to shed blood or witness violence; savage; ruthless　血に飢えた、残虐な
bombard (1)	to flood, attack, or overwhelm with information, questions, or accusations　（質問などで）責め立てる
boost (20)	to increase or improve　押し上げる、増加（促進）する
bottom line (20)	the last line in a financial statement that shows profits and losses; profit　帳尻、収益

boycott (19)	refusing to cooperate or deal with someone or something as an expression of protest　ボイコット
brutally (19)	violently or cruelly; savagely　残酷に、容赦なく
burgeoning (6)	growing or increasing very rapidly; booming 新興の、伸びゆく

C

captive breeding (16)	the practice of trying to get animals kept in zoos to reproduce　動物の園内出産
captivity (16)	the state of being kept in a cage or prison 檻や刑務所に捕われの状態
carnivore (4)	an animal that lives on the flesh of other animals 肉食動物
carpentry (18)	the art or skill of making houses and other things with wood 大工職、大工仕事
caste (19)	a social class based on heredity of historical conditions カースト、階級性
catastrophic (14)	disastrous or calamitous　破滅的な、天変地異（説）の
causal (2)	having to do with the reasons why things happen 原因となる、因果関係を示す
ceremonial (3)	formal; official; ritualistic　儀礼的な、儀式用の
champion (13)	to support or work on behalf of some person or cause （主義など）を擁護する、…のために戦う
chaos (3)	utter confusion or disorder; mayhem　無秩序、大混乱
chronic (15)	serious or lasting for a long time, as a disease; coming back again and again　長期にわたる、慢性の
cite (16)	to state as example or authority　…を引用する、例証する
clarify (2)	to explain so as to make clear （意味など）を明らかにする
claw (4)	the foot or toe of an animal or bird　（鳥獣の）かぎづめ
climatologist (14)	a person who studies weather patterns and conditions 気候（風土）学者
cluster (4)	to gather together; to form groups for warmth and protection 群れをなして集まる、群生（密生）する
coin (2)	to make a new word or expression; to invent （新語・嘘など）を造り出す

collaborate (8)	to cooperate with; to support the enemy during wartime　共同して働く、協力する
colloquial (2)	having to do with spoken as opposed to written language　口語の
colonial (19)	concerned with a country's overseas possessions　植民地の
colony (4, 17)	a large group of animals; a country where people from another country have settled and which is ruled by that country　植民地
combustion (6)	the burning of fuels for heat and energy　燃焼
common (13)	typical of the lower classes; coarse or unrefined in manner　並以下の、品のない、労働者階級の
communal (4)	tending to live together in groups or communities　共同社会の
compassion (16)	a feeling of sympathy or understanding for others' problems or situations　憐れみ、同情
compel (19)	to force someone to do something; coerce　人に無理やり…させる
committed (20)	loyal; determined to succeed　献身的な、ひたむきな
composition (5)	arrangement of artistic parts to make a satisfying whole　構成、創作、作品
comprehensive (10)	including everything that is needed to make a satisfying or effective whole　すべてを包含する、包括的な
comprise (12)	to include or make up; contain; amount to　（部分）から成る、（団体・組織）を構成する
concentrate (10)	to focus or direct one's actions or thoughts towards a common goal or aim　集中する
conceptual (12)	conceived of or imagined in the mind　概念（形式）の、抽象的な
concession (17)	a piece of land offered by one country to another country in return for payment or other benefits　租借地
condemn (19)	to criticize or accuse very strongly; find guilty　責める、とがめる
confess (8)	to admit to a crime or other act of wrongdoing; own up; acknowledge　（悪事など）を白状する、認める
conflict (7)	tension caused by opposing sides or forces; opposition; friction　闘争、対立、衝突
connotation (3)	a suggested meaning or idea　言外の意味、含意

conquest (16)	victory; triumph over an opponent or enemy　征服、勝利
conscientiousness (13)	the habit of always doing a good job; meticulousness　良心的なこと、誠実
console (13)	to try to soothe someone's grief or loss; to comfort in time of trouble or need　慰める
contemplation (9)	deep, careful thinking; reflection; meditation　熟考
contend (13)	to express an opinion; assert; avow　（強く）主張する
contradiction (12)	something that isn't what it seems to be; an inconsistency or anomaly　矛盾
contradictory (3)	inconsistent; seemingly opposed　矛盾した、反対の
conversion (12)	changing from one state or position to another　転換、変換
convert (6)	to change from one state or position to another　転換する、変換する
convey (2)	to communicate or show in words, pictures, or gestures　伝える
convincing (2)	very persuasive and believable; definitive　信じられる、人を納得させる
correlate (4)	to show or establish a relation between certain elements or factors　関連（関係）づける
corruption (8)	dishonesty or wrongdoing, especially that committed by leaders and officials; political wrongdoing　汚職、不正
courage (9)	bravery; valor　勇気
coward (3)	a person who lacks courage or bravery　臆病者
cowardice (9)	not acting bravely or courageously　臆病、小心
critical (1)	carefully exact and thoughtful; keen; sharp　批評の、批判の
crude (11)	lacking refinement, tact, or taste; barbaric　粗い、粗雑な
cruel (11)	aiming to cause pain and suffering; ruthless; heartless　残酷な
crush (13)	to overwhelm or oppress; defeat　（反対勢力など）を粉砕する、…を鎮圧する
cultivate (12)	to grow or foster; promote　耕す、育成する、啓発する
curfew (19)	a law requiring people to be off the streets and in their homes before a certain hour of the evening or night　夜間外出禁止令
curiosity (2)	a desire to know and learn; a high level of interest in something　好奇心

curricula (18)	courses or programs of study offered by a school or university　curriculum（全教科課程）の複数形
curtail (19)	to limit or stop; curb　短縮する

D

dazzling (3)	very impressive; bright　見事な、目もくらむほどの
debt (13)	the state of owing money; money owed　借金
debunk (8)	to prove that something is false or ridiculous; expose（人・思想など）の正体を暴露する
deceive (11)	to fool or cheat; mislead　だます、欺く
decelerate (10)	to slow down　減速する
deception (11)	an act of fooling or cheating　だますこと、詐欺
declining (20)	coming or going down; being reduced in number; getting worse　下落しつつある、衰えつつある
deem (11)	to judge; to have as an opinion　…だと考える、思う
delicate (13)	easily hurt or damaged; tender　きゃしゃな、傷みやすい
delusion (1)	a false belief or opinion; illusion　思い違い、妄想
demean (16)	to debase or make fun of　…の品位を下げる、卑しめる
denial (15)	the inability to see or recognize one's own problems or faults　否定、拒絶
dense (10)	highly concentrated; thick　濃い
deplorable (3)	very bad; terrible; capable of being seriously condemned　嘆かわしい、ひどい
depression (14, 15)	a prolonged period of slow economic growth or activity; a personal feeling of deep sadness and hopelessness　不況、憂鬱
descent (6)	a falling or coming down; a person's hereditary or genetic background　家系、血統
descriptive (2)	having to do with writing or speech that paints a picture in words　記述的な、叙景的な
despair (3)	a feeling of hopelessness; dismay; discouragement　絶望
detectable (11)	capable of being seen or found; verifiable　探知可能な
detention (19)	being held in jail or prison　留置、監禁
deteriorate (18)	to grow worse or less; decline　悪化する
device (10)	a tool or piece of equipment　装置、仕掛け
devise (10)	to create or make; invent　工夫する、発明する
devour (13)	to consume hungrily or passionately　むさぼり食う

diffract (3)	to change the direction of light by passing it by or through something　分散する、屈折させて散らす
digest (1)	to take in or absorb mentally　消化する
digestion (18)	the process by which food is changed into energy in the body　消化
dignitary (16)	a person of high rank or importance　高位の人
dignity (15)	the state of having personal value and importance; self-respect　威厳、気高さ
diligence (13)	the capacity of a person to work hard; industriousness　勤勉さ
diminish (1)	to become less in number or strength; decline　減少する
discipline (12, 13)	a field of study or research; behavior, self-control, or training that results in moral or intellectual improvement　学科、学問分野、訓練、規律、けじめ
discredit (8)	to prove false or unworthy of belief or respect; debunk　…を嘘だとしてはねつける、信用しない
discriminate (3)	to see or understand the differences between things; to separate or distinguish　区別する、相違を見分ける
dislocation (16)	a feeling of being in the wrong place　位置を変えること、秩序の崩壊、混乱
disinfectant (17)	a chemical that destroys bacteria and other organisms that cause disease　殺菌・消毒剤
dismantle (19)	to take apart piece by piece; to tear down or raze　分解する、破壊する
disorder (15)	a physical ailment or disease; syndrome　不調、病気
dispassionately (12)	objectively; without letting personal feelings interfere or cloud one's judgment　客観的に、冷静に
disperse (4)	to spread or distribute over a wide area　四方に散らす、普及させる
disposal (14)	getting rid of; throwing away　処分、始末
disruption (14)	the state of being thrown into confusion or disorder; interference　混乱、中断
dissident (19)	a person who disagrees with or protests against a government policy　反対者、反体制者
dissimilar (2)	not alike; different; not the same　似ていない
distinct (9)	separate; clearly different　別の
distinguish (3)	to tell the difference between things; separate in one's mind　見分ける

distinguished (13)	refined in manner and appearance; highly respected; sophisticated　洗練された、気品のある、高く尊敬される
distort (5)	to lie or give false information with the intention of misleading others （事実・心理・動機などを）曲げる、誤り伝える
distress (11)	serious concern or worry; anxiety　悩み、嘆き
distribution (4)	the state of being spread over a wide area　分布
diversity (2)	variety; assortment　多様性
divine (12)	having to do with God or gods　神の、神々しい
divulge (8)	to reveal or show; expose　あばく、暴露する
docile (18)	obedient; teachable; tractable　従順な、御しやすい
docudrama (1)	a TV program or movie that dramatizes a factual event　ドキュメンタリー・ドラマ
dogma (9)	a strong belief or opinion, especially one that the believer thinks is absolutely true; ideology　教義、定則、ドグマ
domination (19)	the state of controlling or being controlled absolutely or powerfully　支配、統治
dominant (10)	having the most influence or power; superior; leading　支配的な、優勢な
doomed (16)	being headed for a sad or unhappy future or end; about to die　破滅する運命にある
downtrodden (13)	occupying a low position in society because of poverty and oppression; poor; down and out 踏みつけられた、しいたげられた
dreary (13)	dark; dismal; bleak　もの寂しい、憂鬱な
ductile (18)	capable of being bent or shaped 延性のある、どんな形にもなる

E

earnest (17)	serious; conscientious; high-minded まじめな、真剣な、熱心な
elaborate (13)	highly detailed; complex　精巧な
electromagnetic (3)	having to do with the electrical field of force 電磁石の、電磁気の
element (7)	feature or characteristic 要素、（学問の）初歩、（芸術・科学などの）基本、原理

elude (6)	to escape notice; to be difficult to see or determine …の目をのがれる、…に発見（理解）されない
emblematic (3)	symbolic of; representative of　象徴的な
embrace (20)	to accept an idea or belief willingly and wholeheartedly; espouse　抱擁する、喜んで受け入れる
emerge (12)	to come out; to appear or come into existence　現れる
emit (11)	to give or throw off; send out　出す、放つ
empirical (9)	based on fact; relying on observation or experiment 経験による、実証可能
encapsulate (3)	to express in a few words; to summarize　要約する
enclosure (16)	a place (cage or fenced area) surrounded on all sides where things are kept or contained　囲い地
encompass (12)	to include or comprise; to make up　包含する、取り巻く
encounter (12)	to come across; to meet by chance　出くわす、遭遇する
endangered (14)	about to become extinct; dying out; threatened with death 絶滅の危険にさらされた
endeavor (5)	to try very hard; attempt　…しようと努める
enlightened (16)	having advanced intellectual or spiritual insights 啓発された、賢明な
enlightenment (3)	the state of being spiritually or mentally advanced 啓発、啓蒙
enroll (15)	to join; to sign up for; to become a member of （会員・受講生などとして）登録する
ensuing (17)	following; subsequent　続いて起る
entity (18)	a being or living thing; a thing or object　存在物、実体
epitome (3)	a representative example; a model　典型
equivalent (14)	equal or identical to; the same as　同等の
etymological (8)	having to do with word origins and changes over time in word usage and form　語源の
evaluate (1)	to judge; assess; critique　評価する
evolve (2)	to change gradually over time; develop 徐々に発展する、進化する
exacerbate (19)	to make worse or more serious; intensify　悪化させる
excavate (17)	to dig a hole, usually a very large one　掘り起こす
excel (11)	to do very well; to be excellent at　秀でる
exhausted (13)	extremely tired; worn out　大変疲れた、疲労困憊した
exhibit (11)	to show or display　展示する、公開する

exploit (16)	to use someone or something in a selfish or immoral way; to take unfair advantage of　利用する、(人を) 私的目的で使う
expose (11)	to reveal or display for all to see　さらす、触れさせる
exposition (7)	writing that aims to provide information about a subject or topic or to explain something difficult or unfamiliar　論評、解説的論文
extinction (16)	the condition of no longer being in existence; disappearance from the earth of a living thing or species　絶滅

F

facilities (20)	equipment or buildings used for a specific purpose　設備、施設、機関
faulty (1)	not correct; containing an error or defect　欠陥のある、誤った
feces (4)	semi-solid waste matter eliminated from an animal or person's body　排泄物、大便
fellow (18)	having the same characteristics or conditions; being of the same group or occupation　仲間、同僚
fertilizer (4)	a substance used to help crops like vegetables and flowers grow　肥料
fib (11)	a lie, usually not a very serious or damaging one　(たわいない) 嘘
financial (8)	having to do with money　財政上の、金融上の
finite (6)	limited; not endless　限界のある、有限の
flashback (15)	an intense mental image or feeling of reliving a past event　幻覚の再発、フラッシュバック
fluctuation (14)	the condition of changing or rising and falling quite often or regularly　変動、高下
forage (4)	to look for food in nature　食料をあさる、捜し回る
foremost (20)	ahead of all others in rank or position; of the highest importance　一番先の、主要な
forgery (8)	the act of producing something counterfeit or not genuine, like a painting or another person's signature; something that is counterfeit　偽造、偽造品
formalize (19)	to make official or legitimate　正式なものとする

formative (13)	capable of growth and development 形態形成の、発達の
formulate (10)	to make or think up; invent （考えなど）を練り上げる、組み立てる
fossil fuel (6)	an energy source like gas, coal, or oil ガス、石炭、石油のような化石燃料
foster (9)	to help to grow or develop　育む
fragment (8)	a piece or shard of something　破片、断片
fraught with (15)	filled with certain things or features …に満ちた、…をはらんだ
freighter (17)	a ship that carries cargo　貨物船
frequency (3)	the number of repetitions per unit of time of an electric current　頻度、振動数、周波数
fulfillment (20)	satisfaction; contentment　遂行、実行、満足感、達成感
fundamental (7)	basic; essential　基本的な
fundraising (20)	collecting money for a certain cause, purpose, or charity 基金調達、寄付金集め
futile (18)	worthless; useless; in vain　無駄な、無意味な

G

gargantuan (17)	huge; gigantic　巨大な
generate (2)	to produce or make　生成する
generosity (9)	the quality of being willing to freely share with or give your time, money, and labor to others　寛大さ
genetic (15)	having to do with heredity　発生の、遺伝子（学）の
geographical (17)	having to do with the earth's natural features and national boundaries　地理学（上）の、地理的な
geothermal (6)	having to do with the internal heat of the earth　地熱の
glacier (14)	a permanent ice and snow formation on a mountain　氷河
globalization (12)	the process of making the countries of the world more interdependent　国際化
gradually (1)	slowly; a little at a time　徐々に
grave (14)	very serious; severe; critical　厳粛な、重大な
gravity (6)	the natural force of attraction possessed by a planet, moon, or other heavenly body　重力
greedy (20)	wanting or taking more than you really need or deserve; selfish; grasping; avaricious　貪欲な、欲張りな

guilt (11)	the state of being found responsible for a crime or other wrongdoing　罪、罪責
gullibility (8)	the condition of believing things too easily; easily deceived or cheated　だまされやすさ

H

habitual (4)	done regularly, often unconsciously 習慣的な、常習的な
hail (8)	to acclaim or greet with great enthusiasm; cheer; welcome 歓呼して迎える、歓迎する
hallucination (15)	the mental occurrence of seeing things that aren't really there; delusion　幻覚症状、幻覚
halt (14)	to stop suddenly; terminate （急に）停止する、中止（中断、停止）させる
hands-on (18)	practical; not theoretical; involving active participation 実際的な、実用向きの
hamper (14)	to hinder; interfere; get in the way of …の邪魔をする、阻止する
harmony (12)	a pleasing or successful combination of elements; balance: accord　和
haul (17)	to carry or transport ぐいと引っ張る、手繰る、（車・貨車）で運ぶ
harvest (9)	to bring in or gather a crop; to reap 収穫する、取り入れる
hibernate (4)	to sleep through the winter, like a bear or other animal 冬眠する
hierarchy (19)	an arrangement or series in which each element or member is arranged or graded by rank, from low to high 階層制度、ヒエラルキー
hollow (4)	empty on the inside　（物の中が）空の、空洞の
hostage (15)	a person held by one side in a war or conflict who is used as a means to gain some advantage　捕虜
humiliation (13)	deep shame or embarrassment; chagrin; mortification 屈辱、不面目
hydraulic (17)	moved by or operated by a fluid like water or oil 水力式の、水圧（油圧）式の
hypothesis (10)	a possible explanation for something that can be tested for further proof; supposition; theory　仮説

I

ignite (14)	to light a fire; to cause to happen　点火する
ill-temper (9)	anger; irritability; crankiness　不機嫌、短気
illusion (9)	a false idea or mistaken way of seeing reality; delusion; false impression　幻想
immeasurable (6)	very large in number or effect; limitless; vast 計り知れない、広大な
impeachable (8)	said of illegal or immoral behavior or actions that could cause a public official to be removed from office 弾劾されるべき、告発されるべき
imperative (20)	essential; absolutely necessary　避けられない、必須の
implication (12)	a suggested or hinted meaning; inference; connotation 含意
impose (18)	to use force or authority to apply a rule, standard, or idea; compel　押しつける
impressionistic (1)	having to do with the way a person sees things rather than with the way things are; subjective; personal （事実・体系によらず）印象（だけ）に基づく
imprison (13)	to put in jail or prison　投獄する、収監する
impulse (13)	a sudden, often unconscious urge or wish to do or obtain something; whim; caprice　衝動
inanimate (7)	not living; said of things like rocks, furniture, tools, and so on　無生物の
inaugurate (17)	to set in motion; to introduce or originate; to kick off （新事業・政策など）を正式に開始する
incidentally (3)	by chance; by the way 偶然に、ところで、ついでながら
inconsolable (3)	deeply sad or upset; grief-stricken （慰めようのないほど）悲嘆にくれた
incriminating (11)	said of evidence that proves a person's guilt beyond a doubt; inculpating　有罪を証明するような
indispensable (3)	essential; said of something that cannot be done without 欠くことのできない
ingenuity (6)	genius; creativity; imagination　発明の才、創意
inherent (5)	having to do with that which is naturally one's own; characteristic; intrinsic　本来的な、内在的な
initiate (8)	to start or cause to happen; set in motion; kick off 始める、着手する

injustice (13)	unfairness; moral wrong　不当、不法、不正行為
innocence (3)	the state of being free from sin or corruption, often through lack of knowledge of evil　無罪、潔白
inquiry (9)	study; research; investigation　研究、探究
insight (18)	shrewd or penetrating observation, or the outcome of such observation　洞察
insomnia (15)	the inability to sleep; sleeplessness　不眠症
inspire (12)	to cause a person to take action; to encourage or motivate　奮起させて…させる
instill (1)	to introduce an idea, belief, or habit into another person gradually; to impart; to teach （思想・感情などを）徐々に教え込む
integral (18)	essential for completeness; basic; indispensable 不可欠な、必須の
integrity (15)	a feeling of personal worth or value; honor; uprightness 高潔、無欠の状態
intensity (3)	strength; power; brightness　強度、強さ、彩度
interplay (5)	interaction; the back and forth movement of action and reaction　相互作用、交錯
interpretation (1)	a possible explanation or version of an idea, event, word, picture, or piece of writing　解釈
intervention (15)	action taken to stop or prevent something; the starting up of medical care or psychological treatment 介在、干渉、（病気などの）治療処理
intriguing (11)	very interesting; fascinating; causing wonder or delight 非常に興味（好奇心）をそそる、魅力ある、大変面白い
invisible (10)	not capable of being seen　目に見えない
irrigation (17)	a system for providing crops with water　灌漑
irritability (15)	the state of being easily angered, frustrated, or upset; crankiness; grumpiness　怒りっぽいこと、短気

J

justify (8)	to explain so as to prove that something is right or fair 正当だと理由づける、弁明する

L

landscape (5)	a photograph or painting showing mountains, valleys, forests, and other scenes from nature　景色、風景
lavish (13)	marked by extravagance and abundance; plentiful; luxurious; generous 気前の良い、浪費癖のある、豪華な
lease (17)	to rent for a certain period of time　リース、賃貸（制度）
legend (4)	a story that may or may not be true and that has been handed down over several generations; a person who is the subject of such a story　伝説
lexicon (3)	a list of words like a dictionary or glossary; a vocabulary 語彙（集）
lethal (17)	deadly; causing death　致死の
livelihood (19)	means of support or making money; a living or subsistence 生計（の手段）
livestock (19)	animals raised or kept on farms or ranches that are sold or used for profit　家畜
loath to (1)	to be unwilling to do something; to be very reluctant …するのに気が進まない、…するのを嫌う
lobby (19)	to try to persuade or influence political leaders to take a certain action or pass a certain law　陳情運動をする
locks (17)	a system used to raise and lower water levels on a canal 水門、閘門
longevity (4)	long life; long duration or length of time　長寿、寿命
luminosity (5)	brightness; the quality of giving off light 光輝、輝かしいもの
lurk (15)	to wait in hiding with the intention of causing harm; to be a hidden threat or source of danger　潜む

M

mammal (4)	animals that feed their young with milk from mammary glands　哺乳類
mandatory (14)	essential; required　義務的な、強制的な
manifestation (5)	a show or display; a piece of evidence or proof 明らかにすること、明示
menagerie (16)	a collection of animals　見世物用動物の群れ

migrate (4)	to move from one place or area to another 移住する、移動する
millennia (16)	thousands of years　millennium（1,000 年間）の複数形
mingle (18)	to mix or combine; bring together 混ぜる、一緒にする、（人）と交際する
miniscule (3)	very small; tiny　非常に小さい、ちっぽけな
mischief (8)	action that can cause harm or hurt, though usually slight or unintended　いたずら
misguided (16)	influenced or caused by mistaken ideas or principles 誤り導かれた、心得違いの
mobility (19)	movement; the ability to move freely from one place to another　移動性、可動性
moisture (5)	slight wetness; drops of water or other liquid　湿気
monopolize (19)	to use or own exclusively　独占する
mortal (16)	causing or about to cause death; fatal; not living forever やがては死ぬ運命にある
mortifying (8)	causing a person great shame or embarrassment　屈辱的な
motivate (8)	to inspire or encourage to action 動機を与える、やる気を起こす
motive (1)	a desire or need that causes a person to do something; incentive; reason for an action　動機
mount (13)	to pile up or accumulate　（数量・程度が）増す
mourning (4)	the state of being very sad or grief-stricken after the death of a loved one　喪
mysticism (12)	the belief in the existence of realities that are not normally seen or felt in everyday experience; spirituality 神秘主義、神秘主義的信仰

N

naturalistic (5)	realistic; painting or writing that gives a detailed, objective picture of reality　自然主義の、写実的な
navigation (4)	the ability to make one's way from one location to another; the act of following a course or path 航海（航空）学、航海（航空）術
nectar (4)	a sweet liquid produced by many plants and flowers 花の蜜

neuroimaging (15)	looking into the human brain by means of various devices and equipment like MRI　神経画像法
nightmarish (7)	very frightening; horrific; horrible　悪夢のような
nocturnal (4)	active at night　夜行性の
notorious (8)	having a bad reputation; infamous; well known for a bad reason　悪名高い
numbness (15)	lack of physical or emotional feeling　無感覚、無感動
nutrition (18)	food and nourishment or the science or study of such　滋養（栄養）物、栄養学

O

objective (1)	shown in a way that does not express one's personal beliefs; unbiased; unprejudiced; dispassionate　客観的な
obligation (9)	duty or responsibility　義務
obsolete (18)	out-of-date; old-fashioned; passé　時代遅れの
official (19)	sanctioned by institutional or government leaders; formal; authorized　正式の
omniscient (7)	capable of seeing and knowing everything; all-knowing　全能の
omnivorous (4)	said of animals that will eat any kind of food　雑食性の
onset (15)	the start or beginning　開始、始まり
opprobrium (3)	disgrace or shame; shameful conduct; severe reproach or criticism　不名誉、恥辱
opt (17)	to choose or make a choice　選択する、選ぶ
option (20)	a choice; the act of choosing; the freedom to choose　選択、オプション
orient (4)	to locate or place in position; to find one's way　方角（方位）を知る、自分の立場（居場所）を見定める、案内する
orphan (13)	a child whose parents are both dead　孤児
outgrowth (2)	a result or consequence　当然の結果
overcome (12)	to be able to successfully handle a problem or situation; to prevail over; to defeat　克服する、打ち勝つ

P

Paleolithic (5)	relating to the Stone Age when man first started using tools made of stone　旧石器時代の
paleontology (8)	the study of the forms of life that existed in prehistoric times　古生物学
passive (18)	not active; motionless; lifeless　受動的な、不活性の
pawn (13)	to sell off valuable items by taking them to a pawn shop　質に入れる
pedagogy (18)	teaching; education　教育（学）、教授（法）
perceivable (3)	capable of being seen or observed　感知できる、知覚されうる
perception (2)	the act or process of seeing; insight or knowledge based on observation and seeing　知覚すること、認知
perpetrate (8)	to commit a crime; execute or pull off a trick, crime, or plot　（犯罪・過失など）を犯す、（悪事）を働く
perpetrator (11)	a criminal　犯人、犯罪者
persistently (15)	repetitively; continuously; over and over again　しつこく、永続的に
pervade (13)	to be present everywhere; to spread or be spread throughout something　広がる、広くいきわたっている
pesticide (14)	a chemical used to kill insects and other animal pests that can cause damage to crops　殺虫剤
physiological (11)	having to do with the body as opposed to the psychological or mental　生理学上の
pigment (5)	a substance used as coloring; color; hue; tint　顔料
pigmentation (3)	skin color　着色、染色、（植物・動物の皮膚の）色
pioneer (12)	a person who discovers something or does something for the first time; one who opens up new areas of thought or study　開拓社、先駆者、パイオニア
plight (16)	a situation or position, usually an unfortunate or dangerous one　苦境、窮地
plug (1)	to advertise　宣伝する、推奨する
plumbing (17)	the pipes, toilets, and other fixtures that provide and dispose of water in a home or building　配管系統（設備）
populace (19)	the people who live in a city, province, or country; population; citizenry　大衆、民衆
pore over (18)	to read or study something very carefully and intensively; to be absorbed in　熟考する、精査する

pose (14)	to present a possible threat or problem （危険などを）引き起こす
poverty (19)	the state of being very poor　貧困
precipice (6)	a very steep side of a high cliff, mountain, or rock　絶壁
precise (2)	exact; specific　正確な
predisposition (15)	the state of being susceptible to something like a disease or other condition; tendency; inclination …しやすい性質、疾病素質
preeminent (7)	superior to all others; outstanding 極めて優秀な、抜群の
preexisting (12)	coming before; already in existence　先在する
prejudice (1)	a negative judgment or opinion formed before one has learned all the facts; bias　偏見
preliminary (17)	prior to or getting ready for the main action or matter at hand; preparatory　予備の、前置きの
preservation (16)	keeping or maintaining in safety or abundance; protection 保存、保護
prestige (3)	high standing or esteem in the eyes of others; admiration; respect　名声、威信
prevarication (11)	avoiding telling the truth or saying exactly what you think 言いのがれ、逃げ口上
primeval (3)	ancient; original; of great age or antiquity 原始時代の、太古の、初期の
principal (19)	main; most important; key　主要な、最重要な
probe (12)	to investigate or examine carefully 精密に調べる、探りを入れる
productivity (20)	the condition of being able to produce or make things in large numbers; diligence; industriousness 生産性、多産性
proffer (16)	to offer for acceptance or consideration; to suggest （意見・助言）を申し出る
profoundly (20)	deeply; with great penetration or learning　深く、深淵に
progressively (5)	increasingly; step by step　漸次、次第に
prohibit (19)	to ban or outlaw; abolish　禁止する、廃止する
prolific (13)	said of artists who produce many works　多作の
prominently (2)	out in the open; easily seen or recognized 目立って、顕著に
propensity (11)	tendency; inclination; bent　傾向、性癖
proper (9)	correct; just　適切な、正しい

prose (2)	non-poetic writing; everyday language without metered structure　散文
protagonist (7)	the main character in a story, movie, or play　主役
purity (3)	the state of being perfectly clean or pure; uncorrupted　純粋さ
purportedly (8)	supposedly; seemingly; reportedly　噂によれば、その称するところによれば

Q

quality (7)	a characteristic or trait of a person, place, or thing　性質、性格、品質
quest (11)	a search; a seeking or pursuit　探究

R

race (3)	ethnicity; a group of people united by geography, culture, and/or skin color　人種
rampant (17)	occurring without limit or control; widespread　蔓延する、はびこった
rape (15)	forcing another person into sexual intercourse　強姦
rat-infested (13)	filled with rats　ネズミがいっぱいの、ネズミが住み着いた
rationality (1)	the quality or state of being reasonable; the ability to think clearly　合理性、良識
ravages (5)	destruction; devastation　損害、惨事
ravine (5)	a deep, narrow valley or gorge　峡谷、谷間
ream (1)	a measure of paper; a very large amount　連（紙の数量単位）、多量
receptacle (19)	a container　容器
refine (12)	to improve or make better　洗練する、さらに精密（正確）にする、磨く
refinement (11)	improvement; perfection　洗練
regime (19)	the government holding power; administration　政治制度、政権、政府
regrettable (3)	causing disappointment; rueful　残念な、遺憾な
regulate (9)	to control or direct according to set rules or standards; manage　規制する、統制する

relegate (10)	to put in a rank or position that is no longer accepted as being true or valid; to assign to a lower or minor position （より低い地位・状態に）格下げする
relevant (2)	having a direct connection to the matter or situation at hand; useful and significant 関連がある、適切な、実際的な価値（重要性）を持つ
remains (8)	a corpse; a dead body　遺体、遺骨
remote (2)	located far away　遠い、遠方の
repeal (19)	to cancel a law or policy　（法律など）を廃止、撤廃する
replicate (16)	to copy or duplicate　…を複製する
reprisal (19)	an act of revenge or retaliation that intends to cause at least as much harm as that received　報復
residue (9)	that which is left over; remainder　残留物、残り
resin (5)	a clear or yellow liquid derived from plants that is used in varnishes and paints　樹脂、松やに
resolution (7)	the ending to a story or play; outcome 解決、複雑なプロットや謎が解明される部分、クライマックスの後の解決部
respiratory (11)	having to do with the lungs and breathing 呼吸の、呼吸に関連のある
response (11)	an answer to a question; reply; reaction　応答、応え
resistance (19)	an act of opposition or protest, particularly against a government in power　抵抗、反抗
restraint (5)	control; limitation　抑制、制止
restore (16)	to return something to a former state or position; revive; renew　復興する、修繕（修復）する
revelation (3)	something that shows the will or truth of God; a divine manifestation　暴露、すっぱ抜き、啓示、お告げ
revenge (8)	to punish someone in return for injury or insult; vengeance 復讐
reverberate (4)	to echo back; to resound 鳴り渡る、残響する、波紋を投げかける
rigidly (19)	strictly; according to the rules　幻覚に、厳しく
ritualistic (3)	having to do with the observance of religious practices and customs　儀式の、儀式主義の
rodent (4)	a small animal like a rat, mouse, or squirrel with large teeth for gnawing　齧歯類
rote (18)	learning by heart; memorization 機械的記憶、機械的な（退屈な）反復

rundown (13)	in poor condition; dilapidated　荒廃した	

S

sabotage (1)	the destruction of property by civilians or the enemy during times of conflict or civil unrest 破壊工作、サボタージュ
sacred (12)	commanding religious respect and worship; holy　神聖な
sacrifice (20)	giving up something for a greater good or goal; surrender; forfeit　いけにえ、捧げもの、犠牲
saintliness (12)	action or behavior characteristic of a saint; virtue; high moral standards　聖人のようであること、気高さ
salient (7)	most characteristic or important; conspicuous; remarkable 顕著な、目立った
salivation (11)	the formation of moisture in the mouth　唾液の分泌
sanitation (17)	systems or measures designed to protect the public from disease　公衆衛生、衛生設備
sanitized (16)	made more acceptable by removing unpleasant or offensive features; not natural （不快なものなどを除いて、話などが）和らげられた
scorn (8)	treating people or ideas with contempt; the act of looking down on　軽蔑、あざけり
sectarian (12)	having to do with a religious or political group or sect; partisan　宗派の、党派の
segregate (19)	to separate according to race or ethnic background; to keep apart　（人種・階級などを）差別する
self-deceiving (16)	not being honest with or about oneself; having a false picture of one's talents and worth　自己欺瞞
self-pity (13)	feeling sorry for oneself　自己憐憫
sensation (8)	state of extreme public interest or excitement 大評判、大騒ぎ、センセーション
sense (7)	meaning; connotation　意味、意図、趣旨
sensitivity (12)	the ability to feel what others feel; understanding; empathy 感受性、思いやり
sentimentality (13)	excessive or exaggerated emotion or feeling, often said of works of fiction or drama　涙もろさ、感傷
sever (20)	to cut or stop; break off　断つ

servitude (13)	slavery; the condition of being owned or controlled by a master　奴隷の境遇
sequence (7)	the following of one thing or step after another; succession; series　続いて起ること、連続
settlement (19)	the act of moving to and remaining or settling in an area or foreign country　移民すること、入植
shattered (5)	broken into many pieces or fragments　粉砕された
singular (13)	special; unique　非凡な、無二の
shrink (14)	to become smaller in size or amount; dwindle; diminish　縮む、小さくなる
skepticism (8)	a doubting or questioning state of mind or way of thinking　懐疑的な態度、疑い
skewed (11)	biased or prejudiced; not objective; slanted　（事実・価値などが）ゆがめられた、歪曲された
slavish (6)	overly dependent; like the behavior or situation of a slave　奴隷のような、模倣的な
sleight-of-hand (8)	trickery; magic　巧妙な早業、トリック
solitary (4)	tending to stay or be alone　孤独な、孤独好きの
soothe (3)	to relieve pain; calm; pacify; console　（痛みなど）を和らげる、なだめる
sophisticated (11)	refined; advanced　洗練された、熟練した
spark off (14)	to start; to initiate or set in motion　始める
species (16)	a class or category of animal　（生物分類上の）種
specific (9)	of a particular kind or nature; certain　明確な、特定の
specimen (16)	a sample or example of something; a representative　見本、標本
spectrum (4)	an array of colors or other objects　スペクトル
speculate (9)	to wonder about something; to reach conclusions despite a shortage of evidence; to guess　思いを凝らす、推測する
spew (14)	to gush forth; to send out; to emit　吐き出す、噴出する
spontaneous (5)	happening suddenly or without planning; occurring from within without external cause or reason　自発的な、自然に起きる
stagnant (17)	foul or stale from standing too long because of lack of movement; often said of water in ponds or lakes　淀んだ
stake (20)	a share or interest in a business or enterprise　利害関係、関心、（企業などへの）出資
static (18)	unchanging; not moving forward　静的な、固定的な

statistical (12)	having to do with numerical facts and figures　統計（上）の
stimulate (3)	to inspire or encourage; arouse; make excited　刺激する、励まして…させる
stockholder (20)	a person who owns shares or stock in a business　株主
strategy (2)	a plan of action; approach; tactic　方策、計略、戦略
stumble across (5)	to find by accident; happen upon　偶然出くわす、発見する
stud (8)	to fill with small objects　ちりばめる、点在させる
subjective (2)	personal; private; not objective; biased　主観的な
submit (3)	to turn or hand in　提出する
substantially (2)	significantly; in a major way　十分に、たっぷりと、相当に、かなり
substantiate (8)	to prove or verify; to offer evidence for something; substantiate　実証する
subtle (1)	so small or slight in connotation as to be difficult to pick up on or understand　かすかな、微妙な、とらえがたい
successor (19)	a person who comes after or follows another person; used especially with people in public office or positions of responsibility　後継者
suffrage (19)	the right to vote in democratic elections　選挙権
suitor (16)	a man who is courting or trying to attract a woman　（男の）求婚者
superficial (16)	shallow; on the surface; trivial　表面的な、うわべだけの、取るに足りない
supernatural (12)	having to do with divine power; miraculous; not of this world　超自然の、天上界の
supernova (10)	an exploding star that gives off an immensely bright light　超新星
supremacist (19)	a person who believes he or she is better than or superior to others　至上主義者
suppression (19)	keeping people from enjoying or exercising their rights and freedoms; limiting people's social and political activities; oppression　抑圧、弾圧
surgical (16)	having to do with operations performed on hospital patients　外科の、外科手術の
susceptible (15)	easily or likely to be affected, especially by an illness or new idea; vulnerable　影響を受けやすい、感染しやすい

suspect (11)	a person thought to have committed a crime; defendant　容疑者、被疑者
sustain (14)	to keep or maintain; continue　持続させる、維持する
sustainable (20)	capable of being continued or maintained at the present level　維持できる、持続可能な
sustained (4)	continued; ongoing　支えられた、維持された
swamp (16)	a region of low land that is usually covered with water　沼地、湿地
swayed (14)	to be influenced or persuaded by　（意見などが）左右された、人の影響を受けた
swelling (10)	the condition of becoming larger or filling out　はれ上がっている状態、増大
symptom (15)	a sign of a disease or other problem　徴候、症状

T

tame (16)	not wild; domesticated　飼いならされた、なれた
tax break (20)	a lower tax rate given as a reward for something　優遇措置、減税
tempera (5)	a painting medium that uses egg yolk or some other binding material to mix with the pigment (color)　テンペラ絵具
tenable (14)	defendable by reason; capable of being maintained or defended in a debate or argument　批判に耐えられる、弁護できる
tentative (14)	temporary; provisional; not yet decided or complete　仮の、試験的な
thermal (14)	having to do with heat　熱の、温度の
tint (5)	hue; color; shade　色、色合い、色調
toil (17)	to work very hard, usually under unfavorable conditions　骨を折って働く
tolerance (9)	the condition of being able to accept, understand, or empathize with the beliefs and practices of others　寛容、許容
torrential (14)	like a flood or sudden downpour of rain　急流、激流のような
torrid (17)	very hot　炎熱の、とても暑い
torture (15)	the act of causing severe pain to another person as a means of punishment or to gain information　拷問

totality (10)	the state of including everything there is 全体（性）、完全（性）
toxic (20)	poisonous; dangerous　有毒な
trait (7)	a characteristic; feature; quality　特色、特性、特徴
transcendental (12)	having to do with the supernatural or mysticism 超自然的な、神秘的な
transmit (3)	to send from one person or place to another 送る、伝える
transparent (5)	capable of being seen through; clear　透明な、明らかな
trap (14)	to capture or ensnare　罠にかける
traumatic (13)	having to do with severe shock or injury to the body or the emotions, usually caused by an accident or act of violence 心的外傷の
treacherous (17)	very dangerous or hazardous とても危険な、油断できない
treatise (16)	a long essay or dissertation dealing with a serious subject 論文
tremendous (5)	very large or great; awe-inspiring すさまじい、ものすごい、恐ろしい
tribute (16)	a gift or payment made to show one's gratitude or admiration　貢物、感謝・敬意の証としてささげるもの
trick (8)	a mischievous act intended to cheat or deceive someone いたずら、わるさ

U

ultimately (1)	in the end; eventually; in the final analysis 最終的に、結局
unavoidable (20)	having to do with that which must be done or paid attention to; inevitable; necessary 避けることのできない、必然的な
uncanny (13)	exceptionally keen and perceptive; almost too good to be true　異様な、不可解な
unconscious (3)	said of actions that are done without thinking; involuntary; not intended　無意識の
underground (19)	political activity not conducted out in the open; secret; clandestine　地下組織の、秘密の、非合法的な（行動）

underlying (10)	basic; fundamental; essential　基礎をなす、根本的な
unifying (12)	tending to bring the parts or elements of something together to achieve a satisfactory or successful whole 統合する、一体化する
universal (11)	true or valid everywhere; general; all-encompassing 普遍的な、全世界の、万人に通じる
unprecedented (14)	never having happened before; new; original　先例のない
untold (3)	beyond the ability to accurately describe or count; many 言い表せない、無数の
upbringing (1)	the training or rearing one receives in childhood; family background　子供時代のしつけ
uproot (19)	to remove from one area and force to move to another area 強制的に退去させる

V

valid (1)	true; authentic; just; well-grounded 妥当な、正当な、根拠の確かな
validate (8)	to prove real or true; authenticate …が正しいことを証明する
variable (14)	changeable; not constant or permanent 変わりやすい、不定の
vast (10)	very large; huge　広大な、広漠とした
venomous (8)	poisonous; extremely cruel　悪意に満ちた、有毒な
verbal (2)	having to do with words and speech 言葉の、言葉による
verge (4)	edge; outer or upper limit　縁、端、境界
versatile (5)	having many talents or uses; flexible 多芸の、何にでも使える
vertebrate (4)	an animal with a backbone　脊椎動物
veterinary (16)	having to do with the field of animal medicine 獣医（学）の
viable (6)	capable of being effective or successful; doable; practicable 実行可能な、成功しそうな
vice (9)	moral wrongdoing; sin　　（道徳・宗教上の）悪
virtue (9)	correct or proper behavior; moral excellence; goodness 美徳、徳、善

virtually (10)	almost but not quite; for all practical purposes; nearly 実質的には、ほぼ、ほとんど
vital (17)	important; essential　肝要な、重要な
vividly (3)	in such a way as to create a clear mental picture 生き生きと

W

weighty (2)	serious; important; profound　重大な、重要な
wholeheartedly (13)	with great enthusiasm, devotion, and dedication; eagerly 真心をこめて
wickedness (3)	evil; cruelty; deviltry　邪悪、不正、悪意
witness (15)	a person who sees a crime being committed or an accident taking place　目撃者
woe (19)	a problem; difficulty; personal trouble; worry 苦悩、災難、悲痛な出来事

Z

zoological (16)	having to do with animals or the study of animals 動物学の、動物に関する

編著者紹介

ジム・クヌーセン

40年以上日本で生活し、活動している。
ワシントン州立大学で政治学 (1971) と英文学 (1975) の学位を取得。英国サセックス大学で、20世紀英文学の修士号 (1978) を取得。他に高校・大学向けの100冊以上の英文テキストの著者でもある。

生井　健一

早稲田大学国際教養学部教授。ジョージタウン大学大学院博士課程修了（Ph.D.）。専門は理論言語学、英語教育。著書に『音読でたたきこむTOEFLテスト英文法』（南雲堂）、『言語・文化・教育の融合を目指して：国際的・学際的研究の視座から』（共編著：開拓社）などがある。

著作権法上、無断複写・複製は禁じられています。

TOEFL® Test iBTリーディング　実践編		[1-494]
1　刷	2010年　9月29日	
6　刷	2017年12月7日	
編著者	ジム・クヌーセン　Jim Knudsen	
	生井　健一　Kenichi Namai	
発行者	南雲　一範	
発行所	株式会社　南雲堂	
	〒162-0801　東京都新宿区山吹町361	
	NAN'UN-DO Publishing Co., Ltd.	
	361 Yamabuki-cho, Shinjuku-ku, Tokyo 162-0801, Japan	
	振替口座：00160-0-46863	
	TEL: 03-3268-2311（代表）／FAX: 03-3269-2486	
検印省略		
コード	ISBN 978-4-523-26494-1　C0082	
		Printed in Japan

乱丁・落丁本はご面倒ですが小社通販係迄ご送付下さい。
送料小社負担にてお取り替えいたします。

E-mail　nanundo@post.email.ne.jp
URL　http://www.nanun-do.co.jp

Well READ

Well Read オーディオブックは英語を学びたい方や、ゆっくりと読書を楽しみたい方など向けに、年齢を問わず、わかりやすく、楽しい読書とリスニングの体験を提供します。

Well Read オーディオブック・セレクションは、市販のもののおよそ 2/3 の速さで読まれています。単語一つ一つがはっきりと発音されて、話を楽しんでもらえるように、長めの句切りを入れてあります。また、学習効率を最大化できるよう、Well Read オーディオブックにはそれぞれ無料のダウンロード可能な注釈付き完全版 eBook がついてきます。

WELL READ
オーディオブック

今まで無かった英語勉強法とリスニング体験

＊初心者でも分かりやすいゆっくりペース

＊世代を超えた童話や物語を楽しく学ぼう

＊ネイティブの人にもオススメ！

ESL Publishing

http://www.esl-publishing.com
http://www.esl-publishing.jp

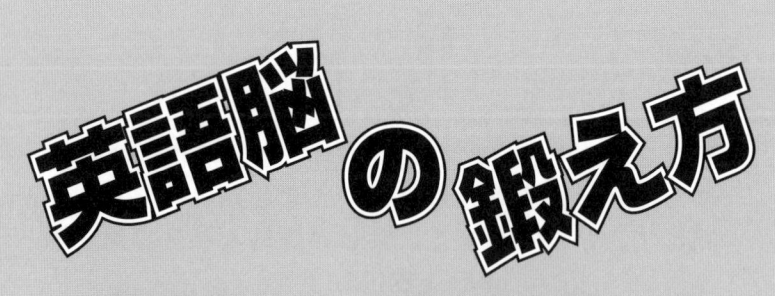

英語脳の鍛え方
―英文を正しく読む18のツボ―

金子　光茂／リチャード H. シンプソン 著
A5判　272ページ　定価1680円（本体1600円＋税）

本書は、どうすれば間違うことなく英語が正しく読めるようになるのか、その技術と実践を示した書物である。

主内容
- 1章　この英文が正しく読めますか？ 翻訳力テスト
- 2章　こまめな辞書引きは基礎の基礎
- 3章　彼、彼女、それ、それらはご法度
- 4章　形容詞は落とし穴だらけ
- 5章　時には必要、補充訳
- 6章　翻訳は原文どおりに頭から
- 7章　国語力への志は高く
- 8章　動詞はふくみも見落とさず
- 9章　名詞の誤訳は誤魔化し利かぬ
- 10章　助動詞をあまく見るな
- 11章　意外に乏しい英語力
- …
- 20章　全章のおさらいテスト
  など

誤訳ゼロへの挑戦

翻訳は昔も今も容易な仕事ではない。誤訳のない翻訳などない、と言っても過言ではない。本書は避けられない誤訳をどうしたら回避できるか、そこに焦点を当て、英語読解力向上を目指す人々のために編まれた指南書である。

南雲堂
NAN'UN-DO

プロジェクトで学ぶ実践ビジネス英語

寺内　はじめ編著

ビジネス・キャッツ
Cats

音声が無料で**ダウンロード**出来ます！
http://business-cats.net

A5判　208ページ　定価1890円（本体1800＋税）

会社を救え、太郎君！

日本とアメリカのビジネス舞台で大活躍。
人工太陽光線開発プロジェクトスタート！

プロジェクトの企画・立案、
プレゼンテーション、クレーム対応までの
あらゆるシーンを網羅。
シミュレーションしながら鍛える
実践型ビジネス英語の決定版！

南雲堂
NAN'UN'DO

南雲堂

宮岸羽合 編著 Miyagishi Hago

英単語レボリューション

Book 1 クラシック　Book 2 ルネサンスI　Book 3 ルネサンスII　Book 4 モダン
Classic　　Renaissance I　　Renaissance II　　Modern

各定価
(本体700円+税)

新書判

便利なハンディー・タイプ！
いつでも、どこでも参照できる！

『英単語ピーナツほどおいしいものはない 金・銀・銅』
に続く新機軸の単語集！

特徴
※音声をインターネットからダウンロード出来ます(有料)

1. コロケーションだから、実力がつく
- 同時通訳者がコロケーション（連語）を覚えて育っていくように、本書はコロケーション重視だから覚えやすい、だから実力がつく。

2. 復習方式
- Classicの動詞はすべてRenaissanceに再登場、Renaissanceの名詞もほとんどがModernに再登場、つまり動詞や名詞は復習しながら覚えられる。

3. 速習対応
- 時間のない人はClassicとModernの2冊だけでも、本書の単語の99.8%をカバー、Renaissance I・IIとModernの3冊なら100%カバー、速習対応。

4. こだわりの例文・コロケーション
- 多くの用例は英語圏の新聞、雑誌、書籍から収録し、3人のネイティブスピーカーがチェック、Google検索でヒット数の少ないものは排除するこだわり。

5. iPodやiPhoneで聴ける
- 用例はインターネットでダウンロード（有料）してすぐにiPod等*で聴ける、時代の最先端を行く英単語集。

*使用環境を満たしていることが条件。iPod、iPhone、iTunesはアップル社の登録商標です。その他の商標はその会社のものです。

6. レベルと対象
- 難関大学入試対応、社会人の英語力向上、通訳・留学の基礎力養成に威力を発揮、TOEFL®やTOEIC®などの英語資格試験対策にも活用できる、英語教師必携。